To Save A Thousand Souls

To Save A Thousand Souls

*A Guide for Discerning a Vocation
to Diocesan Priesthood*

Fr. Brett A. Brannen

VIANNEY VOCATIONS

Rev. Brett Brannen is the Vice-Rector of Mount St. Mary's Seminary in Emmitsburg, Maryland. He is a priest of the Catholic Diocese of Savannah, Georgia, where he served as Vocation Director for ten years.

Vianney Vocations LLC, Valdosta, Georgia 31602
Printed in the United States of America
10 11 12 13 14   1 2 3 4 5

ISBN: 0-615-34551-4

LCCN: 2010920723

Nihil obstat: Rev. Msgr. Steven P. Rohlfs, S.T.D.
Imprimatur: Rev. Msgr. Richard W. Woy, V.G., Archdiocese of Baltimore

Cover photos by Micki Krzynski and Tom Lesser

To Jesus Christ, the great High Priest,
in whose priesthood I have been privileged to share

To live in the midst of the world
Without wishing its pleasures;
To be a member of each family,
Yet belonging to none;
To share all suffering;
To penetrate all secrets;
To heal all wounds;
To go from men to God
And offer Him their prayers;
To return from God to men
To bring pardon and hope;
To have a heart of fire for charity
And a heart of bronze for chastity,
To teach and to pardon,
Console and bless always.
My God, what a life;
And it is yours,
O priest of Jesus Christ.

Jean-Baptiste Henri Lacordaire

CONTENTS

FOREWORD

Chances are, if you're reading this book, you're either considering a priestly vocation, in priestly formation, or helping along someone who is discerning.

Having been there myself, and having known many young men who have embarked along the path of discerning a priestly vocation, I know it to be an experience which is exhilarating, exhausting, captivating, and maybe even terrifying, all at the same time.

With so many competing, sometimes conflicting forces at play in the mind and heart of a young man discerning what God has created him to be, the process of discernment is anything but easy. Nor, perhaps, should it be, because seeking and finding that unique role for which God created each of us — our vocation — is a serious enterprise indeed. It impacts not only the future of the person discerning, but ultimately the lives of countless others with whom he will come into contact over the course of his life.

Any young man endeavoring to discover God's will, especially if that may include the priesthood, does not need pressure of any sort. Fr. Brannen's book makes clear that the Church's interest is helping each individual discern and follow God's true will — because finding that, and living that out, will bring a person the greatest measure of happiness he can expect on this side of eternity. Remember the wise words of Saint Catherine of Siena: "If you are what you should be, you will set the world on fire!"

It's interesting to note that in Scripture, when an angel appears to a human being to bring a message from God, the angel often says, "Be not afraid." Perhaps that's because seeing an actual angel face-to-face can be rather overwhelming. But perhaps it's also because coming face-to-face with the will of God can, at first, be overwhelming too.

What we also see, however, is that when we human beings cooperate with God's will, He opens up for us a future quite beyond what we could ever imagine. Little could Our Lady have known all that would take place—the joys, sorrows, and glories—after she said to the Angel Gabriel, "Let it be done to me according to thy word." And yet, without her cooperation and her trust in God's goodness, the events of our salvation would not have taken place, because our Savior would not have come into the world.

Mary's yes brought Christ into the world, and the yes of every priest brings Christ into the world, continuing on earth the work of our salvation. Truly, there can be no work more consequential than this: to bring Jesus to people and people to Jesus. And as unique and varied as priests may be, I am always struck by at least one commonality among all authentic priestly vocations: they're centered in the Eucharist. Consecrating the Eucharist, changing bread and wine into the Body, Blood, Soul, and Divinity of Jesus Christ—this is at the heart of the priesthood, and is the center and the driving force of everything else a priest is called to be and to do.

Father Brannen has systematically and comprehensively addressed the questions, aspirations, yearnings and even the fears of a young man who feels—perhaps against his initial inclinations—the stirrings of a priestly vocation. Father Brannen is a wise and prayerful priest who has served the Church well in many different capacities, and has witnessed some truly extraordinary instances of God's grace working in individual human hearts, especially through the Catholic priesthood. You will see that for yourself as you read these pages. This is the life to which you may be called.

I've been a priest for nearly thirty-three years. Sure, there have been some tough days, as there are in any vocation. But never would I trade a day of my priesthood for anything else in the world.

Never will I forget the words I heard some years ago from a wise senior priest who, after hearing my confession and granting me absolution, looked me in the eye and said, "In your prayers, don't forget to thank God for all the gifts He's given you, especially the gift of the priesthood, because it's the best gift you ever could have gotten."

So *tolle et lege*—take and read—and be not afraid!

Most Reverend William E. Lori
Bishop of Bridgeport, Connecticut
December 2009

ACKNOWLEDGEMENTS

I wish to acknowledge with gratitude the many priests who have greatly influenced my life and my vocation to the priesthood, thus preparing the way for this book. From the Diocese of Savannah, chief among these are Msgr. Lawrence Lucree, my childhood pastor, who first instilled in me a love for the priesthood; Msgr. John Cuddy, a mentor, pastor, and co-worker; and my good friend Fr. Mark Ross. I also acknowledge post-mortem Msgr. Richard McGinness and Fr. Anthony Manochio, former Rector and Spiritual Director, respectively, of Mount St. Mary's Seminary, both of whom were powerful instruments of God in my own years of priestly formation. May they both rest in peace.

Many thanks to the vocation directors who generously read the first draft of this book and offered wonderful feedback for improvement: Fr. Timothy McKeown, Diocese of Savannah; Fr. Brian Bashista, Diocese of Arlington; Fr. Len Plazewski, Diocese of St. Petersburg; Msgr. Robert Panke, Archdiocese of Washington, D.C.; and Fr. Luke Ballman, Archdiocese of Atlanta. I am also grateful for the suggestions of Fr. John Horn, S.J. and Deacon Jim Keating at the Institute for Priestly Formation. I am thankful for the input of my colleagues here at Mount St. Mary's Seminary: Fr. Dan Mindling, OFM, Academic Dean; and Fr. Frederick Miller, Professor of Systematic Theology.

I must also recognize and thank Bishop William Lori of Bridgeport and Archbishop John J. Myers of Newark for their suggestions, encouragement, and support. I am deeply appreciative of my own bishop, Bishop J. Kevin Boland of Savannah, for his wonderful support and friendship; I am indebted to him in many ways, not least of which is my assignment to work as vice rector of this seminary, a position that has provided the knowledge, experience, and time to write this book.

I am grateful to my family for their love and support throughout this project, especially Colleen Brannen, my sister-in-law, who spent many hours reviewing the manuscript. I thank Sr.

Ellen Marie Hagar, D.C., for her strong support and assistance choosing the title. Thanks to Susie Nield and Paula Smaldone, administrative assistants at Mount St. Mary's, who helped me meet my many editing deadlines.

The Rector of Mount St. Mary's Seminary, Msgr. Steven Rohlfs, has been instrumental in this project. He has been a great friend and has encouraged me from the beginning with his wisdom and advice. He has patiently afforded me the time to work on the book during normal business hours and offered insightful editorial suggestions. I am most grateful for all of these kindnesses.

Finally, I want to thank my editor and publisher, Sam Alzheimer, President of Vianney Vocations. The Holy Spirit brought us together at a fortuitous time: while I was seeking help to publish this book, Sam was forming a new organization, Vianney Vocations, specifically to help vocation directors recruit more priests for the Church. With a stable career, a wife and three small children, this decision was made with great faith and intestinal fortitude. This book would not have been published without his guidance, editing, and expertise. My sincere prayer is that this book and Vianney Vocations will inspire more men to become priests of Jesus Christ.

INTRODUCTION

Does God want me to become a priest? How can I be sure?

How do I know if I have the gifts and abilities to be a priest?

How do I know if I am holy enough?

How do I know that I will be happy and fulfilled?

If you are asking yourself these questions, this book was written for you.

I love being a priest. I have always loved it. I particularly enjoyed the thirteen years I served as a parish priest in my home diocese of Savannah, Georgia. It is hard to imagine a better job in today's Church than being a parish priest.

But becoming a priest—and even discovering whether God wants you to pursue priesthood—can be a very difficult and uncomfortable process, even excruciating at times. As the vice-rector of Mount St. Mary's Seminary, I have witnessed hundreds of men make great progress through years of intensive seminary training and finally be ordained priests. Before coming to work in the seminary, I was the vocation director of my diocese for ten years, and worked closely with men of different backgrounds who were discerning priesthood. I have been privileged to guide these good men as they made the most important decisions of their lives.

Over these past fifteen years, I have read many pamphlets and articles about priesthood, but I always desired a *single resource* I could give to a man who was discerning. I eventually saw that Jesus was calling me to write such a book. I began writing in September 2008, endeavoring to write one chapter per month, and so I was thrilled in early 2009 when Pope Benedict XVI proclaimed the Year for Priests. I saw this as a strong confirmation of God's will. The volume you are holding is my attempt to compile everything I have learned—everything I would tell a man who is considering the priesthood.

Celibacy is always a top concern for men like you. Perhaps you wonder if you're holy enough to be a priest. You may be terrified of preaching in front of a congregation. Maybe you're afraid of what your parents and friends will think about you considering priesthood. You may not know how to get to seminary, or what to expect once you get there. These concerns—and hundreds more—are covered at length in the following pages. This book is simply written and includes many true stories about men just like you.

While my primary audience is men discerning their vocations, this book may also be useful for vocation directors. Hundreds of vocation directors around the world are working extremely hard to raise up new priests for the Church, and I hope they will distribute this book to potential candidates. However, if your vocation director does in fact give you this volume, please understand that your personal relationship with him is critical; no book is a substitute for that relationship. You cannot discern diocesan priesthood without the Church.

An important caveat: this is a book about discerning *diocesan* priesthood. It is not about discerning priesthood in a religious order. Though there are many similarities between these vocations, this is a guidebook for discerning whether God wants you to become an ordinary parish priest. However, this book may be able to help you *exclude* diocesan priesthood, freeing you to continue your discernment with a particular religious order.

Please keep in mind that this is a handbook, which means that some topics will already be familiar to you. For instance, if you have already been accepted as a seminarian, some chapters will be in your past history. Feel free to skip to the chapters applicable to your current situation, keeping in mind that the chapters are arranged more-or-less chronologically, taking a man through the discernment process from beginning to end. You may also find useful the index of questions at the back of the book.

To Save a Thousand Souls. Why did I choose this title? Only Jesus Christ can save souls. Only God has the power to bring people to heaven. But there is an old expression in the Catholic Church: "He who saves a priest saves a thousand souls." It means that if a priest is in danger of leaving his vocation, and someone steps in to help restore his confidence in his priestly ministry, a thousand souls will be saved. Actually, it is a great understatement. The ministry of a single priest affects *many* thousands of people during the course of his lifetime. God uses the vocation of priesthood very powerfully to bring people to Jesus and Jesus to people.

I pray that the Holy Spirit will use this book to inspire more priestly vocations in our country and in our world. I am thrilled that it is being published in the Year for Priests, and I offer it as a gift to the Catholic Church, the Bride of Christ. I love being a priest and I love the Church! May the Lord use this gift as he wills.

As I always said to the young men arriving at my vocation retreats, "I'm glad that you're here. I'm glad that you have come. But now it's time to listen to Jesus. Please check your plans at the door... and let's begin."

December 2009

CHAPTER 1

THIS IS JUST WHAT PRIESTS DO!

"Father, thank you so much. I feel wonderful! I feel so clean!"

I was sitting in the confessional and I had just finished hearing the Confession of a young college student. Several years had passed since her last Confession and she had fallen in many of the ways that are all too common in adolescence and young adulthood. With tears in her eyes, she said to me, "I am sick and tired of sin. I am not happy and I want Jesus back in my life." Afterward, she clearly had experienced the grace and mercy of Jesus in the sacrament of Confession. She said she felt wonderful and clean. I replied, "You're welcome. But this is just what priests do." And then I added, rather piously, "Jesus is the one who died on the cross for us so that our sins can be forgiven. He is the one we should thank." The young girl looked at me thoughtfully and said, "Father, I know that is true. And I love Jesus. But right now, I can't see him. I can just see you."

As she turned to walk out, she stopped and looked back again. "Father, if this is just what priests do, it must be awesome to be a priest."

Most men today, even Catholic men, simply do not have enough information to know whether or not they are called to be a priest. Most men do not really know what priests do nor who priests are. The perception of priesthood given in the secular media—novels, movies, magazines, television—is neither accurate nor adequate. A man cannot make a good decision about anything without good information. In fact, if he has bad information, he likely will make a bad decision.

This truth was brought home to me one day as a young priest. I was teaching in a Catholic school and a young boy raised his hand and asked, "What do priests do all week after Mass on Sunday? Don't you just go back inside your house and read the

Bible all week?" I laughed out loud, as did the sixth grade teacher in the room. I laughed because my life was so busy as a parish priest, and I was working so many hours, the thought of sitting in the rectory and reading all day (even if it was God's word) seemed like a fantasy. As I walked back to my office, I wondered how many young boys, even in our Catholic schools, have no idea what a priest really does. How can a young man realize he is called to something if he does not know what it is?

In almost every case I know, a man is attracted to priesthood because of the example of a specific priest. This was certainly true in my own life. Fr. Lawrence Lucree (now a Monsignor) came to our parish when I was twelve years old and he remained our pastor for ten of my most formative years. Fr. Lucree had two qualities I greatly admired: he was always joyful and he worked relentlessly for the Kingdom of God. Without question, he had more influence on my vocation than any other person. Why? Because I was able to see, by spending time with him, what priests do and who priests are.

As a vocation director, I used to offer what I called "shadow programs." Once I had identified a couple of men whom I considered to be promising candidates, I would invite the two of them to come spend a few days with me in the parish. They stayed with me in the rectory and they simply went with me everywhere and watched everything I did. I made sure that we went to the hospital and nursing homes to visit the sick. We went to the prison. We visited the children in the Catholic school and we worked in the social apostolate. Finally, on Saturday and Sunday, we set up and celebrated the weekend Masses. They watched as I went in to hear Saturday Confessions and as I celebrated Holy Mass for the people. If there was a hospital emergency during those visits (and it seems there often was), I woke them up in the middle of the night to go with me. They watched as I gave the Sacrament of Anointing and Viaticum to the dying. On a number of occasions, these "shadow program" experiences "sealed the deal" for a man who was discerning, and he made the decision to go to seminary. Regardless, men would always leave on Sunday saying, "Father, I had no idea what the life of a priest was really like. I didn't know what a priest did. This will change my discernment." What they meant was that they had more accurate information with which to discern.

These "shadow programs," though I think they can still be used with some modifications, are not much utilized today since the sexual abuse crisis hit the Church. The point, however, is that they were effective because they gave a man good, accurate information about priesthood and the life of a priest. The personal experience of seeing what a priest does, how he lives day to day, and his profound ministry to God's people, was life changing for these men, even if they were not ultimately called to become priests themselves. No book can substitute for that personal experience.

The purpose of a priest is to bring people to Jesus and Jesus to people. How does a priest do this? What exactly is it that priests do? Here are some true stories.

Priests Pray with and for the People of God

I was on call one weekend when my beeper went off. There was a terrible car accident out on the interstate. A young sixteen-year-old girl had suffered a serious brain injury. Even worse, the doctors in the ICU were saying that her brain was swelling and more damage could follow if the swelling continued. The next twenty-four hours were critical. I met her mother and father in the ICU waiting room around midnight. They were terribly distraught. We immediately began to pray. We went in and I gave the young girl the sacrament of Anointing of the Sick and we begged Jesus to save her. We could not stay long in the ICU so we returned to the waiting room and started to pray the rosary. I returned four more times during that next twenty-four hours and we prayed each time. Sometimes I read a Gospel story of Jesus healing a sick person; sometimes we just prayed from the heart. The last time I went in, the parents were radiant. "Father, we just received great news. The swelling has stopped. She is going to survive. And the doctors hope there will not be much damage at all. Thank you. Thank you so much."

This is just what priests do.

Priests Preach the Gospel of Jesus Christ

A priest who is a friend of mine once received a letter from a Catholic family in his parish. "Dear Father, we want you to know how happy we are that God sent you to our parish. When you arrived three months ago, we had already decided to leave the Catholic Church. We had been searching hard for Jesus and for his truth, reading the Bible as a family every day, and trying to grow in holiness. But we did not feel fed in our Church. We enjoyed the preaching much more in other churches and we seemed to learn more. We even attended Bible studies in Protestant churches. The Sunday you arrived was to have been our last Sunday as Catholics.

But you mounted the pulpit with your Bible in your hand! And you encouraged us to bring our Bibles with us to every Mass. Then you preached the Gospel of Jesus Christ and explained the teaching of Jesus on the Holy Eucharist, using the Bible. We had never heard this. We had not realized that we were being fed more profoundly than we could ever know every Sunday in the Catholic Church, both in Word and Sacrament! Father, we were so close to leaving what we now realize is a great treasure: our holy, Catholic faith. Thank you for preaching the Gospel to us. Thank you, thank you, thank you!"

This is just what priests do.

Priests Celebrate the Holy Sacrifice of the Mass

After Mass one Sunday, an elderly woman came up to me, accompanied by one of her grown daughters and asked, "Father, did you see anything unusual today during the Mass?" I replied, "No, but what did you see?" She said, "Father, I don't want you to think that I'm crazy, but I saw angels today during the consecration. I was kneeling and trying to pray and when I looked up, I saw something like white circles of light on each side of the altar. There were four on each side and they were moving up and down, as if in adoration of Jesus. I kept closing my eyes and reopening them, thinking that I was seeing things, but they didn't go away. I even nudged my daughter and told her to look, but she thought I was crazy. She didn't see anything. After you consumed the Eucharist and started giving Holy Communion to the people, the angels disappeared. Father, do you think I am nuts? Do I need to go see a psychiatrist?" I smiled and assured the woman that she was not crazy. I said, "Angels are always present during Mass. Everywhere that Jesus is, his angels are there in adoration and he is certainly present in the Eucharistic sacrifice. Now, why the Lord gave you that special grace of being able to see them, I don't know. But just thank God for the grace and don't worry about it." She left, seemingly satisfied with my answer.

A few days later, I got a call early in the morning from the grown daughter. She told me that her mother had a massive stroke and was taken to the hospital. When I arrived, the entire family of six children was standing around her bed in ICU and they told me that she was dying. The stroke was very severe and there was no way she could recover. I gave her the sacrament of Anointing of the Sick and the Apostolic Pardon and then we prayed the rosary. Finally, I closed with the prayers for the dying. "Eternal rest grant unto her O Lord and let perpetual light shine upon her. May she rest in peace. Amen. And may her soul, and all the souls of the faithful departed, through the mercy of God, rest in peace."

The moment I finished those words, the lines on the heart and brain monitors went straight. Even I was amazed! She died at the very moment we finished the prayers. There was a young doctor standing in the room, an intern, and he spoke to me out in the hall. He said, "Father, I am not a Catholic and I don't even have much religion, but I have to say that is the most amazing thing I have ever seen." I replied, "Jesus is real. He is real."

I often wonder about that holy woman's vision during Mass on her last Sunday on earth. Perhaps it was the Lord's way of telling her that he was proud of the way she had lived her life, raising her children in the faith. I will ask the Lord that question when I get to heaven.

This is just what priests do.

Priests Feed the People of God with the Body and Blood of Jesus

The following story is told about the life of St. John Bosco. He had founded an oratory (an orphanage of sorts) where young boys could come and live. They attended school and were instructed in the Catholic faith. There were so many orphans in Italy that the oratory was filled with several hundred boys almost immediately. Every day began with Holy Mass. One morning, as Don Bosco was celebrating Mass, he looked down on the altar and noticed that the sacristan had made a serious error. He had forgotten to place enough unconsecrated hosts on the altar to be confected into the Body and Blood of Jesus, in order to give Holy Communion to all the boys. Only a few consecrated hosts were in the tabernacle, and by the time he noticed the error, the consecration was finished. It was too late to add more. Don Bosco looked up to heaven, said a quick prayer and then started giving Holy Communion to the boys. He never broke a single host in half and he just kept giving out Holy Communion. Because there were so many boys, the sacristan and everyone else began to realize that a miracle was taking place, a miracle of multiplication. Every boy received the Eucharist and they were all whispering to each other, "It is a miracle. God has done a miracle through Don Bosco."

After the Mass was over, the boys all gathered around Don Bosco in the courtyard, chattering excitedly. One boy asked, "Father, what were you thinking when you realized that God was doing a miracle through you? He was multiplying the hosts."

Don Bosco replied, "I just kept thinking that transubstantiation is a much greater miracle than multiplication, and I see that every day."

This is just what priests do.

Priests Baptize

I will never forget the first time I performed Baptisms in Spanish in my parish. During the Mass, there were to be seven infant Baptisms after the homily. The parents and Godparents had dutifully attended the Spanish Baptism class. The Church was packed with the most beautiful (and numerous) Mexican children. It was a lively scene, to say the least. Children were running up and down the aisle, babies were crying, and one mother was breast feeding her newborn in the front row, without any covering! I was definitely a little out of my comfort zone. But we made it through. *"Juan José Garcia Vasquez, yo te bautizo en el nombre del Padre, y del Hijo, y del Espiritu Santo. Amen."* I anointed the children with the sacred chrism. Then, according to their tradition, we presented them all to the Blessed Mother, Our Lady of Guadalupe, for her protection. They sang songs and they cried and the parents gave out little colorful gifts to everyone present: a tiny homemade rosary in a little egg, a little bottle of holy water from the baptismal font, and many other things. Then they processed around the church holding the newly baptized infants, and they wanted me to walk with them, holding one of the babies. I had never seen anything like it before in my life!

After the Mass, I went out to the farm where they lived for a fiesta. A whole pig was roasting on a spit over an open campfire accompanied by an abundance of traditional Mexican food. Mexican music played and colorful decorations were everywhere. Again and again, I heard *"Padrecito! Padrecito!"* as the different families asked me to bless their homes and gardens. After the meal, I played soccer with the children and had several good conversations with some of the dads (who did not get to Mass very often). It was a great day and I arrived home exhausted, happy and grateful to God for the gift of being a priest.

This is just what priests do.

Priests Witness Marriages

Though I was still a young priest, it was the best marriage I had ever witnessed. The young couple had come to me early in their engagement and happily completed all of the marriage preparation required. Neither of these young people had been to college and they both had ordinary, manual jobs paying the minimum, hourly wage. But they were rich in faith. They both loved Jesus and they loved one another. They were not living together or sleeping together. They wanted a holy marriage, with Jesus in the middle. The Church was decorated only with hand-picked flowers from their family's home and most of the guests arrived in pickup trucks. There was no limousine or special music; they could not even afford an organist. "I, John, take you Susie, to be my wife, to have and to hold, from this day forward, for better or for worse, for richer or for poorer, in sickness and in health, until death do us part." I have never witnessed a marriage where I saw grace in action so powerfully. Jesus was definitely there! Jesus was the honored guest, just like at the wedding feast of Cana.

I spoke to my pastor later about the wedding, "I know that all weddings are not like that. But it was a joy to be there today and to witness the joining of those two souls in the sacrament of marriage."

This is just what priests do.

Priests Visit the Sick

A priest friend was telling me that he was called to the neonatal intensive care unit at the local hospital to do an emergency Baptism. He got the call right after the seven o'clock morning Mass. He had a very full schedule that day: he was scheduled to teach several classes in the school that morning, plus a marriage preparation at eleven o'clock and another meeting at noon. The afternoon was full also. He really did not have time to go to the hospital. And he had not even had breakfast yet! Nonetheless, he grabbed his Baptism ritual, a bottle of holy water, and a stole, and quickly jumped in his car. When he arrived, according to hospital requirements, he had to go through a special hand-washing and then dress in a special mask and gown, all designed to protect premature infants from disease. All this took another fifteen minutes. He finally made it to the incubator where the baby was, only to discover that the parents were not even there.

The nurse said, "Father, they left over an hour ago to run home and shower. They were here all night and wanted to freshen up before the Baptism." He felt great irritation and impatience. He had a full schedule and the children would be waiting in the school. But what could he do? He could not baptize the baby without the parents present. So he just sat in a chair by the infant and he touched the little baby's hand. Immediately, she latched onto his pinky and held it tightly. For the next fifteen minutes, he sat there and prayed for the child and for her parents. He realized that she would have a long road ahead and she needed prayers. He said, "The Holy Spirit communicated to me strongly in that fifteen minutes that nothing else I would do that day was more important than sitting here holding this tiny baby's hand and praying for her while I waited for her parents to return."

This is just what priests do.

Priests Bury the Dead

The couple spoke to me as they were leaving the Saturday Vigil Mass. They were a lovely couple and their twelve-year-old son was with them. He said excitedly, "Father, we're going to get a hamburger at my favorite place and then we're going bowling tonight!" This couple had tried to have children for many years and they spent a lot of money going to different specialists. Finally, they conceived and had a son, but the baby had some complications, including a hole in his heart at birth which took several surgeries to repair. But he was doing great. He was attending our parish school and living the life of a normal twelve-year-old boy.

At nine o'clock that night, a nurse from the hospital emergency room called me and told me to come quickly. I later learned what had happened. While at the bowling alley, the boy had stood up and walked to the lane to bowl. After he bowled his ball down the lane, he turned around, grabbed his chest and fell. The doctors said that he was dead before he hit the ground. His heart had simply burst.

Later that night, I was kneeling in the church with a very heavy heart. I felt so badly for the family and for their suffering. I said, "Jesus, I don't think I have the strength to bury a child right now. I can't do this. Please help me. Please give me the grace to do this funeral and to minister to this family."

I had never seen the Church more packed than it was the day of the funeral. God helped me. He gave me the grace and I made it through the homily. After the consecration and Communion, I remember thinking, "Jesus, it is almost over. Thank you Lord."

The Catholic Rite of Committal at the cemetery is very brief, though it took a long time for all the people to park and make their way to the grave. Once I had blessed the grave and finished the final commendation, the mother looked at me and said, "Father, please open the casket so I can say goodbye." I thought to myself, "Oh no. Please don't do this." But what could I do? How could I deny the request of a mother burying her only child? So I nodded to the funeral director to go ahead and it was just as I suspected. The mother began to scream and cry, hugging her child in the casket. Her husband was there holding her and crying, and the family was all huddled around. It was a terrible, sad, unforgettable moment in their lives—and in mine.

Emotionally, I could not take it and tears poured down my cheeks. The funeral was officially over, so I just turned away and started walking slowly among the graves, acting as if I were looking for a certain name on a tombstone. I was really trying to compose myself. After a few minutes, I suddenly heard Jesus speak to me very clearly. The Lord has spoken to me many times in my life, but there have been only a few instances where his voice and message were so clear.

Jesus said, "Thank you."

And I understood in that instant that he was saying, "Thank you for being a priest. Thank you for burying this child for me, and thank you for ministering to his parents." I knew without any doubt that it was Jesus because his voice totally and immediately restored my emotional and spiritual strength. I went from being heavy-hearted and sad — one of the lowest moments in my life — to being emotionally strong, filled with joy and happiness. I immediately began to thank and praise God, "No Jesus, I should be thanking you. Thank *you*, Jesus, for being my Savior. Thank you for dying for me. Thank you…" But again the Lord communicated to me very clearly and this time he said, "Stop. Be quiet. Right now, I just want you to let *me* thank *you*."

As I walked through the cemetery my heart was full, and I prayed quietly, "You're welcome Jesus. You're welcome. I am so glad that I am a priest."

This is just what priests do.

Priests Instruct Others about Jesus Christ and His Teachings

The Young Married group at our parish had only recently formed and they were a delightful group of young adults, excited about their faith. They had been meeting monthly, having a meal and a social, but they also wanted to grow in their faith. Various speakers were invited to each gathering to discuss various aspects of Catholic teaching. They told me, "Father, we don't care what you talk about. Just teach us about Jesus." I prayed every day that week during my Holy Hour for the Lord to show me what issue he wanted me to address. I began to get a fairly clear message — a message that I did not really want to hear. I felt like the Lord was asking me to talk to these young couples about the Church's teaching on artificial contraception and natural family planning (NFP). Suspecting that the presentation might not be well received by some of the couples, especially since some of the spouses were not Catholic, I was nervous. So I worked very hard to craft a gentle presentation designed to invite the couples to revisit the issue of family planning in their marriages. The couples were respectful and they looked at me and listened politely. I watched their faces for signs of disagreement, anger, or frustration. Clearly, some of them were not very interested.

At the end of the presentation, one couple came up to me and asked if they could talk with me for a few minutes after everyone else had left. They said, "Father, thank you so much for teaching us about contraception and natural family planning. The priest who married us never gave us any information at all about this, even when we asked, and we have always wondered what to do. We want to be good Catholics and we know the Church teaches that contraception is wrong. But we have been using artificial contraception because we did not know that there were any alternatives. We want to learn about NFP right now. Where can we go to learn?"

I gave them the information they needed and asked them to keep me informed. That couple was so hungry for the truth that they contacted the Couple to Couple League and went through the course in NFP. They were so thrilled by the positive difference it made in their marriage that they went through the course to become NFP instructors themselves. They continue to serve the Church in this capacity eighteen years later!

I don't know if that presentation made any difference in the lives of the other couples who were there that night. But it made a tremendous difference in the lives of that one couple—and through their ministry, it impacted many other couples preparing for marriage. Priests instruct others about Jesus Christ and his teachings.

This is just what priests do.

Priests Counsel and Guide the Suffering

A woman I knew had as many problems as Job. She had so much suffering in her life that whenever something new would happen, which was often, I would just say, "Lord, what next? Please give her a break." She would come in from time to time to talk and get advice on the many layers of difficulties in her life: problems with her health, her children, her job, and her husband. She asked me one time, "Father, why does life have to be so hard?" At the end of one of our counseling sessions, the lady said something to me that I will never forget. She said, "Father, thank you for being a Simon of Cyrene for me." I did not know what she meant, so she explained, "When I walked in here today, I was carrying a very heavy cross. It was crushing me. But when I came into your office, I gave you this cross to hold for me while I talked. You simply listened, you cared, and you gave me some good advice. And now, at the end of an hour, you have given the cross back to me. You know that you cannot keep it. But you helped me today, just as Simon of Cyrene helped Jesus with his cross, and for that, I thank you."

This is just what priests do.

Priests Fight for the Souls of God's People

A priest friend told me of something he had done as a young priest back in the 1960s. He was pastor of a church and school in a small town. One day a parishioner came in with some astonishing news. This man worked for the city and he had just learned that a business license had been granted to a pornographic book store, which was to be located on the same block as the parish school. The priest sprang into action, organizing a campaign of letter writing and demonstrations. The mayor's office was inundated with phone calls and letters. Editorials were written in the newspaper. A personal visit was made to the owner of the new book store by a team of parishioners, many of them attorneys, led by the priest. In the end, the store never opened. The people of

God saw this as a threat to the moral well-being of their children and community and they willingly and enthusiastically followed their shepherd in fighting that battle. And they won.

This is just what priests do.

Priests Evangelize; They Bring the Gospel to the World

A missionary priest gave a mission in my parish church when I was a boy. He told a story about a traveling missionary priest in South America who died around 1900. This priest had been sent from Europe to evangelize the native populations and he worked heroically to bring them Christ. Every day, he got on his mule and rode through the mountains from village to village, clothed in his black cassock. He slept on the ground, was bitten by mosquitoes, endured hunger and thirst, and still he struggled on. When he arrived at each village, he would teach and preach the Gospel all day long to anyone who would listen. This was a difficult task because each village had a different dialect. He was largely unsuccessful. Some of the people would listen politely for a while, but very few ever embraced the Catholic faith and asked for Baptism. Months turned into years and years into decades. After thirty years, the priest became very ill one evening in a mountain village. Realizing that he would die, he told the young Indian man who traveled with him from village to village, "I have been a failure. I have tried to bring Jesus to the world but the world has not received him. May the Lord have mercy on me. May the Lord have mercy on us all." The priest died and was buried on the mountain.

About forty years later, in another mountain village in that region, a great, powerful chief lay in his hut awaiting death. As he lay there, contemplating his mortality, he suddenly remembered something from when he was a boy. He remembered a white man dressed in black who visited his village and spoke of a powerful God named Jesus, who had been killed but had risen from the dead. And this white man had said that if you believed in Jesus, and received the cleansing waters, you would live forever. The chief immediately sent runners to the nearest large city with instructions to bring back a man in black—a priest. The priest arrived some days later, quickly instructed the chief in the Catholic faith, baptized him and gave him Holy Communion. Then the chief died.

But he was not only chief of one village, but ten villages, spread all over that region. The law said that the religion of the people would always be the same religion as that of the chief, so they sent for more priests. The priests came and they spent several weeks teaching, baptizing, marrying, and burying the dead. Thousands and thousands of people accepted Jesus Christ and the Catholic faith, and taught it to their children and grandchildren down through the generations. All because of one priest, who worked faithfully and then died, thinking himself a failure.

This is just what priests do.

Priests Defend the People of God from the Enemy

My secretary buzzed me in my office: "Father, there is a woman on the phone who wants to speak to a priest, and she's crying." I didn't know this woman, but she was in desperate need of help, for, as she told me, she had a demon in her home. I quickly learned why I did not know her. She was a Baptist! I asked her, "Have you already called your Baptist minister about this little problem?" "Oh no, Father. I called you straight away! Don't you priests do this kind of thing?" I thought to myself, "Not if I can help it." But I invited her in and she arrived with her two college-aged daughters in tow.

The three women looked terrible. They had not slept in days. They explained to me what had happened. The previous weekend they had a party and played with a Ouija board. They said it was amazing—some spirit had come and started moving the letters on the board, answering their questions. "But the problem, Father, is that when the game was over and our friends went home, the demon stayed. There is some evil presence in our home and we can all feel it. We're terrified. Please help us!" I told them that, first of all, they needed to tell Jesus they were sorry for their actions. They needed his help and they had better first ask for his forgiveness.

We went over to the church and knelt down before Jesus in the tabernacle. You should have seen these three Baptist women praying before the Blessed Sacrament! "Jesus, please forgive us. We are so sorry! We love you. We love you. Please save us. We are so sorry." It was one of the most sincere, beautiful prayers I had ever heard. I knew that Jesus would respond.

Afterward, I gave them a bottle of holy water and told them to go home with these instructions. "First of all, destroy the Ouija board. Rip it up and then throw it away, so no one else can ever use it." I quoted to them the great Padre Pio who said that "the devil is like a great, chained dog. He makes a lot of noise but he only bites those who come too close."[1] Secondly, I gave them some holy water and told them to sprinkle it in every room of the house. Finally, I said to them, "I want you to go to your church on Sunday and pray as a family every night. Call me back if you still have problems." They did call me back a few days later to say thank you. The demon had departed and they were most grateful.

This is just what priests do.

Priests Stay with their People in Good Times and Bad

Fr. Stanley Rother, a priest for the diocese of Oklahoma City, graduated from Mount St. Mary's Seminary back in the 1970s. He was not much of a student and much preferred to work with his hands. He had grown up on a farm and had a strong work ethic. He had a heart for evangelization. Just a few years after he was ordained, he requested assignment to the diocesan mission down in Guatemala. This formerly poor student learned the language of these people in a remarkably short time. He even translated the Bible into their language! He was a great missionary and shepherd.

Soon political and military instability in the country began to cause problems. An encampment of soldiers moved near the outskirts of his village and many of his good, simple parishioners were being kidnapped, tortured, and murdered. Fr. Rother's "crime" was that he buried the dead. He would get into his old pickup truck and go looking in the ditches for his people. When he found a dead body, he would bring it back to the church and celebrate a funeral Mass and burial. For this "crime," he was put on the death list. His bishop called him home, hoping to save his life. He was obedient so he returned home to take a few months of rest on his parents' farm. While there, he was extremely anxious and upset. He told his mother, "A shepherd does not leave his sheep when the wolf comes. I have to go back." With his reluctant bishop's permission, Fr. Rother went back to Guatemala. Soon after, on July 28, 1981, he was shot in the head several times by two assassins who broke into the rectory one night. The people of his parish sent his body back home to his parents, per their request, but they kept his heart in Guatemala. They buried the heart of their priest in the parish church.[2]

This is just what priests do.

Priests Care for the Dying

When I was a seminarian, we had a retreat master who told us the story of a Catholic priest who worked himself to the bone in the Midwest in the early 1900s. He was a circuit rider who rode his horse thousands of miles, going from village to village to celebrate Mass and offer the other sacraments for the few Catholics who lived in the area. Late one afternoon, after he had completed the Holy Mass, one lady said to him, "Father, have you heard about old man Jones? They say he is dying." Immediately, the priest took the Holy Eucharist, his oil stock, and his ritual, and he followed the woman's son, also on a horse, who led him back through the woods many miles. Finally, they arrived at a dilapidated one-room cabin.

When the priest walked in, he saw a cot in the corner. Lying there was an old, black man, emaciated from cancer. He had been a slave, or at least the son of a slave, and his hands were calloused from a life of hard work. He was only skin and bones. When the man saw the priest, dressed in his black cassock, he exclaimed, "Father, I knew you would come!" Immediately, the priest set to work. He heard the man's Confession and then gave him Holy Communion, followed by the sacrament of Extreme Unction (so called in that day). Already the death rasp was audible, so the priest knelt down by the bed, held his hand and began to pray the holy rosary. As evening arrived and the sun went down, the cabin got darker and darker. Suddenly, this weak, cancer-ridden old man sat straight up in bed. He pointed behind the priest and shouted, "I see the Blessed Virgin and she's smiling at you and me!" The priest turned around quickly, but all he could see was darkness. When he turned back, the old man was dead.

The priest said, "I stayed there, kneeling on the floor in the darkness and I held that old man's hands until they grew cold. And I cried, and I thanked God that I was a priest."

The young woman in Confession said: "Father, if this is just what priests do, it must be awesome to be a priest."

Yes, it is.

"Without the Sacrament of Holy Orders, we would not have the Lord. Who put him there in that tabernacle? The priest. Who welcomed your soul at the beginning of your life? The priest. Who feeds your soul and gives it strength for its journey? The priest. Who will prepare it to appear before God, bathing it one last time in the blood of Jesus Christ? The priest, always the priest. And if this soul should happen to die (as a result of sin), who will raise it up, who will restore its calm and peace? Again, the priest...After God, the priest is everything! Only in heaven will he fully realize what he is."[3]

St. John Vianney

CHAPTER 2

THE SACRED POWER OF PRIESTHOOD

"The priest continues the work of redemption on earth... If we really understood the priest on earth, we would die not of fright but of love... The priesthood is the love of the heart of Jesus."[4]

St. John Vianney

Why do we call these men "priests?"

How do priests get this power to forgive sins and to change bread and wine into the Body and Blood of Jesus?

Is a priest's soul changed forever?

What are the promises that a priest must make?

While I was in college, I was once asked by a devout evangelical Christian, "Why do you call your pastors 'priests' in the Catholic Church? In my church, we call them ministers or preachers." I answered the question of this sincere student by pointing him to the Old Testament, where the men of the tribe of Levi were called "priests." But he pointed out in reply, "Those men offered sacrifices of bulls and goats to God again and again for the forgiveness of the people's sins. That is why they were called priests. But that Levitical priesthood was not sufficient for the forgiveness of sins; that is why Christ had to come." I was impressed with his answer. I replied, "Catholic priests also offer sacrifice. Every time we celebrate Mass we offer the one sacrifice of Jesus Christ, wherein he died two thousand years ago and rose from the dead. Catholics believe that the Mass is the perpetuation in time of the one eternal sacrifice of Jesus Christ."

Now that young evangelical Christian raised his eyebrows and shook his head. He said, "Well, I don't believe what you believe—that the Mass is the sacrifice of Christ. But now I do understand why you would call your ministers "priests."

A man cannot discern diocesan priesthood unless he knows what diocesan priesthood is. In the first chapter, I tried to describe what a priest does. In this chapter, I will try to describe who a priest is. This is very basic information about priesthood; it is a theology of priesthood for discernment. For a more complete treatment, read the *Catechism of the Catholic Church* #1533-1600.

A Sacred Power

Fr. John Cihak tells this true story that happened to him some years ago when he was studying in Rome.

"Last spring a brother priest came to the Casa to train for the ministry of exorcism in his diocese. He asked me at the breakfast table one morning to accompany him to a church in the city to observe the work of one of Rome's exorcists. The priest wanted help translating from Italian so that he could better understand the exorcist's extemporaneous words, and the words being hissed or shouted at him. That morning was an extraordinary experience in which my own priestly identity was deepened. About twenty minutes into the session, the exorcist asked the five priests in the room to raise their hands from a distance in a type of epiclesis and to quietly invoke the Holy Spirit over the victim. The reaction was strong. The demons cursed, writhed, begged, raged, whimpered and threatened. A low, sinister voice cried out again and again, "Get them off! You are burning me!" To the demons the hands of a priest seared as though on fire, yet to the victim those same hands soothed as though still wet from holy chrism. The demons were painfully aware of a reality to which we are often blind: these hands are configured to those of the incarnate Son of God. They are His hands. Our chrismed, burning hands reveal the hidden depths of the priesthood He has given us. They remind us of who we are."[5]

Ordination to priesthood is not just an initiation, like joining a club or a fraternity. It is a gift of the Holy Spirit which permits the exercise of a sacred power (*sacra potestas*) which comes from Jesus Christ himself through his Church. The hands of an ordained priest have a sacred power to offer the sacrifice of Christ and to forgive sins in the sacraments (CCC #1537-8). Priesthood is not just being a preacher and a minister, though priests certainly do preach and minister to God's people. It is the administering of a sacred power!

The demons know this even better than we do.

In Persona Christi Capitis

A priest friend once told me this story. One of his parishioners, a daily communicant, invited him to supper. During the supper, the devout Catholic man said, "Father, explain the priesthood to me in thirty seconds or less." The man smiled, knowing that this was impossible. But the priest replied, "That's easy. I will ask you three questions. When you go to Mass each day, do you believe that you are really receiving the Body and Blood of Jesus in Holy Communion?" The man said, "Absolutely. I know it's Jesus!" The priest continued, "When you go to Confession, do you really believe that all of your sins have been completely forgiven, even mortal sins?" The man replied, "Yes Father, I am completely confident that my sins are gone." "Finally, do you agree that only Jesus Christ himself has the power to do these things?" The man stared at the priest and nodded affirmatively. The priest concluded, "Then you know what priesthood is. The priesthood brings the very power of Jesus down to earth out of love and mercy for his people."

A priest, by virtue of his ordination and the sacred power entrusted to him, acts *in persona Christi capitas*, in the person of Christ, the head [of the Church]. Catholics know this is true and witness it daily. For example, when a priest baptizes a baby, he says, "*I* baptize you in the name of the Father and of the Son and of the Holy Spirit." He does not say, "Jesus baptizes you..." At

Holy Mass, the priest says in the first person, "This is *my* body, which is given up for you. Do this in memory of *me*." And in Confession, does the priest say "Jesus absolves you of your sins in the name of the Father and of the Son and of the Holy Spirit"? Of course not. The priest says, "*I* absolve you of your sins..." A priest functions and exists *in persona Christi capitis*. It is really Jesus who is baptizing. It is Jesus who is offering himself in the Mass. It is Jesus who is forgiving sins in Confession. It is the raised hand of Jesus expelling demons from a possessed man. But it is his priest who is saying the words, acting in the very person of Christ (CCC #1548).

"Only Jesus is the true priest; the one who can offer sacrifice for the forgiveness of sins. Every other priest in the world simply shares in his priesthood."

Catechism of the Catholic Church #1545

This identification with Christ is so strong that the Church traditionally calls her ordained priests *alter Christus* (other Christs). When St. Paul writes in Galatians: "I live, no longer I, but Christ lives in me (2:20)," this is certainly true for all the baptized faithful. But when applied to an ordained Catholic priest, this passage takes on a new meaning entirely. Every day, Jesus does powerful miracles through his priests, even if a few happen to be not very holy men. Whether a particular priest is a great saint or a terrible sinner, the sacrament he validly celebrates still takes effect. This is known in theology as *ex opere operato*. It is a Latin expression meaning sacraments confer the grace they signify, regardless of the virtue of the priest (or recipient) of the sacrament.

The story is told that during the life of St. John Vianney, the famous Curé of Ars, a very worldly Parisian lawyer made the trip to the remote village to witness the spectacle about which he had heard — the priest who was a saint. The attorney came back to Paris and immediately began attending Mass faithfully and going to Confession. People asked him, "What did the priest say that convinced you to begin practicing your faith again?" The attorney replied, "Well, I really could not even understand him. He was not a good speaker and his accent was thick. It was not what he said that changed me. It was what I saw. What I saw was God in a man."

To give an extreme negative example, a drunken priest who is also a womanizer and in mortal sin, stumbles through Mass and everyone can see that he is drunk. Nonetheless, he is a validly ordained priest and he says the words of the Eucharistic prayer. He uses the correct matter (bread and wine) and follows the rubrics. The sacrifice of Christ has been offered and the Eucharist has been confected. People likely will come up for communion trying to control their outrage at the behavior of this priest (and rightly so). But Jesus is just as present in the Eucharist at this Mass as he is in a Mass offered by a saintly and devoted priest. Christ always acts in his sacraments if the priest is validly ordained priest and celebrates the sacraments with the correct matter and form.

"How frightful it is to be a priest! How we ought to pity a priest who celebrates the Mass as though it were a routine event! How wretched it is to be a priest without any interior life!"[6]

St. John Vianney

The truths signified by these teachings—*in persona Christi capitis* and *ex opere operato*—are very good news for a man who is discerning priesthood. Why? Well, for one thing, many young men fear that they lack the holiness to become priests. This is good news. The holiness of Jesus is always present in his sacraments and in the work done by a priest, even if the priest might have some personal struggles with sin. And *all priests* struggle with sin, just like *all people* struggle with sin.

There is a riddle which we often tell in the seminary: What do you call the Eucharist that has been celebrated by a holy priest like St. John Vianney and by a selfish and lazy priest in mortal sin? The answer, in both cases, is "Jesus." Nonetheless, a holy priest helps people to enter deeply into the sacred mysteries and to approach the altar inspired (and not outraged).

The priesthood is about serving others and getting them to heaven. Jesus imparts this sacred power to a priest for the sake of others. This is important to know for your discernment.

The Three Degrees of Holy Orders

When I was a seminarian back in 1989, I remember attending a meeting with the bishop and all of the Savannah seminarians at the end of the summer. Each of us, in turn, described what we had done during our summer assignments. One seminarian, who was a transitional deacon, told this story.

> One night, I was in the rectory and it was very late, around midnight. The pastor was out of town on his day off and I was the only one there. The phone rang and it was the hospital calling. There was a medical emergency; a woman was very close to death and the family wanted a priest to come to offer the sacrament of Anointing and to help her prepare for death. I tried to call two other priests in the area but neither of them would answer the phone. So I just went on over to the hospital and anointed her myself.

On hearing this, the bishop gasped. He said pointedly, "You can't do that." The seminarian replied, "I know, bishop, but I'm telling you that I did do it." The bishop said, "And I'm telling you that you *didn't* do it. You can't do it. You don't have the power. You're only a deacon."

Deacons, priests and bishops make up the three degrees of the sacrament of Holy Orders and they are each empowered to do certain actions. All three are received by ordination, but only the bishop has the fullness of the sacrament. Deacons are empowered and entitled to proclaim the gospel at Mass, preach the homily, baptize, and witness marriages. Priests can do all of these things, but they also can celebrate the Mass, forgive sins in the sacrament of Confession and administer the sacrament of Anointing of the Sick. Deacons are not able to celebrate Mass, forgive sins in Confession or to celebrate Anointing of the Sick, since it also forgives sins. To *attempt* to celebrate Anointing of the Sick for the lady who was dying—giving the family the impression that she had received this sacrament—was a very serious pastoral error, in spite of that seminarian's good intentions.

A bishop can administer all the sacraments, of course. Under normal circumstances, he is the only one who can confer the sacraments of Confirmation and Holy Orders. We say that a bishop is the "successor of the apostles," indicating that he is ordained in the long line of Christ's priesthood which has been passed down from the original apostles. Theologians refer to this as Apostolic Succession. The fullness of this sacred power of our High Priest Jesus is found only in the bishop (CCC #1557). A priest shares in the priesthood of Jesus Christ only through his bishop.

Notice that these three levels of ordination must be received in ascending order from deacon to priest to bishop. A certain period of time is required between each ordination called an *interstitio*. For example, there must be a period of six months between ordination to the transitional diaconate and the priesthood. If the priest goes on to become a bishop, it is normally later in life. The Pope chooses men to be bishops who have proven themselves to be capable and faithful after many years of priesthood.

An Indelible Character: Thou Art a Priest Forever

I remember seeing a television show when I was a boy about a parish priest working in a small town in the 1920s. He was a humble, faithful priest and he tried very hard to take care of his parishioners, who made up almost the entire town. Ironically, the mayor of the town and his wife were extremely antagonistic towards the priest and the Catholic Church, even though they were

Catholic. The mayor was constantly opposing the priest's initiatives and the poor priest could not understand why. At the end of the movie, the mayor had a heart attack and he was close to death. The priest was called to administer what was then called the sacrament of Extreme Unction. When the priest went to anoint the palms of the man's hands, which is a required part of the ritual, the sick man turned his hands over for the priest to anoint the back. The priest looked up in amazement! By this action, the mayor was saying that he was also a priest—a priest who had left the priesthood and gotten married many years before. When a priest is ordained, the *palms* of his hands are anointed with sacred chrism. This is why when a priest is receiving the sacrament of Extreme Unction (now called Anointing of the Sick), his hands are always anointed *on the back.* The show ended with the priest realizing why the mayor had always been so oppositional and hateful. He prayed that his brother priest would have peace in Heaven. After all, a priest is a priest forever.

The Catholic Church teaches that priests are signed with an enduring special character at their ordination. The sacrament of Holy Orders, like Baptism and Confirmation, confers an indelible seal on the soul that can never be erased, repeated, or conferred temporarily (#CCC 1582). This is sometimes called an "ontological change," or a change of being.

When you get to heaven, you will see some men there with this mark on their souls and you will immediately know that they were priests on earth (CCC #1581-3). The mayor in that television show was still a priest, even though he had ceased functioning as a priest. His wife said to the pastor after the funeral, "He should never have left the priesthood. He was never at peace."

"If I met an angel of light and a drunken priest walking down the road, I would first kiss the priest's hands and then greet the angel."[7]

St. Francis of Assisi

30

What Happens to a Man Who Leaves the Priesthood?

If a priest decides to leave the priesthood and get married, or if the bishop suspends him for some serious violation of his priestly promises, the man is still a priest and will always be a priest (CCC #1583). However, he is not able to function as a priest licitly because he lacks the faculties. Usually, he cannot celebrate Mass, even in private, and he is not authorized to celebrate any of the sacraments. Yet, in danger of death (*in periculo mortis*), any priest can administer the sacraments. Therefore, if the mayor in the story above had come across a Catholic who was dying, and no "active priest in good standing" was available, he would be authorized to hear his Confession, give him absolution for his sins, to give him the Anointing of the Sick and the Apostolic Pardon. He is, after all, still a priest. The sacred power conferred by ordination does not go away. And the sacraments he gives in danger of death would be both valid and licit, as long as he has celebrated those sacraments with the correct intention and the correct matter and form. This is permitted by the Church because the highest of all laws is the salvation of souls.

"The faithful expect only one thing from priests: that they be specialists in promoting the encounter between man and God. The priest is not asked to be an expert in economics, construction, or politics. He is expected to be an expert in the spiritual life."[8]

Pope Benedict XVI

Priests Are Not "Free Agents"

Priests can exercise their priesthood only in union with their bishop. This is why a priest promises his bishop love and obedience when he is ordained. At every Mass the priest prays for his bishop by name, saying, for example, "In union with Benedict our Pope and *David* our bishop." If a priest is not in union with the pope and his respective bishop, he can neither celebrate Mass nor celebrate any of the sacraments.

A priest must be connected to a diocese; a seminarian cannot even begin to study until he has been accepted by a bishop to study for that particular diocese. This is why we call them *diocesan* priests. A diocesan priest must have the "faculties" to exercise his priestly ministry from his bishop. When a priest is ordained, his bishop gives him a letter stating that he has the faculties to function as a priest in the diocese. If a bishop removes the faculties—which would only happen for some very serious reason—the priest cannot function as a priest in the diocese or anywhere else. He is not in union with the Universal Church, because he has broken with his bishop and therefore, with the Holy Father. Understanding this connection that a priest has with his bishop is critical to a proper discernment of diocesan priesthood.

As a newly ordained priest, I was given a small card called a *celebret*. This card is issued by the bishop or his delegate with a Latin inscription stating that the bearer is "a priest in good standing" in that particular diocese. This card enables me to walk into any Catholic church anywhere in the world and celebrate Holy Mass. I went to Rome shortly after my ordination to priesthood and I loved walking into the ancient and beautiful churches there and showing the sacristans my *celebret*. Usually they were not very interested in reading it because they had seen thousands. They just said, "Yes, yes. Come now, Father. On which altar do you wish to celebrate?"

Vows versus Promises

Diocesan priests do not take *vows* of poverty, chastity and obedience. These are called the Evangelical Counsels and they are vowed by priests, brothers, sisters, and monks who belong to religious orders. The Evangelical Counsels are specifically ordered to holiness; they are meant to facilitate total surrender of one's life to God.

Diocesan priests are also called to live the Evangelical Counsels — because they are ordered to holiness, and thus applicable in every vocation — but they do not take vows in the strict sense of the word. At their ordination, they make *promises* to live celibately for the sake of the Kingdom, meaning they promise not to marry. They promise to pray for God's people every day through the Divine Office. And they promise obedience to their bishop and his successors.

What Do These Promises Mean?

Every person is called by God to live chastely according to their state in life. Since a diocesan priest is not married, he is called to live chastely regarding all genital sexual activity, as any unmarried man is called to do. Neither should he spend time with a woman in a romantic way, because a diocesan priest is in fact married; he is married to the Bride of Christ, the Church, and she deserves and expects his fidelity.

A diocesan priest is also charged to live a simple life, in imitation of the Master, but he does not take a vow of poverty. A diocesan priest can own a car (which is usually an occupational necessity), have a bank account, and other possessions. This is very different from a priest who belongs to a religious order, who may not own anything nor have a bank account. A diocesan priest receives a modest salary, in addition to his room and board, which are all paid by his parish. Normally, the parish pays his health insurance and other benefits as well, so the diocesan priest really does not have to worry about money. He does not need much, since he has no wife or children and pays no room or board. A few priests have received gifts or inheritances from their families. They are free to use or dispose of this money as they see fit, though they would be wise to follow the Gospel admonition to "not let your left hand know what your right hand is doing." When a diocesan priest lives too luxuriously, it can be a cause of scandal to the faithful.

Finally, the vow of obedience taken by a religious is much more extensive than the promise of obedience taken by a diocesan priest. I have been asked by my bishop to change assignments five times in my eighteen years as a priest. For me, this is the primary way that I am obedient to my bishop. A vowed religious, on the other hand, takes on a much more direct call to obedience as a day-to-day endeavor.

As a man discerns diocesan priesthood versus priesthood in a religious order, he must prayerfully consider whether God is calling him to take solemn vows. If he feels very attracted to the Evangelical Counsels, community life, communal prayer, and a focused apostolate like serving the poor, it could be an indication that he is being called to religious life. Diocesan priests typically do not live in community with other priests. Rather, they most often live alone and pray by themselves. And because of the demands of parish life, they cannot focus on only one charism.

The Grace of Holy Orders

A sacrament is often defined as "an outward sign instituted by Christ to give grace." Without question, the sacrament of Holy Orders provides some very powerful graces to the men who receive it.

> The grace of the Holy Spirit proper to this sacrament is configuration to Christ as Priest, Teacher and Pastor, of whom the ordained is made a minister.
>
> CCC #1585

Newly ordained priests often tell me that they actually can feel an internal change after ordination. They find themselves able to do things which they feared during their seminary years. They discover that when they are in a desperate situation — for example, with a family in the hospital after a terrible car accident — the Holy Spirit gives them the consoling words they need to say. When they stand in the pulpit, they can sometimes feel the Holy Spirit giving them confidence and strength, whereas before they had greatly feared preaching. I think that most priests will acknowledge that they have felt the grace of the sacrament of Holy Orders on many different occasions in their lives as priests. It is a configuration to Christ for the sake of God's people.

Having said this, I have also seen seminarians who do not study hard and do not push themselves to grow in prayer and the spiritual life. They might say, "Well Father, the grace of Holy Orders will see me through." They are wrong! Grace builds on nature. A man must work very hard to prepare himself for priesthood. He must pray and study and serve. Priestly formation is a very difficult endeavor. But if a man puts forth this effort, the grace of the sacrament will never be lacking for him in his life as a priest.

I have also seen the grace of the sacrament affect other members of a newly ordained priest's family or his friends. One priest told me that his father decided to become a Catholic soon after his son's ordination. His father had been married to his Catholic wife for thirty-five years and he had raised his children as Catholics. He had silently watched his son go through the seminary, study, pray, and mature. He had attended the ordination and first Mass, saying little through it all. Only a few months after the ordination, after all those years, he began RCIA. This was a special joy for this newly ordained priest.

Holy Orders is one of the two sacraments specifically designed by God to get other people to heaven—to save a thousand souls. Once a man is ordained a priest, the Holy Spirit does not waste any time!

"If we had faith, we would see God hidden in the priest like a light behind glass or like wine mixed with water."[9]

St. John Vianney, The Curé of Ars

Patron Saint of Priests

CHAPTER 3

WHAT IS A VOCATION IN THE FIRST PLACE?

"The only ones among you who will really be happy are those who have sought and found a way to serve."[10]

Albert Schweitzer

Mankind's Search for Happiness and Holiness

Is a vocation about happiness or holiness? Well, both. But I think that most young people are motivated by a desire for happiness, at least in the beginning of their search to know the will of God. All people desire happiness. They want to be fulfilled. This is a desire which God has placed deep within the heart. Yet one of the most common errors people make is to let their lives become consumed by a search for perfect happiness *on this earth*. It is not to be found here. The perfect happiness we all search for, that we yearn for in our hearts, is only to be found in heaven. This does not mean that we cannot enjoy some degree of happiness here on earth, just not the definitive happiness and fulfillment that we deeply desire.

The Irish have a saying, "A bad start is a quick finish." It is important to start the search for happiness with clear thinking. Having a realistic expectation from the beginning about what this world can and cannot offer protects a person from supreme disappointment and despair in later years. As a priest friend of mine used to say in times of difficulty, "This is as good as it gets around these parts."

I emphasize in this book that every vocation is about serving others. God made us for this reason. He desires that we love others more than ourselves and live selflessly. This is the secret to happiness. This is holiness. When a person learns how to serve others and makes this the consuming concern of his life, he is happy.

"I Think You Could Have a Vocation"

As a former vocation director and now seminary formator, it disturbs me to hear someone say about a young man, "I think John could have a vocation." Of course he has a vocation! Everyone has a vocation. What they mean, of course, is that John could be called to be a priest or perhaps join a religious order. But what that person should have said is, "I think John might be called to the vocation of priesthood or religious life." It does a disservice to the person and to the Church to use incorrect language, as if only priesthood and religious or consecrated life are true vocations. Language is important, as it can either illuminate or obfuscate the truth. Clear teaching about the theology of vocation is critical.

I think most people, including most Catholics, have a very vague idea about what a vocation is. They have heard the word mentioned at Mass, usually with reference to priests. They have seen "vocational schools" advertised, where people go to gain a skill to get a job, maybe as a nurse, computer technician, or mechanic. Many think that "vocation" does not apply to them, since they are already married and working. Some people simply have no idea. I am reminded of the conversation in Acts between St. Paul and some Christian disciples he had met in Ephesus. St. Paul asked, "Did you receive the Holy Spirit when you became believers?" They answered him, "We have never even heard that there is a Holy Spirit!"(Acts 19:2) Likewise, I think many Catholics have never heard that there is such a thing as a vocation! Or if they have, many have never taken the idea seriously. This is a problem. So what is a vocation in the first place?

Christ-likeness is the only success recognized by God.

Our Primary Vocation is Holiness

Happiness is doing the will of God. Interestingly, that could also be the definition of holiness. The primary and universal vocation of every person in the world is to be holy — to become like Jesus Christ. Christ-likeness is the only success recognized by God. Or, as St. Bonaventure said: "If you learn everything except Christ, you learn nothing. If you learn nothing except Christ, you learn everything."[11] Interestingly, the people who take holiness seriously are also the people who experience the most happiness here in this life. Why? Because our holiness is preparing us for the supreme happiness of heaven, the true destiny for which we were made, not some glimmer of happiness which we might experience here. Holiness directly leads to fulfillment and human flourishing, and the entire concept of vocation encompasses both.

The first vocation of every baptized person is to become a saint. While that may seem daunting, the good news is that this vocation does not require any discernment. The Church and Sacred Scripture both tell us clearly and definitively that holiness is everyone's primary vocation.

> The Church on earth is endowed already with a sanctity that is real though imperfect. In her members, perfect holiness is something yet to be acquired. Strengthened by so many and such great means of salvation, all the faithful, whatever their condition or state — though each in his own way — are called by the Lord to that perfection of sanctity by which the Father himself is perfect.
>
> CCC #825

Discerning and accepting one's vocation is like building a pyramid. It must be constructed from the bottom up. A man will not be able to know and accept his secondary or particular vocation — marriage or priesthood, for example — until he has been seriously striving towards his primary vocation of holiness. Some have tried to do it in reverse, and almost always have failed.

Our Particular (or Secondary) Vocation: Four Options for a Catholic Man

What I am referring to as our *secondary vocation* is the sense in which we usually hear the word *vocation* used. The secondary vocation refers to the particular state in life in which we are called to fulfill our primary vocation of holiness. This particular vocation normally will have the following characteristics:

~ It has been pre-determined or pre-destined by God

~ It involves a permanent commitment

~ It involves sacrificing oneself to serve God and others

~ It is recognized by the Church as a vocation

~ Its purpose is to help other people get to heaven

For a Catholic man in the Roman Rite (which is the majority of Catholics in the world), there are basically four options:

~ Holy Marriage

~ Holy Orders

~ Religious Life

~ Generous Single Life in Christ

Every Catholic man is being called by God to at least one of these four states in life. I say "at least" because some states in life can overlap; for instance, most permanent deacons are married. In some Eastern rites of the Catholic Church, priests can be married. However, for a Catholic man in the Roman rite whom God is calling to become a diocesan priest, there is ordinarily only one particular state in life: holy orders and a life of cheerful celibacy.

The Vocational Pre-Determination by God

When I was a vocation director, I would visit the Catholic schools in my diocese to teach the children about vocations. I explained to them that before God had even created the world, he knew them and he loved them.

> He already knew your name, he knew every thought you would ever think, he knew how many hairs were on your head, he knew your sins, he knew your good deeds, and he even saw the moment of your death and your entrance into heaven. And God had already decided your vocation before he had even made the world! Or at least, he had already planned to which vocation you would be called. When it finally became time for you to be born, God created your soul to go inside your tiny body, and it was created specifically for that pre-determined vocation.

I call this concept the vocational pre-determination by God, or vocational pre-destination. If God is calling you to marriage, then he prepared your soul and gave you the gifts of body and soul to live out the vocation of marriage. If God is calling you to priesthood, then your soul and body were made with that vocation in mind. This will be an important hint for you as you discern. Look at the gifts God has given to you and where those gifts are best used to build up the Kingdom.

The Ordinary Vocation: Holy Marriage

The majority of men, statistically speaking, are called to the "ordinary" vocation of marriage. I call it "ordinary" not because it is inferior to other vocations, but because it is the most common vocation. In God's plan for the propagation of our race and the building up of the Church, most men (and obviously most women as well) are called to marriage. However, despite the fact that marriage is the most common vocation, *it must be discerned and not just assumed.*

I find it fascinating that the two "vocation" sacraments, marriage and priesthood, are so unique among the seven sacraments for a variety of reasons. How is marriage unique?

~ Marriage is the only sacrament that involves two souls, the soul of a man and the soul of a woman. These two souls are joined together in the sacrament by Jesus Christ in the marriage bond.

~ Marriage is the only sacrament that does not come through the ministry of a priest. The bride and groom give this sacrament to one another (through Christ) when they express their valid, matrimonial consent. The priest is present only as the official witness of the Church.

~ Marriage is an enduring sacrament, but only until the death of one of the spouses. The death of either spouse breaks the marriage bond and ends the sacrament of marriage.

Consider this story told by Pope John Paul II.

Last century there was a talented professor in France named Frederick Ozanam. He taught at the Sorbonne, and he was eloquent and capable. Frederick Ozanam was the founder of the Conference of Charity, which later became the St. Vincent de Paul Society, the Catholic organization which cares for the poor. His friend was the famous writer, Lacordaire, who said: "He is so gifted. He is so good. He will become a priest. He will become a great bishop, this fellow!" No. Frederick Ozanam met a nice girl and they got married. Lacordaire was disappointed and he said, "Poor Ozanam! He too has fallen into the trap of marriage!" Two years later, Lacordaire came to Rome, and he was received by Pope Pius IX. The Holy Father said to Lacordaire: "Come, come, Father. I have always heard that Jesus established seven sacraments. Now you come along and change everything. You tell me that he established six sacraments and a trap! No, Father, marriage is not a trap, it is a great sacrament."[12]

Marriage is indeed a great sacrament. We are told in scripture that the love of a husband and wife for each other is a sign of Christ's love for his bride, the Church.

Many young men move instinctively towards marriage as if it is the only possibility. This is a mistake. God is asking that every young man seriously consider and pray about all the possible vocations. Marriage must be prayerfully and carefully discerned over time, like every other vocation. Some men simply reason, "Well, I'm attracted to girls, so I must be called to marriage." Being attracted to females is an indication that a man is normal and healthy, but it does not necessarily indicate a call from God to marriage. In fact, if a man is seriously considering priesthood, his vocation director will want to confirm that he has a normal healthy attraction to marriage and family. If he does not, he cannot really properly discern or choose priesthood. (This is discussed further in chapter 13.)

Marriage is a wonderful vocation and the one to which most men are called by God. But it must be discerned, not just assumed.

An Extraordinary and Unique Vocation: Holy Orders

Since this is a book about discerning diocesan priesthood, I will obviously spend more time describing Holy Orders than the other particular vocations. In the first chapter, I described what priests do. In the second chapter, I described what priests are. Therefore I will treat the vocation of priesthood here only briefly.

The sacrament of Holy Orders, the sacrament by which a man becomes a priest, is an extraordinary vocation. I call it "extraordinary" not because it is better than marriage but because it is less common. Like Marriage, Holy Orders is unique among the seven sacraments for several reasons.

~ Priesthood is a sacrament that endures forever. It does not end with death. It makes a permanent indelible mark on the soul that can never be erased or ended. A priest still has the mark of a priest on his soul when he is in heaven!

~ Holy Orders is the only sacrament that has more than one degree. The three degrees are deacon, priest, and bishop.

~ Jesus established the sacrament of Holy Orders at the Last Supper when he first celebrated the Eucharist. He told his disciples, "Do this in memory of me" (Luke 22:19). And the Apostles in the early Church laid hands on men before sending them out to preach the Gospel. Holy Orders is the sacrament for bringing the sacraments to the world.

~ Priestly ordination is not just an initiation, like joining a club or a fraternity. It is a gift of the Holy Spirit which permits the exercise of a sacred power (*sacra potestas*) which comes from Jesus Christ himself through his Church. A priest has a sacred power to offer the sacrifice of Christ and to forgive sins in the sacraments (CCC #1537-8).

Priesthood is not just being a preacher and a minister, though priests certainly do preach and minister to God's people. It is the administering of a sacred power!

Diocesan Priest

A diocesan priest is a man who has been ordained *for a particular diocese*. In most circumstances, he is assigned to work in a parish within that diocese, taking care of God's people. This is the great work to which a diocesan priest expends his life. Exceptions to this will be covered in a later chapter entitled "Special Assignments for Diocesan Priests," but most diocesan priests live and work in parishes.

As mentioned, Holy Marriage and Holy Orders are the only two particular vocations that are also sacraments, giving them special importance. The Catechism of the Catholic Church mentions that these are the only two sacraments specifically designed to help others attain heaven (CCC #1534). The other five sacraments are specifically for the good of the person receiving them. Priesthood is about serving others and getting them to heaven! Jesus imparts this sacred power to a priest *for the sake of others*. This is important to know for your discernment.

Religious Life

The call to religious life is another extraordinary vocation. It is not a sacrament of the Church but it is a very heroic, penitential, sacrificial life of service to build up the Kingdom of God. To be theologically precise, it is a higher vocation than priesthood or marriage. It is not a "better" vocation, because what is best for each person is precisely the God pre-determined vocation for that individual. But religious life is a more perfect life in the sense that it is directed to the Evangelical Counsels of poverty, chastity and obedience, which more perfectly reflects the eternal destiny of every person in Heaven. This life was lived, described, and recommended by Jesus Christ himself, so the Church calls this the most perfect life. Living out these radical vows is not for everyone, but it is an extraordinary vocation.

> The religious state is thus one way of experiencing a "more intimate" consecration… In the consecrated life, Christ's faithful, moved by the Holy Spirit, propose to follow Christ more nearly, to give themselves to God who is loved above all and, pursuing the perfection of charity in the service of the Kingdom, to signify and proclaim in the Church the glory of the world to come.
>
> CCC # 916

Men called to the consecrated religious life are called brothers. Besides embracing the three evangelical counsels of poverty, chastity, and obedience, they are called to live in a community with other men, praying, working, sacrificing, and serving together for a specific apostolate of the Church. Men called to religious life might join religious orders such as the Jesuits, the Franciscans, the Dominicans and the Benedictines. There are literally hundreds of different religious congregations in the Church and they each have their own specific charism and ways of living out religious life. Historically, they have each had their own distinctive habit or way of dress, enabling them to be easily recognized as religious brothers of a particular order, though this is not as common today. They have taken formal, public vows recognized by the Church to consecrate their entire lives to Christ in this way. Obviously, women can be called to the religious life also and there are many different religious communities of women in the Church.

Some religious brothers go on to be ordained priests, but they are not diocesan priests. A diocesan priest is ordained for a certain diocese and usually spends his entire life serving in the various parishes of that diocese. Sometimes Catholics who grew up being cared for by religious priests will ask a diocesan priest, "Father, what order do you belong to?" Diocesan priests will often smile and reply, "The Order of Melchizedek," or "The Order of St. Peter." It is a humorous way of saying, "I'm the original kind of priest — a diocesan priest."

Generous Single Life in Christ

It is the plan of God that some men serve the Church by remaining single, dedicated lay Catholics who generously serve in some particular area of need. In my experience, this is one of the most difficult and frustrating vocations to discern. The Catechism mentions that people find themselves in this vocation, though it might not have been their preference.

We must also remember the great number of single persons who, because of the particular circumstances in which they have to live — often not of their choosing — are especially close to Jesus' heart and therefore deserve the special affection and active solicitude of the Church, especially of Pastors.

CCC #1658

Why is this vocation so difficult to discern? I think there are several reasons. A true vocation must involve some type of permanent commitment. You see this in all the other vocations. In marriage, for example, the church offers a sacrament that joins the souls of a man and woman together in the marriage bond for life. In priesthood, the sacrament confers an indelible mark on a man's soul, a mark which configures him permanently to Jesus Christ. In religious life, a man or woman makes perpetual public vows of the three evangelical counsels.

The permanent commitment in each of these three vocations serves to cement the person in a state in life, especially when life becomes difficult. Firmly anchored in their vocations, God helps individuals to grow in holiness and to help get others to heaven. As a woman once said to me, "Father, I love my husband and I consider him and my children my greatest blessings. But they are also my greatest crosses!" Cemented into her vocation of marriage, this woman was describing the challenges of family life that were helping her to grow in personal holiness, even though the sacrament of marriage is primarily ordered to the salvation of the husband and children. But what about a person who is called to the generous single life in Christ? The aspect of permanent commitment is more nebulous.

For the vocations of marriage, priesthood and religious life, the Church offers specific programs of preparation. We offer pre-Cana courses for marriage, seminary for priesthood, and novitiate for religious life. The Church has a developed theology of marriage, priesthood and religious life and offers specific directives as to how these vocations should be lived according to the design of God. But the Church does not offer a training program for the generous single state in life and there is no developed theology. For faithful men and women who are striving to live the generous single life, there is an obvious dearth of information and support. How exactly are they supposed to live? What particular work should they do for the Church? In my experience, single people can become discouraged by this lack of clear direction and support. Usually, these are things that a single person must work out in prayer, experimentation, and spiritual direction. These are all reasons why this vocation is so difficult and frustrating at times.

Nonetheless, it seems clear that a single person, in virtue of the very freedom mentioned above (the lack of being cemented), is in a position to serve the Church in ways that people in the other vocations are not. Therein lies one of the most important reasons, in my opinion, why God calls some people to be single. As a vocation director, whenever I would speak of single life at a parish, it never failed that some man or woman would come up after Mass and say, "Father, thank you for saying that. I've never been married, and people ask me, 'Why? What's the matter with you?' But Father, I do not feel called to marriage or any of the other vocations. My work is to serve the Church in the generous single state." The single vocation is a call from God, a state in life, however one might arrive there. While perhaps not as well-defined as other vocations, it is a legitimate call from God to live one's life and to generously serve the Church in a certain way.

I know of a single man who greatly desired priesthood in his youth and pursued it. Without going into the details, it was not to be. Once that became clear, he prayed and worked very hard to prepare himself for Holy Marriage. He tried very hard to find the right woman. But that also, through a long, painful process of trial and error, was not to be. He went through a period of frustration with God and anger toward the Church. He was such a good man and desperately desired to serve generously. He asked me again and again, "Why won't God show me my vocation? I want to do his will." I counseled this man to use the process of elimination. God clearly was showing him his vocation by excluding the others. Now he needed to work and pray to find the specific, generous work within single life to which God was calling him. And he did find it, in service to the very poor. Today, he is clearly fulfilling all the requirements of a vocation. He is serving others in a way that I believe was pre-determined by God, building up the Kingdom, helping others go to heaven, and growing in holiness in the process! And he has had *to cement himself* into this work, finally realizing that this is where God wants him. He is flourishing in his correct particular vocation.

Please understand that living one's single life selfishly is not a vocation. We all know people who do not marry or do anything requiring a permanent commitment, not because of a call to generous single life, but because of their desire *to always do what they want, when they want, and how they want.* There is a prevalent trend (especially in the U.S.) for young people to grow up keeping all of their options open, making money and spending it on themselves. Being a selfish, self-centered bachelor is not the same as living a generous single life for Christ. It will bring a person great sadness and lead to despair.

"God has created me to do some special service;
God has committed some work to me
which has not been committed to another.
I HAVE A MISSION."[13]

John Henry Newman

Vocation versus Occupation

You will have noticed that professions such as teacher, missionary, nurse, artist, builder, writer, or musician were not mentioned in the above discussion of one's secondary or particular vocation. I call these *occupations* rather than vocations. I know that God has called and given gifts to many people so they can excel in certain fields, professions or occupations. Obviously, some people have tremendous gifts as musicians, for example, and they use those gifts to glorify God. But these musically talented individuals are still first and foremost called to one of the four states in life.

Sometimes people who are wrestling with their vocation will say to me, "But Father, look at me. I'm successful. I make a lot of money. I contribute to society. I am active in my parish." St. Augustine said, *"Bene curret, sed extra viam,"* which means, "He runs well, but off the road."[14] A man is not successful in the true meaning of the word if he is not doing the will of God by living out his respective vocation.

The Pyramid Rule

As a general rule, a man must first discern his particular or secondary vocation (state in life) before he can discern his occupation. Remember, discernment is like a pyramid. One starts at the bottom with the universal call to holiness, then goes on to discern one's state in life. And finally, the Lord shows him how to serve specifically within that particular state in life.

When we discuss vocation, the children in my classes will sometimes say something like, "Father, I am called to be a veterinarian!" What they mean is that they love animals and they are attracted to the idea of helping them. But I draw a pyramid on the board and say, "You may be called to become a veterinarian, but if you try to discern your occupation before your vocation, you can run into problems."

This pyramid schema is helpful to keep in mind while discerning one's vocation, yet we all know that most college students are required to declare a field or occupation (their major) early in their college career, even though they might not have discovered their particular vocation yet.

In the case of a man called to become a diocesan priest, vocation determines occupation. The vast majority of diocesan priests

50

work in parishes and provide pastoral care for the people. That is the occupation of a parish priest. So if that man felt very attracted also to be a doctor, the revelation of his state in life (priesthood) tells him that God does not want him to be a doctor, despite his attraction. Becoming a doctor and becoming a priest are not at the same level of discernment. The vocations of marriage and priesthood are at the same level.

The pyramid rule, therefore, says that a person must first discern his secondary vocation before he can discern his occupation. If God calls a man to become a diocesan priest, that revelation will usually require the man to sacrifice doing something else with his life that he greatly desires to do, such as becoming a journalist or engineer.

Every vocation is a mystery and sometimes the general pyramid rule does not apply. I know a woman who grew up prayerfully discerning her vocation. She felt called to marriage and went to college hoping to find her husband. But she was not able to find the right man for marriage, in spite of her prayers and efforts. College was moving along and she had to declare her major. She began to study to become a teacher, something for which she had always felt an attraction and for which she had obvious gifts. After graduation, still hoping to get married, she found a job teaching in a Catholic school. There was an order of teaching sisters there and she found that she was very attracted to them—to their work, their joyfulness, their sisterhood with one another, and to their holiness. Within a few years, this woman had made the decision to join this religious order of teaching sisters. In this case, the general rule that a person must first discern their particular vocation before they discern occupation did not apply. She had to discern her occupation first, which led to her particular vocation.

"If you learn everything except Christ, you learn nothing; if you learn nothing except Christ, you learn everything."[15]

St. Bonaventure

Does It Really Matter to God if I Get Married or Become a Priest?

Yes. It does.

As a young man, before I became a priest, I was once attending Mass in another city. I was very surprised (and happy) when the priest began to give a homily about vocations. He started out by saying how happy he was to be a priest and he said several other edifying things about the life of priesthood and the other vocations. Then he made this statement: "I don't think God cares which vocation we choose. I think God loves us and says to us, 'You choose. You will please me if you decide to get married, be a sister or brother, or become a priest. It doesn't matter to me. I will still love you.'" I wanted to stand up in the church and yell, "No! Don't tell these people that. That's not true!"

It is certainly true that God loves us infinitely and will continue to love us no matter which vocation we choose. But it is false that the vocation upon which we ultimately decide does not matter to God. He has made us for a specific vocation (state in life) and it matters very much how we respond to that call. If we say no to that call, God will not abandon us or stop loving us. In his loving-kindness, he will go to Plan B, or even Plan C for those of us who are especially hard-headed. But it is an error to think that Plan B or Plan C is just as good as Plan A! To use a common analogy, a round peg is created for a round hole. If one tries to force a square peg into a round hole, one experiences difficulties.

St. Ignatius Loyola writes that every man should try to enter discernment with *a holy indifference*. He should not go to prayer, desperately trying to convince God that he really should get married! Many people try to discern in this way. This is why St. Augustine once said that, "the pious soul prays not to inform God but to be conformed to his will."[16]

Once again, every vocation is a mystery. As already mentioned, there are some circumstances in which a man will be called to both priesthood and marriage, as in the case of a married Eastern Rite Catholic priest. I know of several men who have gone on to become priests after the deaths of their wives. But for most men who are discerning priesthood in the Latin Rite, God is calling to one or the other. And it matters to God which one the man chooses!

An Alternative Discernment Paradigm

Thus far in this chapter, I have described a paradigm that is commonly used by vocation directors to teach others about the different levels of vocation: primary vocation, secondary vocation, and then occupation. It is a paradigm that has helped many people to discern God's will. The Second Vatican Council, however, takes a slightly different approach which I believe can be very helpful to some men who are discerning. I will describe it in the simplest of terms.

The Council Fathers go to great lengths to emphasize that holiness is the essential, primordial vocation of every person. This baptismal vocation to become like Jesus is far more important than any of the secondary or particular vocations, because holiness will be our state for all eternity in heaven. No one goes to heaven unless and until they are holy. The holiness of heaven is characterized by, first and foremost, charity, but also by the Evangelical Counsels of poverty, chastity and obedience. No one in heaven cares about any worldly thing; everyone in heaven is pure in body and soul; and everyone in heaven is humbly obedient to the living God.

Once this is established, the Council Fathers begin to speak of the particular vocations. They outline three possibilities for a Catholic man, moving from the most perfect life to the least perfect life. You will notice there are two options under the lay vocation:

~ Consecrated religious life

~ Priesthood

~ Lay vocation

    - Marriage

    - Single life

Because the consecrated religious life involves the radical commitment to live the Evangelical Counsels of poverty, chastity and obedience, as we will all do in heaven, it is the most perfect life here on earth. A man who is called to marriage should not get upset about this characterization, as if he has been called to something lesser. The absolute best vocation for every person is precisely God's will for that person. Still, to be theologically precise, the consecrated religious life is the most perfect. The vocation of priesthood is not as perfect as religious life, in this sense, because priests (at least diocesan priests) do not vow the Evangelical Counsels. Priests do make a promise of celibacy for the sake of the Kingdom and they promise obedience to their bishop and prayer for God's people.

If a person is not called to religious life or to priesthood, then he is called to do the very important work of evangelizing the world from within the world, as a layman. This important work of the laity is greatly stressed by the Vatican Council Fathers and should not be dismissed lightly. Bringing Christ to the world is not just the duty of priests and nuns. The largest battalion in the Army of Christ is the laity! If called to evangelize the world as a lay person, then a man must discern if he is called to marriage or to generous single life.

With this schema in mind, a man should discern his vocation using the process of elimination from the most perfect to the least perfect. He should first discern if he is called to the most perfect life in the Church, consecrated religious life. One he has eliminated that possibility in his discernment, he should next consider priesthood. If that is not his call either, then he knows he is called to the lay state and he must discern between marriage and single life. Finally, whether married or single, he must discern how God is calling him practically to evangelize the world within his state in life.

"You know how to make God laugh? Tell him your plans."

Author Unknown

Who Will You Bring With You Into Heaven?

I once heard a priest tell his vocation story.

I grew up in a very close, devout Catholic family with loving parents and we prayed together as a family every day. I attended a Catholic school with wonderful teaching Sisters and everything in my life revolved around the Church. I lived in a very Catholic culture. I was the number one altar server, the star student, and a leader in my class. Because of this, and the fact that I loved being around the parish, serving and helping out the priests, everyone would say the same thing, "You will be a priest when you grow up. Won't you?" I heard this constantly from the other kids in my class, from the sisters who taught me, and from the two assistant priests, who were always visiting the classes and interacting with me around the church. But I never heard it from the pastor, which I appreciated. I got tired of people urging the priesthood on me, because I did not especially want to become a priest. I always wondered why the pastor, an elderly Monsignor, never asked me about priesthood as everyone else did, though he was always very kind to the altar servers. One day, as I was coming close to graduation from the parish school, I was assigned to serve the seven o'clock morning Mass and the elderly pastor was the celebrant. Only the two of us were in the sacristy and he vested in silence, mumbling the vesting prayers in Latin and preparing himself for Holy Mass. With just two minutes to go before the Mass began, the Monsignor suddenly turned and said, "John, what will you be doing when you grow up?" I thought to myself, "Oh boy, here it comes. Even from Monsignor." But I replied, "Monsignor, I am still not certain but I am thinking about going into medicine. I would like to become a doctor." And the pastor replied, "Good. Good. And what will you do after that?" I said, "Well, I suppose I will marry and have a family of my own." The priest said, "Good, and what after that?" Not sure exactly where he was going with this line of questioning, I replied, "I guess I will grow old, practicing medicine, and eventually retire. And then I guess I will die and go to heaven." The pastor nodded his head knowingly, thoughtfully, and he was quiet for a few seconds. Then he looked at me earnestly and said, "And who will you bring with you into heaven?" Immediately, he rang the sacristy bell and we walked out to begin the Mass. I thought to myself, "How clever you are, Monsignor. How clever you are." I thought about that comment all during the Mass and many more times during my adolescent and young adult years. "And who will you bring with you into heaven?" It was asking myself that question repeatedly that really turned the tide and convinced me eventually that I should become a priest.

Every vocation is about helping other people reach heaven. I tell this story not to minimize the greatness of the sacrament of marriage, because marriage serves the same purpose! I suppose the young man might have used the same comment made by the pastor to move him towards the vocation of marriage. But the story illustrates the critical point that a vocation is not primarily about self-fulfillment, but about being the instrument of God in saving others.

"What will you do with your life? What are your plans? Have you ever thought of committing your existence totally to Christ? Do you think that there can be anything greater than to bring Jesus to people and people to Jesus?"[17]

Pope John Paul II

Seek and You will Find... and Flourish

The discernment of your correct God-predetermined vocation is the most important decision that you will make in your entire life. It may seem easier or less frightening to make your own plans or to decide your own vocation. But the truth is that the most peaceful place in the world for you is in the perfect will of God. To get there involves a diligent search.

Jesus said, "Ask and it will be given to you; seek and you will find; knock and the door will be opened to you. For everyone who asks, receives; and the one who seeks, finds; and to the one who knocks, the door will be opened" (Matthew 7:7-12).

No one can force you to search for your vocation. It must be your free decision to search, to discover, and to respond. If you choose to search, I promise you that you will find your particular vocation, though it may not be easy. If you choose not to search, you are not likely to find it.

I believe one of the problems in the Church today is that many people are in the wrong vocation. Many people have grown up unaware that they have a vocation, much less that they should be asking God to reveal it to them. And there are many unhappy, unfulfilled, dissatisfied people. As a general rule, *people flourish in their correct vocation!* Flourishing does not just mean they are happy. It means they are steadily growing in holiness, they are fulfilled, and they are becoming the person God wants them to be.

Fr. Brian Bashista, vocation director of the Diocese of Arlington, Virginia, underscores that vocation is less about personal choice and more about discovery.

> A vocation is not so much a choice as it is an invitation and response. A person offers himself or herself to the other. Vocations are always 'other-directed.' They are about love. Love is not so much chosen; it is discovered and then responded to. Even in marriage, a man does not really choose his wife or vice versa. He extends an invitation to her to enter into this vocation and she responds. Every vocation takes two yeses.

As you seek to say yes to God and to discover the vocation in which God wants you to flourish, I recommend this prayer to you. Say it every day, more than once.

> Dear God, I want to want what you want.
> Even if I don't want it right now;
> Even if I am afraid right now,
> I want to want it.
> Help me to want to be what you want me to be. Amen.

Seeking Help from your Vocation Director

The Church realizes that discernment of diocesan priesthood is difficult. For this reason, every bishop appoints a vocation director. Normally it is a priest who is an expert in discernment and can assist men in his diocese through this arduous process. In a word, the vocation director helps you discover and respond appropriately to God's plan regarding your vocation. He is trained to guide a man through the ups and downs of discernment, to help him overcome the fears and to avoid the pitfalls.

Discerning a vocation to diocesan priesthood should never be done alone. Whatever stage of discernment you might be in, I encourage you to go to your diocesan website, find your vocation director, and contact him now. The discernment of your correct God-predetermined vocation is the most important decision you will ever make in your entire life!

"The greatest suffering in the human heart is resistance to the will of God."[18]

St. Catherine of Siena

CHAPTER 4

GOD SAID GO AND I SAID NO

To do anything less than the will of God for your life will bore you!

During the French Revolution beginning in 1789, there was a great persecution of the Catholic Church in France. In 1793, the Reign of Terror began and many priests, nuns, and Catholic lay faithful were murdered because of their allegiance to the Catholic Church. Though they were killed in many different ways, the guillotine became most famous. There was one man who had a horrible hatred for priests and he bragged that he had killed thirty priests with his own hands. His preferred method of execution was to slit the throat. Some years after the Revolution had subsided, this man was old, sick, and dying. His wife, who had remained a practicing Catholic all along in secret, did not want her husband to go to hell, in spite of the terrible things he had done. But he would not hear of discussing religion, much less of repentance. So the wife asked a Catholic priest whom she knew to come. In these post-revolution days, priests still lived in hiding and went about in plain clothes secretly celebrating Mass in the homes of individual Catholics. The plain-clothed priest walked into the man's bedroom and identified himself as a Catholic priest. The old man was lying on his bed, too weak to move, but his face became livid with rage and he screamed, "If I could get up, I would cut your throat!" And the priest calmly replied, "You already did. But God saved me so that I could save you." The priest pushed down his shirt collar to reveal a long scar across his throat, reaching from ear to ear; a scar made by the knife of this very man. The old man was very moved by the magnanimity of this priest. He had tried to kill him. He had slit his throat and left him for dead. Yet now this priest would risk death again to try and save the man's soul from hell. God's grace touched his heart and the old man made his Confession and repented of his sins before he died.

"God saved me so that I could save you." I think there are many priests today who could say these words. There are so many priests who tried to throw away their vocation, to run away from it, either out of fear or selfishness, or both. Archbishop Robert Carlson once remarked at a symposium, "I am constantly amazed at the number of men who are priests who did everything in their power that they would not be." I myself am one of these priests.

The discernment of your vocation is the most important decision you will ever make. It is an art and it must be learned by effort and practice. It is not sufficient just to read about vocations. To discern well, a man must be humble, courageous, and prayerful. He must really desire to know the will of God and he must be willing to work to discover it.

In my experience—in my own life and in helping others—I have found that discernment almost always involves suffering. We should expect this because we are followers of Jesus Christ, who said, "If anyone wishes to come after me, he must deny himself and take up his cross daily and follow me" (Luke 9:23). If you find that discernment is tough and answers don't seem to be forthcoming, know that this is par for the course.

Pope Benedict XVI, speaking to German pilgrims after his papal inauguration, said, "The world offers you comfort. You were not made for comfort. You were made for greatness."[19] We will only appreciate our vocation from God if we have to fight for it, suffer for it, and expend ourselves both to discover it and live it. Our vocation is designed to stretch our hearts and make us great. Because it is not easy, and because it can be scary, many men run from this call for years before they finally realize that they will never be happy outside the will of God for their lives. In fact, to do anything less than the will of God for your life will bore you.

Your Vocation Is an Invitation

What will happen to me if I run away from my vocation?

What are the consequences if I do not accept what God is calling me to do?

What will happen if I pray to know God's will, he tells me that he wants me to become a priest, and then I say "no?"

First of all, will I lose my salvation? Will I go to hell? No. A vocation is a call. It is not a commandment. When a person says no to God by disobeying one of the Ten Commandments, that is called a sin. But a vocation is a request, a petition from God saying, "I love you. I invite you. I am asking you to do this, to help me bring the kingdom of God to fulfillment." Therefore, technically, it is not a sin to say no to your vocation. A person will not lose their salvation, at least on that account alone. If all other things are in order, namely, that a person is a faithful Christian, practicing the teachings of Jesus, and living in a state of grace, then that person still can attain salvation.

Responding to your vocation is a free choice. God will not hunt you down and send you the plagues of Job because you said no to his invitation to become a priest. I have known men who declined God's invitation to priesthood then subsequently wondered if God was punishing them every time something bad happened. But that is not true; God is not vindictive. And there is a difference between the man who clearly knows he is called to be a priest and says no, and the man who has discerned carefully and conscientiously but ends up making an incorrect decision.

Remember that God does not need us. He is omnipotent. He is infinite in power and can build the Kingdom of God without our help. However, because he loves us, he wants us to have the privilege of cooperating with him. God gives us the opportunity as human beings to demonstrate our dignity by graciously saying yes to his call. This is why he invites us to search out, to discover and to embrace our vocation.

Often when I talk in parishes about following one's true vocation, a man will come up to me afterwards and say, "Father, my wife and children are here with me today. When I was a young man, I felt a strong call to be a priest. I know I was called. But the Church was a mess in those days. The ship seemed to be sinking. So I said no. I got married instead. What will happen to me now? What should I do?"

I would always respond, "Be faithful to your wife, love your children, raise them to follow Christ and be faithful Catholics. Be a good, selfless, loving husband and father. Work out your salvation in your chosen state in life, and one day, live forever with Jesus in heaven." What I do not say to this man, only because no good would come from it in that time and place, is that there are consequences of not following one's vocation.

The Consequences of Not Following Your Correct God-Predetermined Vocation

What are these consequences of not following your true vocation? It seems to me that there are at least four, generally speaking.

~ A man will never be as happy and fulfilled in this life if he is living in the wrong God-predetermined vocation.

~ God will not use a man as effectively as his instrument if he is living in the wrong God-predetermined vocation.

~ A man will struggle with some residual sadness of spirit, knowing that God asked him to do something generous and he said no.

~ A man's no to God regarding his vocation can have serious implications on the lives and faith of others.

The First Consequence: Our Own Happiness and Fulfillment

I have seen hundreds of men arrive at seminary to begin their multi-year journey to priesthood. When they arrive, they are understandably a bit nervous, but they are also excited and joyful. They know they are about to begin a process which will end in their ordination as a priest of Jesus Christ! To use a marriage analogy, seminary is like the engagement and ordination is like the wedding. A man who has just gotten engaged is excited; a man who has just gotten married is thrilled.

An extremely high percentage of priests report that they are happy and fulfilled. God made us to be happy and he made us for a specific vocation in which we will achieve the most happiness and fulfillment. If a man says no to his vocation—his God pre-determined state in life—does it not seem logical that this will affect his happiness and fulfillment?

It can be said this way: a man has an ideal, true vocation, the one God intended from the beginning, and he has the vocation in which he ends up. The closer these two vocations are together, the happier he will be. The farther apart they are, the less happy he will be.

The Second Consequence: Our Usefulness to God

A hammer works best when it is used as a hammer. Similarly, God will use you most effectively as his instrument—to get other people to heaven and to give him glory—in your proper vocation. Remember that God is omnipotent. He can do anything with anyone, anytime, under any circumstances. He does not need us. But God *chooses* to use people powerfully who have generously prayed for, accepted, and endeavored to live out their correct vocation. God cannot (in the sense that he usually will not) use you as effectively as his instrument if you're in the wrong vocation.

The Third Consequence: Sadness of Spirit

I remember feeling terrible when my mother or father would say to me, "I'm very disappointed in you." I always preferred a spanking to that verbal punishment. I disliked that someone very important to me was now disappointed in me.

God is the creator of heaven and earth. He sent his son Jesus to die for us. He has been so generous to us. And now he asks us to be generous with him. If a man says no to his call, as he is free to do, he still must live with himself, and may experience a residual sadness of spirit. Remorse for not being generous to people who love us is a heavy enough cross. This is most true with God because he loves us most and we love him most.

We have all made many mistakes in our lives. We cannot change any of them. The past is the past. But what about the future? Starting now, we can be generous to God in everything he asks. It is an invitation, but however we choose to respond affects our spirit.

"Each one of us has some kind of vocation. We are all called by God to share in his life and in his Kingdom. Each one of us is called to a special place in the Kingdom. If we find that place we will be happy. If we do not find it, we can never be completely happy. For each one of us, there is only one thing necessary: to fulfill our own destiny, according to God's will, to be what God wants us to be."[20]

Thomas Merton

The Fourth Consequence: Our Response Can Have Serious Effects on the Lives and Faith of Others.

There is no question that our faith has been handed down to us by other people. Most of us first learned about Jesus from our parents, grandparents, teachers, friends, and priests. Usually, it was people in their correct vocations who had the most powerful spiritual influence on our lives. Think of the people who influenced your faith development. Where would you be right now, if those people had said no to their vocation? Would you be considering priesthood? Would you even be a practicing Catholic? The fact is that our faith-lives are powerfully intertwined in the faith-lives and decisions of others.

Is it possible that some soul or souls might not go to heaven if a person says no to his vocation? This is not a question designed to create a guilt trip. God is infinitely merciful and he gives every person every opportunity to repent, to choose to love, and to go to heaven. Still, the destiny of other souls could depend on one person saying yes. The title of this book is *To Save a Thousand Souls*. Though only God can save, he uses his priests powerfully in this endeavor. If a man is called to priesthood, his answer to God will seriously affect the lives of many others.

"Strange is our situation here on earth. Each of us comes for a short visit, not knowing why, yet sometimes seeming to a divine purpose. From the standpoint of daily life, however, there is one thing we know. That we are here for the sake of others… For the countless unknown souls with whose fate we are connected… Many times a day, I realize how much my own outer and inner life is built upon the labors of people, both living and dead, and how earnestly I must exert myself in order to give in return as much as I have received."[21]

Albert Einstein

Consider the Incarnation. The angel Gabriel visited the Blessed Virgin Mary and asked her if she would accept her vocation—to conceive and bear a Son of the Holy Spirit. Her vocation was marriage and motherhood. Mary was invited to respond to her vocation. She was free to say yes or no. It is true that she had been chosen from all eternity for this vocation, but so have you—for your vocation. It is true that she was given some wonderful gifts which would enable her to live out her vocation, but so have you—for your vocation.

Theologians sometimes ask the question: what if the Blessed Virgin had said no to the Angel Gabriel? Would this mean that the human race would be lost without a Savior, the whole world going down into hell? It is a terrible thing to even ponder. Some people reason that God would have sent the angel to another woman. Perhaps he would have. Others say that since God loves us so much, he would have found another way to save us. The truth is that we just don't know what God would have done had the Blessed Mother refused her vocation. She said yes, and for that, we are all most grateful.

God often chooses to save his people through the collective free choices of other people. He did this through Mary. She said her "Fiat" and Our Savior came to earth. God is still trying to do this through his people, and I think this is especially true of his priests.

Because your parish priest said yes, Jesus comes to you every day in the Holy Eucharist and in the Word. If he were not saying Mass and preaching to hundreds or thousands of people on every weekend, then who would be? Some people reason that since God loves us so much, he would raise up somebody else to be a priest. Perhaps God *is* trying to raise up somebody else; perhaps it is *you*.

God, in his infinite goodness and generosity, always respects our freedom. He will not move without our freely given yes. A vocation is a free choice. But there are consequences when a person says no.

We Are Free, But Sometimes God Exerts Pressure

One of my favorite vocation stories from Scripture is the story of Jonah.

This is the word of the Lord that came to Jonah, son of Amitai. Set out for the great city of Ninevah, and preach against it; their wickedness has come up before me. But Jonah made ready to flee to Tarshish, away from the Lord.

68

He went down to Joppa, found a ship going to Tarshish, paid the fare, and went aboard.

Jonah 1:1-3

God gave Jonah his vocation. He was a prophet called to go to Ninevah to prophesy, to warn the people there that they must repent or be destroyed. But Jonah rejected his vocation, probably out of fear. Then he tried to run away.

The Lord, however, hurled a violent wind upon the sea, and in the furious tempest that arose the ship was on the point of breaking up. Now the men were seized with great fear and said to him, "How could you do such a thing?" They knew that he was fleeing from the Lord, because he had told them. "What shall we do with you," they asked, "that the sea may quiet down for us?" For the sea was growing more and more turbulent. Jonah said to them, "Pick me up and throw me into the sea, that it may quiet down for you; since I know it is because of me that this violent storm has come upon you."

1:4,10-12

It does not behoove us to run away from God or from our vocations. Already we can see in this story from scripture that doing so not only endangers us, but also endangers others.

Then they took Jonah and threw him into the sea, and the sea's raging abated. But the Lord sent a large fish, that swallowed Jonah; and he remained in the belly of the fish three days and three nights. From the belly of the fish, Jonah prayed."

1:15, 2:1-2

From the belly of the fish, Jonah prayed! That line from scripture always makes me laugh. I am sure he prayed very intently! I think I would be praying very hard if I were in the belly of a fish for three days and three nights. I think I would be praying about why God wanted to send me on this mission and why

69

it was so important that he would take drastic measures, such that I would end up in the belly of a fish. Yes, I am sure that Jonah prayed!

> Then the Lord commanded the fish to spew Jonah upon the shore. The word of the Lord came to Jonah a second time: "Set out for the great city of Ninevah, and announce to it the message that I will tell you." So Jonah made ready and went to Ninevah, according to the Lord's bidding.
>
> 2:11-3:3

What a fascinating vocation story: "Jonah made ready and went to Ninevah, according to the Lord's bidding." After the fish finally spewed Jonah out onto the beach, God gave him his vocation again. Jonah was still afraid, yet he realized now that this was very important. He was still free to say no, but the Lord had taught him something in the belly of the fish. Perhaps Jonah reasoned, "If God can keep me alive and safe three days and three nights in a fish, he can take care of me in that wicked city of Ninevah."

> Jonah began his journey through the city, and had gone but a single day's walk announcing, "Forty days more and Ninevah shall be destroyed," when the people of Ninevah believed God; they proclaimed a fast and all of them, great and small, put on sackcloth.
>
> 3:4-5

God did not destroy the people of Ninevah because he loved them. And because his prophet Jonah finally said yes to his vocation and obeyed the Lord, 120,000 people were saved (c.f. Jonah 4:11). No wonder God exerted a little more pressure.

God saves thousands of people through the ministry of the average diocesan priest. The purpose of a priest is to bring people to Jesus and Jesus to people. Priesthood is a powerful vocation which can influence so many souls towards God.

Another great example from Scripture is the conversion of St. Paul in Acts 9:3: "On his journey, as he was nearing Damascus, a light from the sky suddenly flashed around him. He fell to the ground and heard a voice saying to him, 'Saul, Saul, why are you persecuting me?'" When he stood up to go, he realized that he was blind. I find it fascinating that St. Paul, like Jonah, spent three days and three nights in darkness, praying for God's will, before the scales over his eyes were removed. Then he received his vocation to go and preach Jesus Christ to the Gentiles. St. Paul was called to be a priest. He was a bishop. It is not at all an exaggeration to say that hundreds of millions of people have been influenced towards Christ by St. Paul the Apostle. His epistles make up one third of the New Testament! The Church calls him "the apostle," as if there were no other. Hundreds of millions of souls were at stake—no wonder God exerted a little more pressure.

But are you not free to say yes or no? Yes, you are free. But if you are called to be a priest, don't be surprised when God exerts a little more pressure. I am not saying you will be swallowed by a fish or knocked down and blinded like St. Paul. But then again, I don't really know what God is going to do. He is God. He knows best.

"Run if you want. But God is going to get you if he wants you." I said these words to a young high school man many years ago when I was vocation director. I do not remember saying it, but he never forgot it and he reminded me of it later, after he was ordained a priest. He freely answered God's call. This is a great mystery I have seen many times. When you are a priest, you will say, "I was really free. I chose this vocation freely. But God did exert a little more pressure—and I am glad he did."

"You have seduced me Lord and I let myself be seduced."

Jeremiah 20:7

Inability to Make a Permanent Commitment

I once heard a vocation director giving a wonderful homily on vocations at a college retreat. He said jokingly that he had decided to join a women's support group. He explained that at the meetings, the women complain to one another, "The problem with men is that they just can't make a permanent commitment." The vocation director shook his head and said, "I know. I know." It was a humorous way of expressing his frustration with grown men in this society who seem unable to make a commitment. He had obviously been working with some of these men.

A man in his late thirties was discerning priesthood in a certain diocese. The man had been engaged to be married twice, but both times, the man (not the woman) had broken off the engagement in the months closely preceding the wedding. His pastor suggested that maybe the reason he was not peaceful about marriage was because he was called to priesthood. So he discerned with his vocation director. This man eventually filled out an application to join the diocese and to go to the seminary, but then backed out two months before he was to have begun. The vocation director was wondering if this man, who seemed to be an excellent candidate for priesthood in many ways, would ever be able to peacefully make a permanent commitment. Of course, going to the seminary is not a permanent commitment, but he was too afraid to take even this first step. A definite pattern suggested that this man had some emotional or psychological obstacle to making a permanent commitment.

Resistance to commitment is a common condition in our present culture. The United States today could be called the Land of Perpetual Adolescence. People don't want to grow up. Young adults have grown up in a culture that preaches, "Keep all your options open. Don't commit to anything or anyone. After all, something or someone better might come along." The voice of the world is screaming that making lots of money, having lots of toys, and having lots of free time is the good life. The voice says, "Don't give up your freedom." But these are lies. The people who live these supposedly unfettered lives are usually quite discontent.

True freedom comes from sacrificing our own wants and desires to reach a greater good. Sometimes this means you cannot have everything you want. And there are some places you cannot go. But God made us for happiness and for greatness. And our happiness and greatness consist in discovering the plan of God for our life and then committing ourselves to this greater good, despite giving up some things.

Moreover, every vocation entails a certain level of permanence. If you are ordained a priest, your soul will be changed for all eternity; you will be committed to a certain life and mission, under obedience to your bishop. If you are called to holy marriage, then you will marry one woman and be faithful to her until one of you dies. In both marriage and priesthood, permanent commitment is an essential component.

The man in the above illustration may have had understandable reasons for his inability to commit. If he grew up in a broken and dysfunctional family, he may never have witnessed a happy, committed marriage. Perhaps his parents were divorced and went through many other unsuccessful relationships. Perhaps the priest at his parish abandoned the priesthood. Perhaps his siblings and friends got married and divorced. His experience is that permanent commitment is not possible.

I would recommend that this man spend some time with people who have been successful and happy in living out their vocations. He needs to see vocations well-lived in order to be convinced of the possibility of permanence. He also needs to address the problem in spiritual direction and in prayer. If the problem is especially acute, the man may need a few sessions with a good Catholic psychologist. In the end, the inability to commit is a serious problem; it is a major obstacle to discerning his vocation. He would do well to address the problem head-on. If he does not, he risks living a life of indecision and sadness.

"The Lord has a plan for each of us; he calls each one of us by name. Our task is to learn how to listen, to perceive his call, to be courageous and faithful in following him and, when all is said and done, to be found trustworthy servants who have used well the gifts given us."[22]

Pope Benedict XVI

Are There Any Saints in Plan B?

I will often say to our seminarians here at the Mount, "I would rather you be a saint than a priest, if you cannot be both." This is meant as a simple reminder that holiness is the most important vocation of all. If a man comes to seminary and discerns he is not called to priesthood, he will be more holy from the experience. I remember Fr. Benedict Groeschel once saying to a group of vocation directors on a retreat, "The heroes in the church are not the clergy. The clergy are the janitors of the Church. The heroes in the Church are the saints."

If a man is called to be a priest but rejects his vocation (which is Plan A), deciding instead to get married, God does not write him off as a second class citizen! I have described in this chapter some negative consequences of not following Plan A, and I believe that those are generally true. Nonetheless, God never gives up on anyone. The man in this situation should not live his life thinking that he has blown it forever, that he will have to struggle through life with great unhappiness, hoping to squeeze into heaven at the end.

God never stops calling anyone to holiness, no matter what decisions he has made in the past. Yes, it is possible to become a saint in Plan B. Remember that God can do anything with anyone at anytime! God very much wants you to choose Plan A. He wants you to choose the vocation for which he predestined you. But if you do not, he still loves you infinitely and he still wants you to become the saint that you are called to be. If you ask for his grace, it will not be lacking. A man living Plan B is not damaged goods, but his sanctity will require some serious grace and effort.

While there are definitely negative consequences to saying no to your vocation, I am convinced that there are saints in heaven who became saints in Plan B. God never writes off anyone!

CHAPTER 5

SIGNS OF A VOCATION TO PRIESTHOOD AND CHARACTERISTICS OF A GOOD CANDIDATE

God does not always call the best to be his priests, but he does expect the best of those he calls.

God can call any man he chooses to become a priest, anytime he chooses, and under any circumstances he chooses.

And God does not always call the best to be his priests. As in the biblical story of Gideon (Judges 7), sometimes God calls fewer men, or even less talented men, so that when they accomplish great things, people know that the glory goes to God. *God does not always call the best to be his priests, but he does expect the best of those he calls.*

Sometimes you may be surprised by whom God calls, especially if he calls you. You may think, "God, you know me. You know what a sinner I am. You know my weaknesses. You don't really want *me* to be a priest; there are other men who are much holier than me. Why don't you call them?" But of course God does not need advice about his choices. In his divine wisdom, he calls those whom he wants.

If God does call you, he has the power to qualify you for the work of a priest, even if you may think that you are not qualified now. God will never send you where his grace cannot sustain you. In other words, God does not call a man to a certain vocation without giving him the wherewithal to live and thrive in that vocation. God wants priests to live happily, to flourish, and to help others get to heaven, even as he himself works out his own salvation. This means that to be a good priest, a man should have certain minimal characteristics. These are God-given qualities or gifts that are normally nurtured by a good Christian upbringing, but often need to be developed through grace and hard work.

This chapter will identify twenty signs that are either indications of a possible vocation to priesthood or characteristics of a good priest. While I have listed the qualities which I believe are most important, this is not an exhaustive list. There are priests with many good qualities not specified here. However, the absence of a large number of these twenty characteristics may call into question whether a particular man is suited for priesthood.

Let me make an important point. As you examine yourself regarding these indicators, do not exclude yourself from priesthood too quickly. Most candidates for priesthood lack one or more of these qualities, at least initially. You should always get the opinion and recommendation of your vocation director and bishop. In the end, it is your diocesan bishop, exercising a special charism from the Holy Spirit, who will assess whether you have the requisite qualities to become a priest.

Never discern alone! Always discern diocesan priesthood with the help of a good spiritual director, your vocation director, and your bishop.

---

1. A good candidate for diocesan priesthood should know and love Jesus Christ and have a thirst to bring Jesus and his teachings to the world.

A man who wants to become a priest thinks about Jesus frequently and finds himself very attracted to the Lord and to his Kingdom. He is pained by his own sins and the sins of the world because he realizes that Jesus suffered and died on the cross as a result of sin. This man desires what Christ wants for the world: the fulfillment of the Kingdom of God that brings peace, justice, mercy, and the holiness and salvation of every person. This man wants to evangelize the world!

A good candidate strives to have a real, personal relationship with the Lord Jesus. This means talking with him, listening to him, and trying to become like him. The Lord is the center of his life, or at least he strongly desires the Lord to be the center of his life. A man can't be a priest if he doesn't love Jesus.

2. A good candidate for diocesan priesthood should be a believing, practicing Catholic.

A good candidate attends Mass faithfully every Sunday, and even during the week when possible. He studies the teachings of the Church and believes them wholeheartedly, even the ones he has trouble understanding. He has a deep belief in Jesus' presence in the Holy Eucharist and he loves the Word of God, the Sacred Scriptures. He tries to go to Confession regularly. This man has a loving relationship with the Blessed Virgin Mary and respects and prays for the Holy Father. In general, he is attracted to all things Catholic.

Often a man will struggle to understand certain Church teachings because he has not had the opportunity to study them. But a good candidate has the humble attitude that he still has much to learn—which is precisely the purpose of seminary.

3. A good candidate for diocesan priesthood should be striving to live a life of prayer.

A priest is a man of prayer. He should have a very close, intimate relationship with God. If a priest is to be *alter Christus*, another Christ, he certainly should know Christ well. This man feels drawn to prayer, both private prayer and liturgical prayer, even though the intensity of this desire varies from time to time. He likes to spend time with God and he feels peaceful in prayer, even though he may not understand all the different methods of prayer recommended by the saints.

I remember once asking a devout young candidate about his prayer life and he responded like this.

I think about God all the time. I love him and want to spend time with him. I attend Mass often throughout the

79

week. I make it a point to visit Jesus in the Blessed Sacrament frequently and sometimes I stay a long time because I feel so close to God there. I often pray the rosary and read my Bible. All of this makes me feel different from my friends. But I'm still not sure if I'm praying enough. Father, what do you think?

I assured this man that he was doing quite well! Clearly this young man was being called by God into a deep, intimate friendship, even if he ultimately was not being called to priesthood. Most candidates I encounter are not praying as much as this fellow, though some are. Regardless, a man's prayer life develops tremendously during seminary because he has the guidance of a spiritual director and is influenced by a prayerful seminary community.

4. A good candidate for diocesan priesthood should live and desire a life of service to others.

This life of service is exemplified in the Spiritual and Corporal Works of Mercy.

Corporal Works of Mercy: To feed the hungry, to give drink to the thirsty, to clothe the naked, to shelter the homeless, to visit the sick, to visit those in prison, and to bury the dead.

Spiritual Works of Mercy: To convert the sinner, to instruct the ignorant, to counsel the doubtful, to comfort the sorrowful, to bear wrongs patiently, to forgive injuries, and to pray for the living and the dead.

A man who is united to Jesus Christ in prayer will experience a desire for service that results in concrete charitable acts. Service springs naturally from prayer; it is a result of becoming more like Jesus.

A candidate should be able to tell his vocation director how and when he has been generously serving others. Most of the candidates in our seminaries have spent time serving the poor. Some gave up significant periods of their lives to serve in intensive, full-time youth ministry programs. Others have taken mission trips or worked with Habitat for Humanity. In essence, they sacrificed themselves to bring Jesus Christ to others or to alleviate the suffering of others.

If a man has no history of service at all, this is definitely a growth area for him. If a man sits at home all day and watches television or plays video games, he is probably not ready to begin seminary. A priest is called to serve others, not to be served.

5. A good candidate for diocesan priesthood should have a desire to be a priest.

A man who will eventually become a priest should feel an attraction to do what a priest does and to be who a priest is. This attraction may come and go in different spiritual seasons, and it is stronger at some times than at others. But for a man truly called to priesthood, the feeling just won't go away. He might want it to go away and he may try to make it go away, but the desire will remain and it will keep re-surfacing like a submarine.

There is an important difference between an intellectual appreciation for priesthood and a desire for priesthood. Any faithful Catholic man will have an intellectual appreciation for priesthood. Simply recognizing that a priest functions *in persona Christi Capitis*, (in the person of Christ, the head of the Church) and that he transforms bread and wine into the Body and Blood of Christ should give anyone immense respect and admiration for the priesthood. But admiration is not the same as *desire* to become a priest.

A man who is really called by God sometimes fantasizes about saying Holy Mass, hearing Confessions or preaching. He catches himself thinking about it. One priest said it this way:

> I can remember as a young man in high school sitting in
> Mass. Rather than listening to the homily (as I should have

been doing), I was making up a homily that I would have preached were I the priest. Then I would realize what I was thinking, shake my head, and think, "What am I doing?" I can also remember "playing Mass" as a child with my brothers and sisters. But, as they are fond of reminding me, it was always my idea.

A good candidate feels an attraction for priesthood, though he will often say that he doesn't know why. I remember a young man saying to me:

Father, with all due respect, the life of a priest just doesn't look exciting to me. The only thing I ever see my priest do is say Mass on Sunday. He drives a beat-up car. He's old and not particularly charismatic and certainly not an interesting preacher. It's not that I don't love him and appreciate him being our priest; I do. It just doesn't look very adventurous or exciting. So here is my question: why am I so strongly attracted to priesthood? I just don't understand.

I told that young man that he is attracted to priesthood because Jesus Christ, the Savior of the world, had placed that attraction in his heart. And whether or not he was particularly impressed or inspired by his local pastor, he was being attracted to the priesthood of Jesus, who offered himself on the altar of the cross to take away the sins of the whole world. Now that is impressive and inspiring! The young man agreed.

I am often asked this question: if a man has all the other signs and qualities of a good candidate, but he does not feel a desire to be a priest, should he go to the seminary anyway? Should he give it "the old college try"? Some men reason like this, "Father, I don't want to be a priest. But I know the Church needs priests. I think I have at least the minimal qualities, and I suppose I should do it for the Lord. After all, he died for me."

The Church will survive without that man becoming a priest, I can assure you. I would hesitate to recommend that a man move forward to seminary if he does not have at least some desire to be a priest. The desire may not be especially strong. It may come and go. It may surface at unexpected times, especially after significant "Jesus Experiences" like a powerful retreat, the death of a loved one, or just a sober moment of honestly asking oneself, "What will ever become of me?"

I have witnessed exceptions to the generally sound rule that a candidate should have some level of desire to be a priest. I have seen a few candidates come to seminary out of a desire, "to do my duty," and the desire to be a priest grew in them tremendously after they arrived.

In the early Church, there are precedents of men being ordained who did not actively pursue ordination. The story is told about how God miraculously led St. Ambrose to his vocation. Ambrose was the governor of Milan, and in that capacity was called upon to quell a riot that had broken out over the Arian heresy in the early Church. After he very diplomatically resolved the immediate dispute, a little child in the crowd started calling out, "Ambrosius... episcopus, Ambrosius... episcopus" (Ambrose for bishop). The crowd then insisted that Ambrose agree not only to be a priest but to be their new bishop.[23] And he turned out to be a phenomenal bishop! St. Gregory the Great was also made a priest and bishop by the acclamation of the people.[24]

The Eastern Church has a joke of sorts about this:

Some men are called by God (*theocratie*)
Some men are called by the people (*democratie*)
Some men call themselves (*autocratie*)

Men in the latter group are the dangerous ones! These men may have a desire to become priests, but for the wrong reasons. They need the priesthood more than the priesthood needs them. We don't need autocratic men who call themselves to priesthood. A priest is called by God and by the Church to serve others and he experiences a holy desire for priesthood.

6. A man who is called to become a priest often will have that call validated by other people.

The Holy Spirit often works through the *sensus fidelium* in the people of God, who can often sense a vocation to priesthood in a young man. I am reminded of the story told about Michelangelo during the carving of his marble masterpiece, *David*. A young boy would come every day and watch him work. The carving of this magnificent work of art took a long time and the young spectator persevered. When it was finished, Michelangelo turned to the boy and asked, "What do you think?" The boy just shook his head and said, "I have only one question. How did you know that guy was in there?"

Many seminarians report that people frequently told them, "You really should be a priest. I can see it in you." Or perhaps people would ask, "Have you ever thought of becoming a priest? I think you would make a good one." Remarks of this kind are strong indications, especially when they come from different people under different circumstances, completely unsolicited.

In every parish there is a wonderful group of people whom I call "the holy women of Jerusalem." They are the sweet elderly ladies who are present for daily Mass, for Holy Hour, for novenas, and for every funeral. These saintly people are strong intercessors and every parish is blessed to have them. They are often the first to recognize a priest's heart in a young man and mention it to him.

One's peers can offer insight, too. Seminarians often tell me that, during their high school or college years, they were the designated "counselor" among their friends. Their friends came to them when they wanted to discuss a problem. These men would just listen and try to give some good practical advice, always sprinkling in a little faith. They say, "Father, I don't know why they came to me. I guess because I was a little more mature than the rest and a little more religious?" If people feel safe confiding in a person, it is an indication of trustworthiness. They can see goodness and kindness. They can see a priest's heart.

I remember one seminarian telling me the story about the night he was set up on a date during his college years. He liked the girl very much and was quite hopeful that she might be a potential girlfriend and even a future wife. During dinner, the conversation turned to religion and she told him that she was a Catholic. He was thrilled with this news, thinking even more that this relationship might have some potential, and he began to share just a little bit about his faith. Suddenly, this very beautiful young woman looked at him intently and said, "Are you thinking of becoming a priest? I think you would be a good one." This young man went to pray at the church the next day and said to the Lord, "Leave me alone. I can't even go on a date without someone seeing a priest in me!"

Most young men I have guided through discernment were tired of other people telling them they would make good priests. Whether or not a man ends up becoming a priest, this is still a great compliment. People are saying that they can see Jesus in him, that they can see him functioning *in persona Christi Capitis*.

7. A man who is called to become a priest will find his calling validated in Sacred Scripture.

I can remember one fellow telling me, "Father, I have stopped reading the Bible." I responded, "What? You can't do that. The Bible is God's word. Why did you stop?" he told me, "Because every time I open it up, it talks about priesthood. And I don't want to hear it."

The Bible is the living word of God and speaks to us. Many of the saints found their vocations by reading a single line from Scripture. For St. Francis of Assisi, it was the words of Jesus to the rich young man from Matthew 19:21: "If you wish to be perfect, go, sell what you have and give to the poor, and you will have treasure in heaven. Then come, follow me." St. Francis never looked back. He gave away everything and followed Christ as he understood the call at that time in his life. For St. Augustine, who had a very difficult and long journey coming to Christ, it was Romans 13:14: "Put on the Lord Jesus Christ and make no provisions for the desires of the flesh." I think St. Augustine can be a great patron saint of a man's discernment, as he really struggled with chastity and indecision. For Blessed Mother Teresa of Calcutta, it was the words of Jesus from the cross in John 19:28: "I thirst."

Don't play "Bible Bingo." Maybe you have heard of it before. Bible Bingo is when a man asks the Lord a question and then closes his eyes, opens up his Bible and puts down his finger on a page. Whatever verse he reads, according to this unwise practice, is God's answer. I do not recommend that you ask Jesus if he wants you to become a priest and then play "Bible Bingo" for the answer.

Sacred Scripture is the living power of God. It has the power to change a man's life, to shake his world, to re-route the course of his life. Praying with Sacred Scripture is critical in vocational discernment. Do not be afraid. Fear is always from Satan, who does not want anyone to read the Bible! At the same time, not everyone who looks to Scripture will immediately find validation of a priestly vocation. God just as easily can use the Scriptures to convey to a man that he is *not* called to be a priest.

8. A good candidate for diocesan priesthood is striving to live a life of virtue.

A virtuous life should spring naturally from a life of prayer and intimacy with Jesus. A man should be conscious of his sins and bothered by them. He should be trying very hard to live out the supernatural virtues infused at his Baptism: faith, hope, and charity; and to develop the intellectual virtues of prudence, justice, temperance, and fortitude. He should be a man who is completely honest, truthful, has self-control, and tries to practice chastity within his current state in life. He is courteous, responsible, and dependable. The primary vocation of "Christ-likeness" must be lived before determining one's secondary vocation.

I remember hosting a vocation discernment group in my diocese one evening and we began to talk about the reality of sin in our lives. We were discussing mortal and venial sins and someone mentioned that missing Mass on Sunday is a serious sin. One sincere young man raised his hand and asked incredulously, "You mean it is a mortal sin to miss Mass on just one Sunday?" I assured him that it was a grave obligation and, barring sickness or other extenuating circumstances, he was required in justice to attend Mass every Sunday and it would be mortally sinful if he did not. The man whistled out loud and said in front of the whole group, "Father, can I go to Confession?"

Now the fact that this young man did not have sufficient knowledge—one of the three required conditions for a mortal sin— saved him from committing a mortal sin by missing Mass on Sunday. When I told him this he was relieved, but then I added, "Now you know. Knowledge is power!" Like this man, many men admit that they have not had sufficient moral instruction, illustrating why proper catechesis in the Church is so important.

I am not saying that a man has to be a living saint before he can become a priest or even go to the seminary. Our quest for holiness is a life-long process. But a man must be able to show that he is *sequela Christi,* following Christ. He must be striving to live a life of virtue and he must show some success in this endeavor over an extended period of time.

Men who were living profligate lives have told me that they felt a called to priesthood! They recognized this seemed crazy. Amazingly, they felt a call to priesthood even while mired in sin, and they wanted me to reject or discourage them. They wanted me to say, "You are not called. You are a sinner. You can never become a priest. Go away." But instead I told them, "God is calling you to actively pursue your primary vocation of holiness. Until you get this part of your life in order, you will be unable to make a decision about priesthood or any other vocation." When speaking to these men, I have sometimes thought that the desire to be a priest while living immorally may be an even *stronger* sign that a man is being called to be a priest.

John the Baptist's message should ring in a man's soul: "Repent! The Kingdom of heaven is at hand!" He should go to Confession, cleanse his soul, and then pray again about his vocation. He then will be able to hear God's call much more clearly.

Men who are discerning should take heart; nearly every seminarian and priest I know can describe a time in his life before seminary when he was not living very virtuously. Seminarians will often talk about their L.B.S., or Life Before Seminary. But most vocation directors will require a man to be living a life of Christian virtue over an extended period of time, perhaps two years, before beginning seminary.

9. A good candidate for diocesan priesthood should have good people skills.

Pastores Dabo Vobis, the great document on priesthood by Pope John Paul II, says in #43:

> In order that his ministry may be humanly as credible and acceptable as possible, it is important that the priest should mold his human personality in such a way that it becomes a bridge and not an obstacle for others in their meeting with Jesus Christ the Redeemer of humanity.[25]

Good human formation is critical for today's priests. Because a diocesan priest takes care of people every day he needs good people skills. He should have good conversation skills and be able to make friends easily. His personality should be hospitable. He should be approachable, even to total strangers. This is not to say that every priest must be a boisterous extrovert, but he must like people and like to be around them. If a man has no friends, finds himself in awkward silence during conversation, and feels intimidated by people, he will probably have a difficult time in diocesan priesthood.

The way a man interacts with people depends both on his personality and on his family and social relationships while growing up. I personally think one of the reasons why the majority of priests come from families with multiple children is because in a large family, a child simply has to interact with others, both those he likes and those he does not.

I have closely observed men who were socially underdeveloped and concluded that improvement in this area is exceedingly difficult. Certainly some progress can be made in seminary formation, but it requires an immense effort on the part of the man. I have known seminarians who are painfully shy. They would sit at the dinner table with a group for two hours and never say a single word, unless asked a direct question. A man like this must be able to grow out of this extreme timidity if he is to minister to people as a priest.

Your personality and your family are two important gifts God has given to you. God always gives the gifts you need to live the vocation to which you are called. Some men tend toward introversion and can still become excellent priests. But if you struggle in this area, speak with your spiritual director and vocation director about it. They can advise you regarding how to improve your social skills and abilities. They also will help you determine if you have at least the minimum qualities required in this regard to do the work of a diocesan priest.

10. A good candidate for diocesan priesthood should have above-average intelligence.

In most U.S. parishes, the majority of Catholic people sitting in the pews on Sunday have college degrees and many have advanced degrees. No priest can assume he is the smartest or most educated person in the Church, nor can he assume that people will accept everything he says as law. If a priest is not able to speak intelligently about many subjects, he will not be respected when he mounts the pulpit to speak about Jesus Christ and how to live the Gospel in the modern world. People repeat what their priests say, so if a priest says something that betrays his ignorance or lack of education, it will negatively affect his ministry.

Consequently, priests are required to complete both college-level and masters-level studies. A good candidate for priesthood should have a proven academic record indicating a sufficient intelligence and a solid study ethic, beginning in high school and moving into college. Ideally, every man should arrive at major seminary (the last four years of theology before ordination) with a balanced education and a college degree. The degree may be from a Catholic college, a college seminary, or a secular university.

A man may major in any field he chooses, such as business, education, or biology. However, it is important that he completes core courses in a wide range of subjects such as math, science, history, politics, psychology, music, art, law, and economics. A traditional liberal arts education is important because a priest must be conversant about many topics.

After college, the academic work gets even more difficult. Unless they go to a college seminary, most men these days study six years after college before being ordained. This includes two years of pre-theology (philosophy, Latin, etc.) and then four years of masters-level Catholic theology. I describe this system in detail in chapter 14, but my point here is that a man must be able to succeed in these courses.

If a man is academically weak and has to work very hard just to get average grades, he still can become a priest, though seminary will be a challenge for him. Today's seminaries have many structures in place to help average students succeed. Some of the best priests the Church has ever known were not the best students. St. John Vianney, the patron of priests, is just one example of many.

I remember a young man who came to me with all the signs and qualities of a good candidate. He made a wonderful first impression. He was extremely likeable and friendly, and was a wonderful conversationalist. He was generous in serving others.

He loved the Lord and the Church, and he was extremely prayerful. He was psychologically and emotionally stable. When he told me he was certain that God was calling him to become a priest, I was thrilled. The diocese needed priests like this man! But I noticed that he rarely ever spoke about school, even though he was college-aged. I had to press him to discover that he was not in college at present and that he had not graduated from high school. He had dropped out in his senior year, knowing that he was going to fail. He told me finally that he had a very severe learning disability and that his IQ was very low. His parents had never pushed him to do anything about it. He was now working at a hardware store. I did spend some time with him and we enlisted the help of some specialists to evaluate his educational capacity. It was heartbreaking to see every test come back worse than the last. All the educational experts told us he might be able to get his high school diploma with a lot of work, but he would never be able to do college-level work, much less master's-level theology. This man told me, "Father, I know that Jesus is calling me to be a priest. I feel it in my heart." And I had to say to him, "No, he is not. I'm sorry. God never calls us to a vocation without giving us the wherewithal to live out that vocation. And he has not given you the minimal academic abilities to learn what a priest has to know." I was able to work with this young man to help him find some wonderful religious communities, as he had the qualities to become a saintly religious brother or monk. But he was not called to be a priest.

11. A good candidate for diocesan priesthood must be physically, emotionally, and psychologically stable.

How physically healthy does a man have to be to become a priest? Diocesan priests work very hard and they must have the physical health necessary to do this work day after day. It is not usually manual labor, but it is exhausting nonetheless. Every priest can attest that celebrating three Masses on a Sunday takes work. Not only does he prepare and preach the homily at each

Mass, but he also attends to many other needs: greeting the people after Mass, hearing a quick Confession just before Mass, solving a problem in the choir, running to the hospital, or fixing the air conditioning. All of this leaves a priest exhausted by nightfall on Sunday evening! Good health is required. If a man has a physical handicap, it cannot be so debilitating as to impede him from doing the ordinary daily duties of a priest. Being able to drive a car is almost always essential.

I have known priests who lived with very painful and difficult illnesses, but they still did outstanding priestly work. I know one priest who is 95 percent blind but is one of the most energetic and pastorally effective priests in his diocese! Nonetheless, he admits it is very hard for him. I know others who are crippled with arthritis, some who have diabetes, and others who live in constant pain from some other ailment. If a priest is terribly obese, this can also be a debilitating factor; it is something which must be addressed in seminary formation.

Every vocation director requires an extensive physical examination as part of the application process to determine if a man has the physical ability and endurance to do what an ordinary priest does every day.

While physical health is an important quality, emotional and psychological health are equally important in the life of a priest. However, because of our culture, many men arrive in seminary today carrying significant psychological and emotional baggage. Today's families are fractured in staggering proportions and divorce has touched nearly all seminarians in one way or another. Many of our present seminarians grew up in single-parent households or in what sociologists call "blended families." Some of our seminarians these days have significant "father wounds" caused by absent or abusive fathers, whether that abuse was physical, verbal, emotional, or sexual. Others suffer from depression or anxiety. These difficulties can drag them down and keep them from becoming the selfless priests that God is calling them to be.

I am not suggesting that the majority of the men entering seminary today have these types of problems. In fact, in my experience, the truth is just the opposite: the majority of seminarians today are in fact very emotionally and psychologically stable when they arrive. But there are a number of men who will need some assistance to deal with one or more of these issues. This is their cross. They did not choose it. It is not a sin. It is not their fault, but it is their problem. If a man is to live his life as a priest, which is an outward-looking life caring for others, he will have to address this inner turmoil before ordination. If it is severe, it will need to be evaluated and addressed before coming to seminary.

12. A good candidate for diocesan priesthood should be joyful and have a good sense of humor.

Dealing with fallen human nature (our own and others') can be frustrating at times, so a priest must have a sense of humor. He needs to be able to laugh at himself and to be joyful in the Good News of Jesus Christ, even as he is dealing with the sad realities of sin and death. The human personality of the priest is very important because it is a bridge to Christ. Priests who never laugh and smile are not attractive to people and they are often deemed unapproachable. Oliver Wendell Holmes once said, "I might have become a clergyman had not so many clergymen I knew looked and acted so much like undertakers."[26]

I read once that the average adult laughs approximately seventeen times per day, but the average child laughs over two hundred times per day. I feel sure that this is at least one of the reasons why our Lord Jesus exhorted us to become like little children in order to enter the Kingdom of God. As a vocation director, I often said, "In the job description for priests, joy is required." Blessed Mother Teresa of Calcutta writes in the Constitutions of the Missionaries of Charity: "Joy is a net of love by which we can catch souls for God."[27]

We call the Gospel the *Good News* of Jesus Christ. A priest should act as if the news he proclaims truly is good! He is a messenger of the best news that the world has ever known:

> For God so loved the world that he gave his only Son, so that everyone who believes in him might not perish but might have eternal life.
>
> John 3:16

In my role as vice rector of a seminary, sometimes it is necessary to call a man into my office for a chat. If a man is extremely intense, never smiles or laughs, and walks around in his own tightly-wound world, rarely looking up and meeting the eyes of those around him, I will call this man in and say, "As vice rector, I have some very important and sophisticated theological advice for you." "Yes, Father, what is it?" I say, "*Chill out!* And do it now!"

Sometimes the man will say, "But Father, this is just who I am. I am an intense person." And I will say, "No! This is not just who you are. The priest is not his own. If you want to be a priest of Jesus Christ, then you will have to change who you are in this regard, with God's grace. You have to learn to relax and smile."

A dour man will not be approachable to people in the parish unless he learns to look at people around him, smile, laugh, and show that he has the joy of Christ. This is what a truly human person does. I remember the famous documentary about Blessed Mother Teresa of Calcutta created by Malcolm Muggeridge—the film that first made Mother Teresa famous. At one point, it showed Mother Teresa getting into a car as she was leaving one of her convents. She rolled down the window, pointed at a certain sister and said, "Somebody make that sister laugh!" She certainly understood the importance of joy in living the religious life. Many convents of the Missionaries of Charity have a sign on the wall with a quote from Mother Teresa: "Joy is the infallible sign of the presence of God."

Pope Benedict XVI recently said, "The greatest poverty in the world is the inability to live our lives with joy." And Blessed Julian of Norwich once wrote: "The greatest honor and glory you can give to almighty God, greater than all your sacrifices and offerings, is to live your live happily, joyfully, because of the knowledge of his love."[28]

In the seminary, we watch our men to see if they laugh, if they smile often, and if they show joy. In light of the psychological and emotional pain mentioned above, some men will have a more difficult time doing this than others. Nonetheless, laughter is good medicine.

13. A good candidate for diocesan priesthood has a "priest's heart."

When I say "heart" in this context, I am describing what is also called the soul. I can remember when I was a vocation director giving a talk on vocations, often some young man would come up to me afterwards and say something like, "Father, that was a great talk on vocations! When you were talking, my heart was really burning." I would always reply, "If your heart was burning, it was not because of my talk. The Holy Spirit is the only one who makes a man's heart burn, and he does it especially when he is calling that man to something great. You could be called to be a priest."

In the gospel account of Christ's post-resurrection appearance on the road to Emmaus, this is exactly the feeling that the apostles described: "Did not our hearts burn within us as he talked to us on the road and explained the Scriptures to us?" (Luke 24: 32) These were apostles; they were priests! A man who is called to become a priest will report this "burning heart" sensation on more than one occasion.

A priest's heart is modeled after the Sacred Heart of Jesus, full of kindness and compassion for others, like the Good Shepherd. In Scripture, we read that Jesus felt compassion for the people because "they were like sheep without a shepherd" (Mark

6:34). Regardless of how tired the Lord was, he healed the sick, he fed the hungry, and he taught people about God. Jesus always sacrificed himself for the people he loved.

You can tell a lot about a person's heart by simply watching him, listening to him, and observing what he says and does. If a man is overly strict with himself and others, or if he seems to lack mercy and kindness for sinners, or if his speech is cynical and caustic, then there is reason to believe his heart is not ready for priesthood. I believe that a "priest's heart" is one of the best indicators for a vocation director that a man is pursuing priesthood for the right reasons. The people of this world desperately need the goodness, love, and mercy of Jesus, especially when they are suffering. This is priesthood. The purpose of a priest is to bring people to Jesus and Jesus to people. Priests can provide that Good like no one else can!

A candidate for priesthood should ask himself these questions: Do I really love God's people? Do I feel genuine compassion for them in their sufferings and in their sins? Am I willing to spend myself, to empty myself in order to forgive them, to heal them and to bless them?

St. Isaac Jogues, S.J., was tortured and martyred by the Mohawk Indians in 1646 near present-day Auriesville, New York, because he went to them again and again to bring them Jesus. He had been captured and tortured before, but he finally escaped and returned to France where he was considered a hero! However, his heart would not allow him to stay away. Knowing he would probably die, he returned to America and immediately went back to the people that God had sent him to serve. This time he did not escape. The Native Americans who killed him were very inspired by his bravery and love, even in the midst of torture. After they killed him, they ate his heart hoping to receive his strength and courage.[29] They recognized the heart of a priest.

14. A good candidate for diocesan priesthood has self-possession and self-mastery.

Most priests in parish ministry would recognize familiar elements in this story.

> I had finished a wedding Mass in the afternoon and stopped by the parish hall to make a brief appearance at the reception. Everyone seemed to be having a wonderful time. I happened to engage a man in conversation who had been celebrating with more than a few drinks. He had become quite talkative, and slurred his words a bit when he told me, "Father, I used to be a Catholic, but thirty-five years ago, when my mother was dying of cancer, I called a priest to come give her the Last Rites. That priest yelled at me because I called him at home after nine o'clock. I have never been back to Mass in these thirty-five years and neither has my family.

Now, I do not know the specifics of this situation. I have no idea who that priest was or what was going on in his life thirty-five years ago. I do not know what else had happened between this priest and this particular family. Perhaps the man standing before me was unreasonable. I don't know any of these things. But I do know that this man's faith was obviously very weak at that time, hanging by a thread, and that the priest's unkindness and lack of self-mastery damaged the Church.

Because a priest is an *alter Christus*, people expect more from him. They expect him to be like Christ, and they have a right to that expectation. That is why Jesus calls and equips us to become priests in the first place. As a retreat master said in one of our annual seminary retreats, "The three most important qualities in the life of a priest are: Be kind. Be kind. Be kind." People are always going to be in very different places spiritually. Some have a very strong faith, and a curt, unkind word from their pastor after Mass will be easily shrugged off and forgiven: "Father must be having a bad day. Jesus, please be with him today." But the same word to people of weaker faith will send them off angry and bitter. They will tell at least ten others the story of the priest's rudeness, and you can bet they won't be at Mass the next Sunday.

Self-mastery can make all the difference in a priest's work. Consider this story about St. Clement Marie Hofbauer, the patron of Vienna.

> St. Clement began orphanages to care for the children on the street. He had to beg money to buy food for the children. One day he entered a saloon where there were some godless ruffians playing poker and drinking whiskey. He went up to a poker table where he saw a huge stack of money and he took off his hat and begged, "May I please have something for my orphans?" One of the men turned, cursed him horribly and spat right in his face. St. Clement Hofbauer calmly took out his handkerchief, wiped his face and then said, "That was for me. Now, may I please have something for my orphans?" The men at the table became very nervous. They did not know how to respond to self-mastery like this. They had never before seen such self-control. One of the men laughed loudly, grabbed the huge stack of bills and gave them all to the priest. St. Clement's self-mastery had won the day. [30]

Self-mastery means that a priest has good impulse control and he is able to control his anger and all of his emotions. He is in control of what he says and how he says it, conscious that people are very sensitive. He understands the proverb, "A word is a bird. Once it flies away, it cannot be recaptured."

Self-discipline and self-mastery also indicate a man who is dependable. He is able to wake up on time, keep his scheduled appointments, and in general to do the things that are expected of him. Procrastination, tardiness, and lack of responsibility are all signs that a man does not yet possess the required self-mastery to be a priest.

Many times during my years as a vocation director, I would be working men who would suddenly stop returning my calls or miss appointments. They would not call to cancel an appointment or apologize for missing it. They just missed. This was a good indication that this man still lacked self-mastery. Admittedly, this was probably triggered by fear or cold feet. After all, speaking with the vocation director for the first time about the possibility of priesthood can cause a considerable amount of anxiety or stress. Nonetheless, a man with self-mastery will have the courtesy to return phone calls or cancel appointments.

The spiritual life is a battle and it demands mastery over one's will. A vocation director and seminary do not expect a man to be perfect in this regard in order to be accepted. Priestly formation is a process precisely designed to help a man grow in self-mastery, selflessness, and holiness.

15. A good candidate for diocesan priesthood must show stability in lifestyle.

Priesthood is a lifetime commitment. The sacrament of Holy Orders imparts an indelible ontological mark on the soul which lasts forever. The Church needs priests who will go where they are assigned and remain there—at their battle station, so to speak—taking care of God's people. Walker Percy, the great Catholic writer, once wrote of the parish priest: "He is one of the heroes of the modern age."[31] He could see the priest standing at his battle station on the front lines, faithfully fighting for Christ and his people against the onslaught of the world, the flesh, and the devil. He could see priests blessing and strengthening people through preaching, teaching, and the sacraments.

If a man changes jobs, locations, and parishes very often, without any good reason, this is a concern. If he does these things and then tries to justify them by blaming the boss or the pastor — everything and everyone except himself—this is a sign that he will be unable to commit to the life of a diocesan priest.

I remember hearing of a young man who had been to five different colleges in five years. He still had not graduated. When asked about this, he went into a long, unsatisfactory explanation.

The bottom line was that he could not be still. His vocation director explained that seminary was six years in the same place and priesthood required even more stability. The diocese needed some evidence that he could stay put that long. He was asked to come back (with his college degree intact) when he could show that he had lived in the same place, doing the same thing, for at least two years. He never returned.

The people of God need pastors; they need shepherds. They need and deserve a Father who will be dependable, loving, strong, and present. The world is unstable and there are many people who are not dependable and trustworthy. A priest has to be like a rock.

A good candidate for priesthood cannot have wanderlust. I sometimes hear people speak about their priest, saying, "He's never here. He's always leading a pilgrimage here or doing a retreat there. It seems he is always doing good things in other places but we need a priest here, with us, to stay put and take care of us day in and day out." Diocesan priests must do what they need to do and what they promised to do, not just what they want to do.

Developing this virtue of stability can certainly be done but it must be substantially present prior to beginning seminary studies.

16. A good candidate for diocesan priesthood should be a Christian gentleman.

To be the most effective priest possible, a man should have a certain degree of social polish. He should be a man who has excellent table manners and a neat appearance. He is always dressed appropriately but not so lavishly as to draw undue attention to himself. He has good hygiene, he is courteous and patient with others, and he uses correct grammar when speaking. He understands and respects appropriate boundaries with both men and women. In a word, he is a Christian gentleman.

Public propriety is a term we use often in seminaries. It means that a man understands what is fitting and proper in this culture and in this society.

I can remember a family in one of my parishes who told me about the night that they invited their priest to a very nice family dinner. They had fine china on the table, champagne glasses, a delicious meal and several non-Catholic family guests. About half way through the meal, the priest took his linen napkin (which was not in his lap) and loudly blew his nose into it while sitting at the table! They were absolutely mortified. The Catholic family was terribly embarrassed by their priest in front of their non-Catholic relatives. They never forgot it and they never really respected that priest as much in the future. The priest was actually extremely holy and his homilies were superb, but his lack of manners and public propriety lessened the effectiveness of his ministry.

In our culture today, many young men grow up in families where they were never taught these things. This does not make them bad people, but the deficiency must be remedied. The personality and overall persona of the priest must be a bridge to Jesus Christ. If a man has never learned good manners, proper hygiene, and over-all public propriety, he should take the time to do so immediately. It will benefit him greatly in life, whether or not he ever becomes a priest.

17. Events in the life of a good candidate will sometimes point towards priesthood.

Perhaps you have heard the expression, "Sometimes in the winds of change, we find our true direction."

I remember meeting a priest who told me that he was drafted into the army in the early 1970s and sent to Vietnam. He was not even practicing his faith, though he went to Confession and started praying once he got there. He recalled the day he was in a foxhole with two of his best friends and a mortar exploded near them. He was in the middle of his two friends. They were

101

both killed, yet he survived with minimal injuries. Later, he asked the Lord, "Why? Why did they both die that day, yet here I am still alive? What do you want from me?" This was the first time he had ever asked God that question and he eventually got an answer. He ended up in the seminary and he is a priest today.

As part of the seminary admissions committee, I have the privilege of reading the autobiographies of many new seminarians every year, and I am always amazed at the ways God has orchestrated the events of their lives. Some of these events involved the death of a loved one, the birth of a handicapped brother or sister, the inexplicable loss of a job at a critical moment, the painful divorce of their parents, or retreats, pilgrimages, or mission trips.

One of the more unusual stories I have heard involved a young man who had considered priesthood, but decided instead to pursue his dream of becoming a game warden. Yet he had told the Lord, as he wrestled back and forth between becoming a priest or accepting a job, "Lord, you know I have always wanted to be a game warden and all the doors have opened for me. If you don't want this, and you want me to become a priest, then send me a clear sign." He had to take a lie detector test as part of the application because it was a law enforcement position. He had been told that the polygraph was really just procedural; they basically had already admitted him into the program. It turned out that he failed the lie detector test! He told me, "Father, I didn't lie about a thing!" He was absolutely shocked when he failed, and so were the other game wardens. Failing meant waiting a year, reapplying, and taking the lie detector test again. But the man said, "No thanks. I'm applying to seminary."

I call these kinds of amazing events "idiot-proof signs." But while powerful conversions—from heinous sinner to saintly priest—make for dramatic vocation stories, many men are not called in this way. Many men never had one single event or incident that made them realize their vocation. Rather, the Lord gently guided them to make little steps along the way. For example, a young man found himself fascinated by the work of his parish priest, which led to him becoming an altar server. His spiritual life deepened through prayer and the reception of the sacraments. His faith was increased by high school youth group mission trips and retreats. He found himself desiring prayer and he was thinking about Jesus more and more. He liked being around the parish and felt fulfilled there. He began reading about apologetics; his religious opinions became stronger and better informed. He started going to spiritual direction. He taught Bible school every summer and started teaching Religious Education. This man cannot point to one single significant event that made him realize his vocation. But the many small steps that he took, cooperating with God's grace, added up to an "idiot-proof" sign.

Caution: be careful about looking too hard for a single sign that you should become a priest! It is wiser to use the many different signs that result from your overall process of discernment.

"This voice of the Lord calling, however, is never to be expected as something which in an extraordinary manner will be heard by the ears of a future priest. It is rather to be known and understood in the manner in which the will of God is daily made known to prudent Christians."[32]

Presbyterorum Ordinis

---

18. A good candidate for diocesan priesthood is able to accept both success and failure peacefully.

First of all, *success* is not a Gospel word. Mother Teresa of Calcutta insisted that her call was to faithfulness, not success. This is true for all of us working in the Lord's vineyard.

Nonetheless, we are all human and we like to see good fruit coming from our efforts. A seminary spiritual director I knew used to say, "There is nothing worse than a proud priest." Some men have been given significant pastoral gifts and they do realize a lot of apostolic success in their preaching and teaching. They receive lavish praise about every homily and they might even come to expect it from the people. These priests would do well to heed the famous Spanish maxim, "Prosperity is the most dangerous situation of man." Accepting success peacefully and humbly is an important thing for a priest to learn. Those men with significant pastoral gifts must work very hard spiritually to depend on the grace of Jesus Christ at all times and not on their own natural gifts. In the end, we can do nothing without God's grace.

On the other hand, working with Jesus to save souls is a tough business and many of our pastoral endeavors will not succeed. I remember once speaking with a priest who lamented that he had tried very hard to promote priestly vocations in his parishes. He prayed publicly for vocations, he invited young men constantly to consider priesthood, and he tried hard to cooperate with the projects of the diocesan vocation office. Yet not one man had gone to seminary from any one of his parishes in thirty years. He was a very fine priest and his people loved him. He was understandably disappointed by this lack of "success."

A good candidate realizes that Jesus has already won the war. He will work hard for the Kingdom and he will use the gifts that God has given him, but when some things fail, he will not lose his peace. This requires humility, trust in God and a constant purifying of one's motivations. He will feel privileged to work for God's glory, whether or not a particular pastoral endeavor bears any observable fruit.

19. A good candidate for diocesan priesthood should have a healthy psycho-sexual development and orientation.

Psycho-sexual development is discussed at greater length in Chapter 13, so it will be treated here only briefly. A healthy man should have a normal sexual attraction for adult females and this attraction should be under the control of the will. It is preferable that he have some normal chaste dating experiences, though this is not absolutely required. A man should not be addicted to pornography, masturbation, or any type of aberrant sexual behavior. If he has ever been sexually active with a woman, then he should have a lengthy period of sexual sobriety prior to making application to seminary. If a man has had some same-sex attraction, this does not automatically exclude him from becoming a priest. However, because same-sex attraction is a disordered attraction, a more careful analysis of this man's psychosexual development and identity is indicated. In general, a good candidate will have shown evidence of his capacity to live a chaste, celibate life.

20. A good candidate for diocesan priesthood is truly open to the will of God for his life.

A good candidate yearns to do the will of God. He thinks about Jesus and ponders God's will when making decisions in his life. He truly believes that happiness is doing God's will, wherever it may lead. Arriving at this spiritual attitude is not easy. On the contrary, it involves a long, drawn-out spiritual battle in a man's heart. As one seminarian said, "Father, every morning I completely abandon myself and my will to the perfect will of God. Then I spend the rest of the day taking it back!"

As a young priest, I can remember visiting the classrooms in our Catholic school regularly and teaching the children about vocations. I strongly encouraged them to pray daily about this major life decision and to listen carefully for the voice of God. During vocations awareness week, the Knights of Columbus sponsored a vocation poster contest for the smaller children and an essay contest for the older ones. I was selected to read the essays and judge the winners. I will never forget what one fifth-grade girl wrote at the end of her essay.

> In conclusion, I do not yet know my vocation. I have asked Jesus to tell me but he has not told me yet. I do not know if he wants me to get married or be a sister but I don't really care. I love Jesus Christ so much and I trust him so much that I will do anything he asks. The end.

I almost fell out of my chair! I thought to myself, "Now here is the kind of faith, love, and trust that will change the world for Christ!"

And yes, she won the contest.

Discernment Exercise

Examining oneself using these twenty qualities or signs is a good way to begin one's discernment of priesthood, but it should not be done in a vacuum. There are many other ways to discern. Your vocation director needs to be a part of this process.

On each of the twenty points below, rate yourself on a scale of 0 – 5. A rating of 0 means you do not possess the sign at all. A 5 indicates that the sign is very evident in your life. The highest possible score is 100. Be completely honest with yourself and rate yourself fairly.

_____ 1. I love Jesus Christ and I have a thirst to bring Jesus and his teachings to the world.

_____ 2. I am endeavoring to be a believing, practicing Catholic Christian.

_____ 3. I am trying to live a life of prayer and I desire a life of prayer.

_____ 4. I am trying to serve others and I desire a life of service to others.

_____ 5. I feel a desire to be a priest, though it is sometimes stronger than at other times.

_____ 6. I have had others tell me that I should be a priest or that I would make a good priest.

_____ 7. Prayerful reading of Sacred Scripture leads me to believe I might be called to be a priest.

_____ 8. I am endeavoring to live virtuously.

_____ 9. I like to be around people and I have sufficient social skills to engage others.

_____ 10. I have enough intelligence to complete graduate-level coursework and function as a priest

_____ 11. I think that I have the physical, emotional and psycho-logical stability to become a priest.

_____ 12. I am joyful and I have a good sense of humor.

_____ 13. I think that I have a "priest's heart," as described in this chapter.

_____ 14. I believe that I have the self-mastery to be a good priest.

_____ 15. Generally speaking, I have demonstrated stability in life style.

_____ 16. People who know me would say I am Christian gen-tleman.

_____ 17. I have had events happen in my life that seem to be signs pointing towards diocesan priesthood.

_____ 18. I am usually able to accept both success and failure without losing my peace.

_____ 19. I believe that I have a healthy psycho-sexual develop-ment and orientation.

_____ 20. I am trying to be truly open to the will of God for my life.

_____Total

Tally your score and e-mail it to your vocation director and your bishop and ask for their feedback. I promise you that they will be happy to hear from you and happy that you are considering priesthood. But remember: this is only one instrument of discernment, to be used in conjunction with the many other tools described in this book.

I encourage you to try to develop the qualities that need strengthening. Speak with your spiritual director about them. This will make you a much better Catholic man, even if you are not called to become a priest.

"It became clearer and clearer to me that there is more to the priestly vocation than enjoying theology, indeed, that work in the parish can often lead very far away from that and makes completely different demands…The yes to the priesthood meant that I had to say yes to the whole task, even in its simplest forms.

"Since I was rather diffident and downright unpractical, since I had no talent for sports or administration or organization, I had to ask myself whether I would be able to relate to people – whether, for example, as a chaplain I would be able to lead and inspire Catholic youth, whether I would be capable of giving religious instruction to the little ones, whether I could get along with the old and sick, and so forth. I had to ask myself whether I would be ready to do that my whole life long and whether it was really my vocation.

"Bound up with this was naturally the question of whether I would be able to remain celibate, unmarried, my whole life long… I often pondered these questions as I walked in the beautiful park of Furstenried, and naturally in the chapel, until finally at my diaconal ordination in the fall of 1950 I was able to pronounce a convinced yes."

Pope Benedict XVI

CHAPTER 6

DEVELOPING A SPIRITUAL PLAN OF LIFE

---

*"Do not conform yourselves to this age but be transformed by the
renewal of your mind, that you may discern what is the will of God,
what is good and pleasing and perfect."*

Romans 12:2

I knew a man who was discerning priesthood for several
years. He worked as a manager for a fast food restaurant and he
excelled in his job. He was also very bright and finishing a master's degree. He wasn't dating anyone and had not dated for
some time. He and I had talked many times about priesthood and
he always admitted that God was probably calling him. But he
would not go to seminary. He just could not bring himself to fill
out the application and take that next step. And he could not explain to me why he would not go. One day, his boss, who owned
many restaurants, called him with a proposition. He told him that
he had another restaurant in a city about one hour away and this
restaurant was not doing well. He wanted this man to move to
this new city and take over the management of this failing restaurant, for an increase of salary. The man who was discerning did
not really want to move away from his own city, as he had many
friends and felt settled. So he agreed to take over the new restaurant, but decided that he would make the one hour drive each
morning and evening instead. Within a few months, this man
called me to say that he was ready to go to seminary. He filled
out an application, was accepted, and began seminary that fall. I
asked him, "What happened? What happened that helped you
finally make a move?" He told me that during his long commute
he had decided to pray the rosary to know his vocation, once in
the morning and again in the evening. He said, "Father, I had not

been praying. That's why I could not make a move. Once I started praying faithfully and consistently, I knew that I could no longer delay seminary."

Bishop Robert Carlson, when he was bishop of Sioux Falls, South Dakota, once said, "The biggest problem in my diocese is not between priests who are liberal and priests who are conservative. It is between priests who pray and priests who do not." If a priest is not praying every single day, then he will very quickly be led astray. His people will see clearly that he is not praying by the way he comports himself, the way he preaches, celebrates Mass, and the way he interacts with others. In the same way, if a man is not praying every day, then he is really not discerning his vocation. Many men have made this mistake. The development of a spiritual plan of life is an essential when discerning diocesan priesthood.

Obviously, the more a man knows and loves God, the more clearly he will see how he is to serve God in this life. Therefore, the best remote preparation for every vocation is always the basic Christian formation one receives (or should have received) as a child. Trying to discern your secondary vocation before learning and living out your first is like trying to do algebra or geometry before taking elementary mathematics. You must know how to add, subtract, multiply, and divide before you can use these skills in more advanced mathematics. Similarly, you must learn to practice the basic Christian virtues of faith, hope, love, obedience, fortitude, trust, and generosity before discerning a vocation that requires these virtues. Without this groundwork, one cannot understand what a vocation is, much less freely choose it and live it out.

The concept is simple but that does not mean it is easy to implement. Knowledge of our secondary vocation always comes with living our first. As a young man said to me once, "Father, I don't practice Christianity seriously enough to discern priesthood." I replied, "Well said! And now you know exactly where God is calling you to start!"

Jesus is the Pearl of Great Price

> When Jesus went into the region of Caesarea-Philippi, he asked his disciples, "Who do people say the Son of Man is?" They replied, "Some say John the Baptist, others Elijah, still others Jeremiah or one of the prophets." He said to them, "But who do you say that I am?" Simon Peter said in reply, "You are the Messiah, the Son of the Living God." Jesus said to him in reply, "Blessed are you, Simon son of Jonah, for flesh and blood has not revealed this to you, but my heavenly Father. And so I say to you, you are Peter, and upon this rock I will build my church, and the gates of the netherworld shall not prevail against it. I will give you the keys to the kingdom of heaven. Whatever you bind on earth shall be bound in heaven and whatever you loose on earth shall be loosed in heaven.
>
> Matthew 16:13-19

Who do you say that Jesus is? Simon Peter had to answer this question with conviction from deep within his heart before Jesus would give him his vocation. Would you not agree that our first Pope needed to be convinced that Jesus Christ is God before he could begin his sacred ministry? Jesus is the pearl of great price. As Pope John Paul II said, speaking at World Day of Youth, "Jesus is the answer to which every human heart is the question." But do *you* believe this? Have you fallen in love with this Jesus so much that you are ready and willing to give your life for him? Until a man is completely convinced that Jesus is the pearl of great price, he will not have the faith and generosity to answer his call.

I have spoken to many men through the years about priesthood who immediately began to talk about the sacrifices: "Well, I don't think I can give up sex. I am not sure I want to make all those sacrifices that you priests make." When Jesus stood up and solemnly declared "I am the Way and the Truth and the Life" (John 14:6), he was well aware that many would respond, "No! I want it my way. This is my life." Obviously a man who responds

111

like this is not yet convinced that Jesus is the Lord of Lords and King of Kings.

He who is constantly counting the cost is really asking if it is worthy of the price!

Do you know who Jesus is? Do you believe he is the answer to which every human heart is the question? Do you believe Jesus is worth every sacrifice required?

Are you convinced of this?

The Dual Method of Learning Christ

If I were teaching a course about the life of George Washington, I would assign you ten books to read describing everything we know about this founding father of the United States. The syllabus would require you to read those ten books in their entirety and you would be responsible to know all the information within them. Periodic tests would confirm your knowledge. Thus you would learn about the parents of George Washington, his birth, his education, military career, political career, and religious beliefs.

Now at the end of a year, if you read those ten books and came to class every day, would you know George Washington? No. You would know a great deal *about* him, but you would not know him. But what if I could raise George Washington from the dead and have him come into our class every day for a year? You would be able to talk with him, ask him questions about what you had read, and listen to his answers. At the end of a year, you would know George Washington well. You would understand much more about his personality, his character, and his beliefs. You would know him as a person, not just as an historical figure.

Jesus Christ is the Son of God and he is alive. It is possible to know him *as a person*. This means that we must study and read about him. However, it has often been observed that "knowledge makes a bloody entrance." It requires effort. We must know everything we can about his life and teachings, beginning with the Gospels. St. Jerome wrote: "Ignorance of the scriptures is ignorance of Christ."[33] We must know the teachings of Jesus Christ as handed down to us; we must study and know the Catechism of the Catholic Church. Finally, we must spend silent time with him every day in prayer. In this way, we will know not only facts and stories about Jesus, but Jesus himself.

As in the analogy with George Washington, it is important to talk to Jesus about the things we have been learning about him and his Church. In the seminary, we often say to the seminarians, "It is important to pray your theology." This means a man should take what he learns in class into the chapel during his holy hour and talk to Jesus about it. In the seminary, should you go there, you will spend an enormous amount of time in these two endeavors: study and prayer. But you must begin now, or you will never get there!

Do you know your Catholic Faith? Do you know Jesus in a personal way? Are you spending a significant amount of time trying to communicate with God in silence every day? Falling in love with Jesus Christ is the essence of Christianity. And you can't fall in love with someone you do not know. You might ask yourself this question: if other people knew the details of your relationship with Jesus, would they say that he is your best friend?

I recommend to all men discerning their vocations to start teaching the faith to others. Volunteer to teach religious education class, vacation Bible school, or RCIA. Offer to lead a Bible study for your parish. Standing up in front of others and teaching them about Jesus is a strong significant motivator to learn more about him! When a man has to articulate the teachings of the Catholic Church and field questions about these teachings, it helps to interiorize them.

A Jesus Experience

The truth of Jesus resonates in our souls. As we learn the truth, we quite naturally begin to love it and desire to live it. Often men who are called to become priests can remember a certain moment when God became very real to them. I call this a "Jesus Experience." As I hear the vocation stories of seminarians, I am amazed at the extraordinary Jesus Experiences that they have had. Usually one of the three transcendentals touches a man's soul: the good, the true, or the beautiful. Sometimes it is the love of Christ that he experiences, or especially if he is mired in sin, Christ's great mercy and forgiveness.

My first memorable Jesus Experience happened in eighth grade. Our pastor took five altar boys to spend the weekend at the Monastery of the Holy Spirit, a Trappist Monastery in Conyers, Georgia. I did not really want to go. I would have preferred to stay home and play with my friends. But my mother informed my brother and me that we were going! It was the first time I had ever witnessed monastic life and I was very impressed. I will always remember being in the church in the early morning singing the Psalms with the monks. I was struck by their impressive-looking habits, their bald heads and long beards, and their kindness. On Saturday night, after supper, I went back into the church to spend a few minutes in prayer. It was empty. The monks had gone to bed since they would be up again for 4:00 a.m. matins. I wanted to pretend to be a monk, to try it on for size, and I went up into the choir stalls to sit where they sit. I can remember feeling a sense of deep peace and, though fully awake, I simply sat in the presence of Jesus without saying a word. Very solemnly, I felt that God loved me greatly and that he had made me to do a special work for his Kingdom. I could feel Jesus, the truth, filling my whole being. Time passed without my realizing it, and when I looked at my watch, two hours had gone by! I had never prayed for two hours straight in my life. That night I realized that not only did God love me deeply, but also that I loved him deeply.

He had given me a tiny glimpse of his goodness and I was capti-
vated. I did not yet know my vocation but I did say to the Lord
before I left the church, "Okay, Jesus. Whatever it is that you
want, I'm in."

Whether you have a dramatic "Jesus Experience" like this or
just gradually come to know him and his love for you, it is essential to develop a personal, loving relationship with Christ, as you
progress in discerning your vocation. The purpose of a priest is to
bring people to Jesus and Jesus to people. As we often say in the
seminary, *"Nemo dat quod non habet"* (One cannot give what one
does not have). A priest cannot bring Jesus to others if he does
not know him.

I have seen young people go on a retreat and come back totally transformed. They tell me with great excitement how God
made himself real to them and they experienced his love and
goodness. I can remember some of our high school students
spending a summer serving in the Bronx with the Missionaries of
Charity. They would spend their summer helping the sisters run
a day camp for inner-city children. There was no air conditioning
and it was a rough part of town. The youth would always come
back from that experience and say, "That was the hardest thing
that I have ever done—and the greatest experience of my life. I
met Jesus!"

It seems to me that these Jesus Experiences most often happen when a person has given up a weekend or a significant
amount of time specifically to try to grow closer to Jesus. It most
often happens on a retreat, pilgrimage, or mission trip. God is
never outdone in generosity, but he won't force his way into your
life. He must be invited.

I am not suggesting that everyone must have an emotional,
cathartic spiritual experience in order to have a personal relationship with Jesus, even though quite a few do begin this way. Many
men simply develop this relationship over time and gradually
come to have a deeper love and commitment to the Lord. Their

Jesus Experience is the synthesis of quietly walking with Jesus throughout their lives, not one single cathartic event.

"Ask and it will be given to you; seek and you will find; knock and the door will be opened to you. For everyone who asks, receives; and the one who seeks, finds; and to the one who knocks, the door will be opened."

Matthew 7:7-8

If you are not able to remember a significant Jesus Experience in your life, don't worry. But if you are not sure that you have a personal loving relationship with the Lord, I recommend making a retreat. But be careful: not every retreat is the same. Speak with a priest whom you trust or ask your vocation director to recommend a certain retreat. Then attend this retreat and ask Jesus to reveal himself to you. Jesus will come to you and reveal himself if you ask, whether in a powerful emotional moment or quietly over time.

Developing a Spiritual Plan of Life

Coming to know Jesus in this dual method described above requires developing a spiritual plan of life. What is this all about? We humans are habitual creatures. Sometimes our habits are good and sometimes they are bad, but we do like habits. Aristotle once observed that habits can sometimes be stronger than nature itself.[34] We all tend to go to bed, get up, eat, work, and pray at a certain time each day. We can call this a general plan of life; people function best when this plan is stable. It is important to take control of one's plan of life and to make sure it is healthy, balanced, and *directed*. A famous Chinese proverb says, "If you do not change your direction, you will very likely end up where you are headed." Our plan of life should be moving us in the direction where we want to end!

In the same way, you will need to establish a very specific and well-directed spiritual plan of life. This plan will be primarily directed toward two things: growing in holiness and discerning your vocation. A spiritual plan of life must be *reasonable* and *achievable*, according to the demands of your present state in life. I can remember a young man who came to me once for spiritual direction. After giving him some basic ideas, I asked him to write down some things that he would like to do each day for his spiritual plan of life. He came back with this list: I will get up every morning at 4:00 a.m. to begin my prayers. I will pray twenty decades of the holy rosary. I will fast three days per week. I will pray in the Church two hours a day. I will read one book of the Bible every day..."

The list went on and on. While I admired the enthusiasm of this young man, his list was completely unrealistic. He was a senior in high school, studying hard, playing sports, and was involved in many other healthy activities. Had I allowed him to attempt that plan of life, he would have quickly failed in many of the spiritual exercises, gotten discouraged, and probably thrown out the whole thing. Satan can tempt people to try to live a life of heroic virtue and prayer before they have lived a life of basic virtue and prayer. He wants them to try to run before they can walk. He does this, knowing that they will become discouraged and then stop trying. Satan wants people to see holiness as impossible.

I helped this young man to craft a much more realistic spiritual plan of life and he was quite successful in living it. What would a good spiritual plan of life look like for a high school man?

~ I will pray for 20-30 minutes each day in my room.

~ During my prayer time, I will read the Mass readings of the day.

~ I will pray five decades of the rosary each night before bed.

~ I will go to daily Mass three times per week, as my schedule permits.

~ I will meet with my spiritual director monthly and go to Confession at least monthly.

~ I will pray before the Blessed Sacrament in church (or go to an adoration chapel to pray) for one hour each week.

~ I will pray three Hail Marys every day to know and accept my vocation.

~ I will attend the vocation discernment retreats sponsored by the vocation office.

I asked him to make his goals very specific. For example, he might have written: "I will pray from 9:00 to 9:30 in the evening, sitting in the blue chair by the window with the phone, computer and television turned off. I will talk to Jesus in my own words and spend at least half of the time trying to listen to him." Notice that the goal describes time, place, and other logistics. Specificity increases accountability. When this young man would come for spiritual direction, and I would ask him if he had been faithful to his prayer for the last month, he could answer with certitude. Often, the answer would be something like, "I prayed my 30 minutes, my appointment with God, approximately 85 percent of the time since our last meeting." I would reply, "Great work! I know Jesus is pleased. Now next month, let's make it 100 percent!"

How Do I Spend This Prayer Time?

Your spiritual director will work with you on different ways to pray and he will help you find the ways that help you the most. I always encourage my spiritual directees to talk with Jesus in their own words. Prayer is a conversation, not a lecture. A conversation involves both talking and listening. Remember that

God already knows what you are going to say to him in prayer, but you do not know what he wants to say to you. "This is my beloved Son. Listen to him" (Mark 9:7).

How to Have a Conversation with Christ

The following passage has been re-printed thousands of times in pamphlets and quoted on web sites. The author is unknown, but the wisdom is timeless. Keep in mind this guidance as you converse with Jesus.

~ You do not have to be clever to please me; all you have to do is want to love me. Just speak to me as you would to anyone of whom you are very fond.

~ Are there any people you want to pray for? Say their names to me, and ask of me as much as you like. I am generous and know all their needs, but I want you to show your love for them and me by trusting me to do what I know is best.

~ Tell me about the poor, the sick, and the sinners, and if you have lost the friendship or affection of anyone, tell me about that, too.

~ Is there anything you want for your soul? If you like, you can write out a long list of your needs, and come and read it to me.

~ Just tell me about your pride, your touchiness, self-centeredness, meanness and laziness. Do not be ashamed; there are many saints in heaven who had the same faults as you; they prayed to me, and, little by little, their faults were corrected.

~ Do not hesitate to ask me for blessings for the body and mind, for health, money, success. I can give everything, and I always do give everything needed to make souls holier.

~ What are your needs today? Tell me, for I long to do you good. What are your plans? Tell me about them. Is there anyone you want to please? What do you want to do for them?

~ And don't you want to do anything for me? Don't you want to do a little good to the souls of your friends who perhaps have forgotten me? Tell me about your failures and I will show you the cause of them. What are your worries? Who has caused you pain? Tell me all about it, and add that you will forgive and forget, and I will bless you.

~ Are you afraid of anything? Have you any tormenting, unreasonable fears? Trust yourself to me. I am here. I see everything. I will not leave you.

~ Have you no joys to tell me about? Why not share your happiness with me? Tell me what has happened since yesterday to cheer and comfort you. Whatever it was, however big, however small, I'd like to hear about it. It was I who prepared it for you.

~ Ask me to show you your true vocation. Pray to know my will for your life and pray with confidence and trust. Give me your yes now for whenever I ask the question. I promise that I will answer the question of your vocation for you clearly, when the time is right.

~ Well, continue on your way. Get on with your work. Try to be a little quieter, humbler, kinder, and more submissive; and come back soon. I am always here, eager and happy to talk to you.

Your spiritual director will help you learn to pray and develop a consistent spiritual plan of life. And because you will be meeting with him and reporting on your prayer life, he will help hold you accountable to your spiritual duties. Remember, if you are not praying faithfully, every day, then you are not really discerning.

I am constantly amazed at the number of men who are priests who did everything in their power that they would not be! Like that man in the opening story of this chapter, if a man is not praying, he is doing everything in his power not to be a priest. Satan will easily be able to lead this man away not only from his vocation but away from his life's work of holiness.

"To lose one's way is nothing more than the giving up of prayer. Whoever does not pray does not need the devil to lead him off the path. He will throw himself into hell."

St. Teresa of Avila

CHAPTER 7

THE IMPORTANCE OF A SPIRITUAL DIRECTOR

In my experience, men who enter seminary with a history of spiritual direction are more prepared for seminary life. Those who have never had spiritual direction begin immediately when they arrive at seminary.

The Program of Priestly Formation emphasizes that spiritual direction is an essential aspect of seminary discernment (#127-135). St. Bernard of Clairvaux underscored its necessity when he said, "He who is his own master is the disciple of a fool!"[35]

As I read the applications and the autobiographies of the nearly fifty new seminarians beginning their studies each fall, there is a consistent thread: any man who *did* have a regular spiritual director experienced tremendous spiritual growth and discernment progress. Here is a typical story.

In my second year of college, at the advice of my vocation director, I found a great priest who became my spiritual director and I began to meet with him once a month. My spiritual life was immediately transformed! My prayer life grew, I began to serve others more consistently, and my sins began to diminish. He taught me about prayer, gave me great books to read about Jesus and priesthood, and sound advice about growing in holiness. I became excited about holiness as I began to see it as actually possible. The voice of God started coming through with greater clarity. Having someone to talk to about my fears and uncertainties brought me peace. I also learned about the devil. Discernment is not easy and Satan was actively trying to confuse and frustrate me. Once I started meeting with a spiritual director, I learned how to recognize what he was doing and to rebuke him.

Discernment can be tricky and confusing, and Satan is very involved in trying to discourage priestly vocations. For this reason, any man who is seriously discerning priesthood (especially if he is college-aged or older), should try to find a spiritual director.

The first purpose of the spiritual director is to help a man construct a spiritual plan of life and hold him accountable to it. Then, once he is praying faithfully, using the sacraments, and growing in virtue, the discernment of one's vocation becomes a regular topic of discussion. He also will guide the man to good books or resources to aid his discernment.

I am often asked by my spiritual directees, "Father, how do I know that my prayer is working? How can I be sure that I am doing it right?" Charity is the litmus test of prayer. I always ask, "Are you more kind? More gentle? More humble? More patient? Do you think about Jesus more during the day? Do you see your sins diminishing?" As long as a man can answer, "Yes, I think I am growing in charity. I can see myself getting better," then the spiritual plan of life is working.

Remember that prayer does not change God. He is immutable. The purpose of prayer is to change *us*, and this will usually be in small ways. St. Augustine wrote, "The pious soul prays not to inform God but to be conformed to his will."

Internal Forum vs. External Forum

The spiritual direction relationship is in the internal forum, meaning that it is extremely confidential. A man can bear his heart and soul to his spiritual director, confident that whatever he says will never be repeated. The internal forum of spiritual direction is not the same as the the seal of Confession, which is absolutely inviolable in all instances, but it is still sacrosanct.

A man discerning priesthood should go to Confession, preferably to his spiritual director, at least monthly. Don't make the mistake that many pious young men make. They want so much to *impress* their spiritual director that they confess to him only when they have not committed certain sins, when they are "proud of their sins," so to speak. They have another confessor in a far away parish for when they fall, for example, in the area of pornography or masturbation. Don't play this game! Tell your spiritual director everything. If there is something you don't want to tell him, tell him that thing first! He needs to know your virtues and vices in their entirety in order to help you. Hide nothing from him. The relationship is completely confidential and secure.

Please remember that your vocation director operates in the external forum, so he should not be your spiritual director or hear your Confession. This can be disappointing for some men, because your vocation director is likely to be a priest whom you would *desire* to be your spiritual director. In many ways, he is well-suited for the task: he loves the priesthood; he is prayerful and holy; he understands the process of discernment; he is joyful and approachable. This is why the bishop named him vocation director in the first place! But nonetheless, he should not be your spiritual director.

Let me explain. Should you decide to apply for seminary, the vocation director is responsible for evaluating you and sending his report to the bishop and the seminary. In making this evaluation and report, it is too difficult to distinguish what he learned in the internal forum (Confession and spiritual direction) from what he learned in the external forum (the interview and application process). Thus, because he needs to speak to the bishop about you, it is best that he operate only in the external forum.

In contrast, your spiritual director does not talk to anyone about you, not even to the vocation director. The only exception is that you can give permission to your spiritual director to write a letter of recommendation for you, should you apply to seminary. But without your permission, he will say nothing.

Let me be clear. You must talk to your vocation director about sensitive things. You must be completely honest with him about yourself so that he can make the best decision regarding your candidacy. When the time comes to apply, tell him every-thing. Hide nothing! Just don't go to Confession to him.

Finding a Spiritual Director

"Father, I have asked four different priests to be my spiritual director and they have all refused. How can I discern a vocation to diocesan priesthood if I can't get a diocesan priest to help me?"

Many young men have told me how frustrating it is to find a good spiritual director. The reason is that most priests, especially the good ones, are already well occupied. Spiritual direction takes a great deal of time, and their parish duties sometimes have to take precedent. A good spiritual director is a great gift from God and I believe that the Holy Spirit will help a man find the best spiritual director for him. But he will need to pray for this per-son — and then begin a search. God can't drive a parked car; you have to start moving. But how should you go about finding a spi-ritual director?

First, identify the prospects. If you are discerning priesthood, ideally you should try to find a priest to work with you. You might consider starting with your own pastor or one of the priests in your parish. One of the best ways to find a spiritual di-rector is to contact your vocation director and ask his advice. He will know the priests in the diocese who are gifted in this area. The truth is that some priests are simply not very good at spiri-tual direction, specifically for those discerning their vocations. It can frustrate a man greatly if he is going to spiritual direction but not really being directed! It can make him give up on the whole endeavor. So be careful. Ask your vocation director for the names of several priests who are good spiritual directors for men dis-cerning priesthood. Ask seminarians and priests for the names of priests renowned for giving spiritual direction to men discerning priesthood. Ask seminarians who their spiritual directors are. Ask which priests have the reputation of producing many semi-narians from their parish. Once you have identified several priests who might be good potential spiritual directors, the next step is to interview these priests. How does one do this?

Here is some advice on how *not* to begin. Don't call the priest and say, "Father, will you be my spiritual director?" Many priests will reply, "No, I cannot take on another directee right now. I have too many other obligations." Instead call the priest and say, "Father, I am trying to grow in holiness and to know God's will for my life. I might be called to be a priest. Can you meet with me to discuss this? I need some guidance." Most priests will grant a single appointment for such a request. During this appointment, you can honestly discuss your strengths, weaknesses, sins, and vocational discernment. Ask for his wisdom on how you should proceed. He will ask you many questions and interview you to see how to advise you. The truth is, you are interviewing him as well so as to determine if he is the right spiritual director for you (and he is quite aware that you are doing this). Did you feel trust and rapport during the session? Did he give advice that helped you? Is he the kind of priest that you would like to become, if you are called to be a priest? Is he joyful and prayerful, faithful to the Magisterium and the teachings of the Church? This is the kind of spiritual director you want.

At the end, if you feel that he might be a good fit, ask him if he would consider seeing you again about these things in the future. Don't make an appointment yet, but just leave the door open. Get his e-mail address so you can more easily make another appointment later. Then make an appointment with another priest and repeat the process. Developing this relationship with a priest by a first appointment will often persuade that priest to take you on as a directee. I know this well because I have been persuaded in this manner on many occasions to take on yet another young man as a spiritual directee to help him discern his vocation.

I have described here how to find the "ideal" spiritual director, but we have to remember that "beggars can't be choosers."

We often have to accept the person who is willing to take us on as a directee, and this person may not be a priest. Once a man goes to seminary, the Church insists that he have a priest for a spiritual director and these priests are specially selected and trained for this purpose. A seminarian may not have a lay person, a sister, or anyone except a priest once he begins his seminary formation. But in the interim, remember that a non-ideal spiritual director is better than no spiritual director at all.

God will direct you to the person who will really help you but you must make an effort to find that person. I know a man who tried unsuccessfully to find a priest spiritual director for nearly a year. The doors just kept closing. The priests that he wanted were unable to say yes and there were not many priests within a reasonable distance. He finally asked the permanent deacon in his parish for an appointment and received wonderful spiritual direction every month for several years until he entered seminary. I often say that the Holy Spirit will guide you to the right people to help you find your vocation. But you have to make the effort to find those people. God can't drive a parked car. Move!

To Guide, Not Command

In my opinion, a spiritual director's job is to guide, advise, teach, forgive, and encourage. His job is not to command or to pressure a young man to go to seminary with a guilt trip. A spiritual director should not insist on anything as a condition for his services, except that the man pray faithfully. A few men have told me that their spiritual director commanded them under obedience to do this or that. While there may have been a time in the Church when spiritual directors commanded this type of complete obedience, I do not think this is healthy.

If your spiritual director talks all the time and never listens to you or asks you questions, if he is not talking about Jesus, or if he makes you feel uncomfortable by overly-aggressive direction, something is wrong. If he is not a good fit, then change — and don't feel guilty about changing. If you feel uncomfortable with a spiritual direction relationship, pay attention to your instincts. On the other hand, don't run from your spiritual director because he is telling you the truth! I have seen men make the mistake of thinking, "This spiritual director is really challenging me to grow spiritually, and that makes me feel uncomfortable." If this is the discomfort you feel, deal with it and thank God for a good spiritual director.

What Would I Talk About in Spiritual Direction?

If you have never been to regular spiritual direction, you might be wondering how it works. "What would I say? What would we talk about?" These are the types of things that you would cover in spiritual direction.

~ Your spiritual director will help you develop a spiritual plan of life, as outlined in the last chapter.

~ He will help you trace your spiritual and moral history and your family history. Self knowledge is important for discernment.

~ Talk about your prayer. What are you experiencing? Is your prayer dry and difficult or is it exciting and stimulating? Ask advice about how to pray better.

~ Talk about your strengths and weaknesses, virtues and vices. Identify your dominant defect and work to correct it. Go to Confession to your spiritual director regularly.

~ Is there anything about yourself that you suspect is not quite right and which will be important in your discernment? Are you scrupulous about your sins? Are you depressed or anxious a lot? Do you have any obsessions or compulsions? Do you have a problem with anger? Do you suffer from internal turmoil which affects your ability to live your life peacefully?

~ Tell your spiritual director everything about your sexuality. Do you masturbate and entertain impure thoughts? Do you have any same-sex attraction or any other aberrant attractions? Do you look at pornography? Have you ever been sexually active? Are you now sexually active? Were you ever sexually abused or have you abused another? Do not be embarrassed or afraid. Tell him everything and you will be able to move forward in peace.

~ Talk about what excites you in life, what you dream about and think about most, what terrifies you and why. Describe your fears and ask how to pray through your fears.

~ Talk about your relationships with other people, your family, friends, women, etc. Are these relationships healthy and do you have appropriate boundaries? What can you do to improve them?

~ Check the litmus test of prayer: Are you growing in charity? Are you more patient, more kind, more loving, more merciful, and more forgiving of others? Do you trust Jesus more? Are you growing in generosity? Would most people who know you say you are a kind person? Have others noticed you becoming more kind and selfless?

~ Do you love Jesus more, think about him more, and think about his Kingdom?

~ Is there anyone you have not forgiven? Is there anyone you have injured or offended whose forgiveness you need to ask? Do you have difficulty forgiving others easily or asking forgiveness?

~ How are you serving others? Ask your spiritual director if he thinks you are doing enough in this regard.

~ Ask your spiritual director to teach you different ways to pray so as to find the ways that help you most. Ask him to teach you how to do *lectio divina* (prayerful, meditative reading of Sacred Scripture). Ask him to recommend books for spiritual reading.

~ Finally, speak with your spiritual director about vocational discernment. Which vocation seems to be most attractive to you now? What are your fears? Have you received any signs or has anything happened in your life that makes you think you are called toward priesthood? Toward marriage? Toward religious life? Are you confused or are things becoming clearer? How are you praying about your vocation? What are you doing concretely to discern? Are you truly "open" to whatever God might ask you to do or are you having trouble surrendering your will to God? Are you moving toward your vocation for the right reasons? Are you fighting against God or running from him? What does God want you to do right now?

Living a Life of Prayer

Your spiritual director always should ask first about your prayer life. He will ask if you have been faithful to your spiritual plan of life and if you are talking to Jesus every day. Remember, if you are not talking to Jesus, you are not really discerning.

The following observations about prayer were originally written by Fr. Tony Manochio, former spiritual director at Mount St. Mary's Seminary.

~ To be a good Christian, prayer is necessary on a daily basis. Our God is a living God, with whom we must converse.

~ Real prayer begins when the most difficult thing to do is to pray.

~ When it comes to prayer, we are all beginners, no matter how long we have been praying.

~ The secret of a prayer life is perseverance, every day, no matter how difficult or dry.

~ One of the hindrances to prayer is impatience, the anxiety to become a person of prayer instantly.

~ Prayer does not change God. He is unchangeable. Prayer is to change yourself.

~ You can read all the books in the world on prayer, but prayerfulness requires actual prayer—and patience.

~ It is very important to set aside the same time and place every day to pray, and to be very faithful to your appointment with God.

~ Morning is the best time for prayer (for priests especially), but it requires discipline and going to bed at a reasonable hour. Of course, some men are simply not morning people, so your prayer schedule should be discerned with your spiritual director.

~ Never judge prayer by feelings. Go to prayer for God, not for his gifts. The dry times in prayer are vital to a mature prayer life. You simply have to be faithful, no matter how you feel.

~ Never cut corners on your time for prayer. Stay the full time. Twenty to thirty minutes is minimal. Eventually, you will need more time. Do not be stingy with the Lord as far as your time is concerned.

~ Be totally honest in spiritual direction. Be honest about your sins, your relationship with God and with others.

~ Good spiritual direction can only take place when there is faithfulness to prayer. Otherwise, it can turn into a gripe session or a social get-together.

~ Spiritual direction is a grace-filled event, guided by the Holy Spirit, who is the true director. The hearts of both the director and directee must always be open to the Spirit.

~ The spiritual director should pray daily for his directee, and the directee should do likewise.

~ To grow closer to Jesus Christ, it is essential to have a close and loving relationship with Mary, his mother and ours.

Every young man who is serious about holiness and seriously discerning a vocation to diocesan priesthood needs a good spiritual director. He who is his own master is the disciple of a fool! Do not delay any longer. Contact your vocation director for the names of good priests, beg the Holy Spirit to guide you to the right person, then make an appointment. If God wants you to become a priest, he will provide the right people and the right resources to help you.

CHAPTER 8

HEARING THE VOICE OF GOD

---

*"Then the Lord said to Elijah, 'Go outside and stand on the mountain
before the Lord; the Lord will be passing by.' A strong and heavy wind
was rending the mountains and crushing rocks before the Lord – but
the Lord was not in the wind. After the wind, there was an
earthquake – but the Lord was not in the earthquake. After the
earthquake, there was fire – but the Lord was not in the fire. After the
fire, there was a tiny whispering sound. When he heard this, Elijah
hid his face in his cloak and went and stood at the entrance of the
cave."*

1 Kings 19:11-13

Now that we have discussed developing a spiritual plan of
life and finding a spiritual director, we must now talk about *to
whom* we should be listening. Many voices shout for our attention, so we have to be able to distinguish among them. God almost always speaks in a small, still voice as he did to Elijah,
though there are some notable exceptions. St. Paul was knocked
down and struck blind. Only then could he hear the voice of Christ saying, "Saul, Saul, why are you persecuting me?" (Acts 9:4)
God spoke to Moses in thunder and lightning from the mountain
and the Israelites were terrified. They said to Moses, "You speak
to us and we will listen; but let not God speak to us, or we shall
die" (Exodus 20:19). Personally, like the Israelites, I prefer the
small, still voice.

I had a friend who went to the Holy Land many years ago on
a pilgrimage. He told me this story.

> One day, I was standing in the main street of a little vil-
> lage, looking out towards the country. I saw a shepherd

coming into the town with about twenty-five white sheep following him. I had never seen a real, authentic shepherd so I watched with interest. Then I looked in the other direction and saw another shepherd coming into town. He also had about twenty-five white sheep following him. The two shepherds knew one another and greeted each other with a laugh. The two of them began to walk side by side down the main street heading towards the Church, in an animated conversation. Of course, their sheep got all mixed up! I was very concerned about this and wanted to shout, "Can't you see that the sheep are all white and they are getting mixed together. You'll never be able to separate them." But I said nothing. I just watched and learned. At the end of the street, the two shepherds waved to one another and one went to the left and the other to the right. They began to call their sheep using a certain voice, a sound that I had never heard before. The two calls were very distinct. And I watched in amazement as every sheep separated and followed his own shepherd. The shepherds never even looked back. They knew that their sheep would follow their voice!

My friend told me that for the first time, he understood the teaching of Jesus in the Gospel of John, "I am the Good Shepherd, and I know mine and mine know me" (John 10:11). The passage also says, "When he has driven out all his own, he walks ahead of him and the sheep follow him, because they recognize his voice. But they will not follow a stranger; they will run away from him because they do not recognize the voice of strangers" (John 10:4).

Why did those sheep in that story know their master's voice? The shepherd spent an enormous amount of time with those sheep. Shepherds would often spend weeks at a time out in the wilderness with their sheep. Thus to recognize the voice of Jesus, our Good Shepherd, we have to spend a lot of time with him, both in silent prayer and with his Word, the Sacred Scriptures.

In a nutshell, vocational discernment is the process of asking God a question and listening patiently for the answer. "Jesus, what do you want me to do? Do you want me to be a priest? I want to want what you want. Jesus, are you speaking to me?" Understand, however, that God can answer these questions in many different ways.

The Four Voices of Discernment

We have to learn to distinguish the voice of God from the many other voices and noises in the world. There are four primary voices of discernment: God's voice, the world's voice, our own voice, and Satan's voice. These later three correspond to the traditional description of the enemies of God: the world, the flesh, and the devil. Because God usually prefers to speak in his *still, small voice*, we will have to find a time and place for silence if we want to hear it. It is not that God cannot speak loudly and clearly, above any obstacle. He certainly spoke loudly to the Israelites in the Book of Exodus! But he usually prefers to speak quietly and gently, especially with regard to one's vocation. Why? A vocation is an invitation, not a commandment. It is a request. A loud, terrifying voice would be a mandate, not an invitation, causing a person to respond out of fear, not out of love. God does not want this. He wants you to want to hear his voice and to know his will. He does not want to force you, and he will not force you.

Noise is a great obstacle to hearing Jesus, who is meek and humble of heart. Finding time every day for silent prayer, silent listening, is critical. Jesus' desire to tell us our vocation is much greater than our desire to know it, but we must be willing and able to hear it. We must show the Lord through our fidelity to prayer that we desire to know his perfect will regarding our vocations. Let's look at these four voices more closely.

The voice of God will always exude confidence, love, and peace. It will say, "I love you infinitely, no matter what you do or what you decide." As St. Thomas Aquinas points out, God does not love us because we are good; he loves us because he is good.[36] His voice will urge us to desire goodness, to hate evil, to love other people, to repent when we sin, and to show compassion and mercy to others. Many times in my life, I have heard the voice of God through a sudden unexpected thought, "Why don't you go visit Margaret Jones. She has been so sick lately and she could really use some encouragement and prayer." I had not thought of Margaret in a long time, but the Lord was telling me that she needed a visit.

When I was a vocation director, the Holy Spirit would sometimes speak to me by suddenly filling my mind with a thought to check in on a certain young man who was discerning priesthood. "Call him right now!" the Lord seemed to say. When the young man would pick up the phone, he would say, "I can't believe this, Father. I was just praying to God that he send me a sign that I should go to the seminary, and here you are calling me." Or a man would tell me that he received a letter from the vocation office inviting him to a retreat on the very day he finished his novena to St. Therese of Lisieux, a novena asking God if he should go to seminary. Such events happened again and again during my ten years as a vocation director.

The voice of God can come to us at different times of the day, and not only during prayer. We can recognize his voice easily when he tells us that he loves us, that he wants us to love him, to love others, to serve others, and to repent of our sins. These are the things we would expect God to say! The challenge is when he tells us unexpected things. It is hard to be sure of the answer when we ask questions like:

~ Should I ask that girl out on a date?

~ What should I do to help my parents with their troubled marriage?

~ Which college should I attend?

~ Who should I ask to be my spiritual director?

~ When should I contact my diocesan vocation director?

~ What is my vocation?

But keep asking these kinds of questions and keep *actively listening* for the answers. Sometimes God does not immediately answer our questions for serious reasons: because we are not yet ready to hear the answer; because we are not yet able to act on his answer; or because it is just not yet the time for us to know this information. This can be frustrating. But be patient!

A Need-to-Know Basis

I often say to seminarians that God gives us information like in the military, "on a need-to-know basis." If you are diligently pursuing the will of God for your life, I promise you that God will speak this information clearly to you at the proper time. Your job is to be disposed to the Lord's voice, prepared for when God speaks to you about your vocation. God knows when the time is right. Just keep saying to Jesus, "Speak Lord, your servant is listening. I want to want what you want."

"There are only three kinds of persons; those who serve God, having found Him; others who are occupied in seeking Him, not having found Him; while the remainder live without seeking Him and without having found Him. The first are reasonable and happy, the last are foolish and unhappy; those between are unhappy and reasonable."[37]

Blaise Pascal

I once spoke to a seminarian who told me that, during college, every time he prayed he would begin to think about priesthood. I asked him, "What did you do?" He replied, "I stopped praying!" For several months, this young man would continue to go to Mass on Sunday but he refused to pray. He had a girlfriend and he was making plans to marry her. But avoiding prayer did not work for long; he could not stay away from Jesus. He loved him too much. So he eventually started praying again, and once again, he started thinking about priesthood. He eventually entered the seminary. Many young men play these kinds of games. Thankfully, our God is a very patient God!

Is This Really God Speaking?

What about the other three voices? Many young people have asked me, "Father, when I am praying and asking God questions, how can I know if it is really God answering me or if it is just my own mind?" It is a very good question. My recommendation is that when a new thought occurs during prayer, ask yourself, "Who is speaking to me now? God, the world, myself, or Satan?" Use the process of elimination. For example, you may find yourself thinking frequently about being rich, famous, and powerful. But you know that Jesus teaches the opposite: "Blessed are the poor in spirit; the meek, the humble, they shall inherit the earth." Clearly your desire for money and power is not the voice of God, which leaves three other possibilities.

Remember that Satan has been described as the prince of this world, so his voice will always be echoed in the voice of the world. We hear this voice of the world and the devil and see its message everywhere we look. This is why the Missionaries of Charity often quote Blessed Mother Teresa of Calcutta as having called the television "Satan's tabernacle in our homes." So many people sit before this tabernacle five to six hours per day listening to the voices of Satan and the world. This can render God's still, small voice all but inaudible. Give God his time in silence and you will hear him speak clearly! Ask the Holy Spirit to give you this gift of "voice discernment."

Satan the Liar

God's voice is most easily identifiable when he tells you that he loves you and that he wants you to trust him, which makes you feel peaceful. Satan's voice most often will cause anxiety and fear. Remember that Satan is very wicked and cunning. St. Ignatius Loyola, in his fourteenth rule of the discernment of spirits, offers a sound insight about Satan's tactics.

> The enemy of our human nature studies from all sides our theological, cardinal, and moral virtues. Wherever he finds us weakest and most in need regarding our eternal salvation, he attacks and tries to take us by storm.[38]

Just as a military commander looks at the enemy line and finds the weakest point, Satan studies your weaknesses and knows just when and where to attack. For example, if you are a person who finds it hard to trust, perhaps because of a past family issue, Satan will speak to you constantly about this issue. He will encourage you to distrust everyone, especially God: "Look at what has already happened to you. God can't be trusted. Trust yourself only. Do what you think is best. Don't ask God anything."

This inability to trust God is a serious obstacle in discernment, and Satan uses it often. Recognize this voice and rebuke it. For example, you may find yourself thinking and feeling fearfully about priesthood, "I can't do that. I like girls too much. I could never stand up and preach a homily in front of all of those people. I am afraid that I am not holy enough." This is likely the voice of Satan, who uses fear as his greatest weapon. He will try to add his influence to your own disordered voice.

You may become apprehensive because you think you must be a priest on your own power, using your own abilities. No! You can only live a vocation to priesthood through the grace of God. This line of thought demonstrates that you are looking at yourself and not at Jesus (the first error) and you are listening to your own voice and not the voice of Christ (the second error). This is why you are not confident and you are filled with fear. St. Paul says, "I have the strength for everything through him who empowers me" (Philippians 4:13). God will never send you where his grace cannot sustain you.

Rebuke It, Correct It, or Obey It

When a person identifies which voice is speaking, he should do one of three things: rebuke it, correct it, or obey it. If it is the voice of God, obey it. If it is the voice of Satan or the world, rebuke it. But if it is your own voice, you need to decide if it is speaking the truth. Sometimes it will be true, and at other times it will be deceiving. If your own voice is saying to you, "I will never be happy as a priest. I will always be miserable because I am not married and because I cannot do what I want," then you need to correct this voice. The truth is that you will be most happy doing nothing less than the will of God for your life, whatever it might be.

If you are serious about hearing the voice of God, especially regarding your vocation, you need to minimize other voices and maximize the voice of God, who speaks in a small, still voice. The Blessed Virgin Mary was not listening to her iPod when the Archangel Gabriel came to her with a message from God! As a woman of silence, she clearly heard the voice of God.

Once, when presenting this idea at a retreat, a young man responded, "Well, if an angel came to me like Gabriel did to the Blessed Mother, then the voice would be clear. I would answer God's call then and accept his will." I reminded him of the words of Jesus in the parable of Lazarus and the rich man. When the rich man—who was in hell—was begging Abraham to send someone from the dead to warn his brothers, Abraham replied, "If they will not listen to Moses and the prophets, neither will they be persuaded if someone should rise from the dead" (Luke 16:31).

Angels are coming to you all the time. Jesus has risen from the dead! The voice of God is coming to you all the time. Eventually you must give an answer. Mary did: "I am the handmaid of the Lord. Be it done unto me according to thy will."

"Lord, Jesus Christ, Good Shepherd of our souls, you who know Your sheep and know how to reach man's heart.... Stir the heart of those young people who would follow you, but who cannot overcome doubts and fears, and who in the end follow other voices and other paths which lead nowhere. You who are the Word of the Father, the Word which creates and saves, the Word which enlightens and sustains hearts – conquer with your Spirit the resistance and delays of indecisive hearts. Arouse in those whom you call the courage of love's answer: 'Here I am, send me!'"[39]

Pope John Paul II

Prayer before the Blessed Sacrament

During the time young Samuel was minister to the Lord under Eli, a revelation of the Lord was uncommon and vision infrequent. One day Eli was asleep in his usual place. His eyes had lately grown so weak that he could not see. The lamp of God was not yet extinguished, and Samuel was sleeping in the temple of the Lord where the ark of God was. The Lord called to Samuel, who answered, "Here I am." He ran to Eli and said, "Here I am. You called me." "I did not call you," Eli said. "Go back to sleep." So he went back to sleep. Again the Lord called Samuel, who rose and went to Eli. "Here I am," he said. "You called me." But he answered, "I did not call you, my son. Go back to sleep." At that time Samuel was not familiar with the Lord, because the Lord had not revealed anything to him as yet. The Lord called Samuel again, for the third time. Getting up and going to Eli, he said, "Here I am. You called me." Then Eli understood that the Lord was calling the youth. So he said to Samuel, "Go to sleep, and if you are called, reply, 'Speak, Lord, for your servant is listening.'" When Samuel went to sleep in his place, the Lord came and revealed his presence, calling out as before, "Samuel, Samuel!" Samuel answered, "Speak, for your servant is listening."

1 Samuel 3:1-10

This wonderful Old Testament story teaches us at least three very important things about hearing the voice of God. First, every man who is discerning diocesan priesthood should spend silent time regularly before the Blessed Sacrament. Just as God spoke to Samuel *in the temple*, where the Ark of God was present, he will speak to you powerfully before the Blessed Sacrament. This is the Holy of Holies, the very presence of Jesus Christ, body, blood, soul, and divinity. Would you not expect to hear his voice most clearly there?

Second, learning to hear and distinguish the voice of God is an art, acquired only through effort. "Samuel was not familiar with the Lord, because the Lord had not revealed anything to him as yet." We must *practice* silent prayer and listening to God.

Finally, when a young man is first learning to discern the voice of God, he especially needs a more experienced person to guide him. Eli was Samuel's spiritual director: "Go to sleep, and if you are called, reply, 'Speak, Lord, for your servant is listening.'"

I always recommend that a man discerning priesthood should spend a minimum of one continuous hour per week before the Blessed Sacrament. Find a Eucharistic adoration chapel where the Holy Eucharist is enthroned in the monstrance and sign up for an hour. If that is not available to you, then just go and sit in the church before the tabernacle. Ask the Holy Spirit to turn up the volume on the voice of God and to deafen you to all the other voices!

I Tell You, I Do Not Know You!

St. Vincent de Paul was born of peasant parents in a little village near Dax, France with three brothers and two sisters. His father could see that he was both pious and intelligent and he made many sacrifices to send him to school to become a priest. In that day, the life of a priest was a very privileged life. St. Vincent was sent to Paris to study for the priesthood and he had been there for a few years, very much enjoying everything about it. One day, his father arrived unexpectedly. He had walked all the way from Dax (two hours by bus, even today). He had come to visit his son, and he was hungry and exhausted, his ordinary peasant clothing covered with the dust of travel. Another seminarian answered the door and could not believe that this dirty peasant was Vincent's father. He went up to St. Vincent's room and said, "There is a peasant at the door who says that he is your father. But that cannot be true. Is it?" St. Vincent was enamored by education, prestige and fine dress, so when he saw how dirty and poorly clad his father was, he said, "I do not know him." To his own father, who had made so many sacrifices for him, who loved him so much and had walked that great distance to see him, St. Vincent said, "I do not know him." His poor father was devastated and walked away sadly.

St. Vincent was ordained a priest at the extraordinary age of twenty and soon after, he entered a crisis of faith. He admits that, in his early years, his ambition was to be comfortably well-off, which he achieved. He was chaplain to Queen Margaret of Valois and received the income of a small abbey. One day, he was celebrating holy Mass and when he lifted up the chalice, he heard a voice very clearly say, "I tell you, I do not know you." His crisis of faith no doubt stemmed from his treatment of his father and this experience at Mass but mostly it was caused by *the way he was living his priesthood.* He had been studying to become an ecclesiastic, not a priest of Jesus Christ. He did not know the voice of Christ and he was not listening for it, as there were so many other voices speaking loudly. He was empty and depressed. As he later acknowledged, nothing is worse than a priest who knows his theology but does not know Jesus.[40]

During this crisis of faith, St. Vincent de Paul disappeared for three years. He suffered greatly during that time, and when he returned to Paris, he was a different priest. He immediately traveled to Dax to ask his father's forgiveness for denying him. He began to live his entire life in service to the poor, no longer as an ecclesiastic. St. Vincent de Paul later did great work in the formation of seminaries. He wrote: "There is nothing more perfect than the formation of a good priest."[41]

I think one of the reasons St. Vincent focused on priestly formation was because initially he was not formed into a good priest. He had never learned to hear the voice of Jesus, until he heard those horrible words that day at Mass, "I tell you, I do not know you." Learning to recognize the voice of God is not an optional exercise for a priest.

Sin Deafens Us to the Voice of God

Blessed Mother Teresa of Calcutta always said that the soul is the window through which we can see God and hear his voice. If a person is living his life in serious sin, then this window will not be clear. The window needs to be cleaned. If a man is struggling to hear the voice of God, I always ask him how long it has been since he last went to Confession.

Strive to live a life of Christian virtue, go to Confession regularly, and keep that window of communication open and clean. The voice of God will be much more perceptible.

Private Revelation

The primary locus of private revelation is the human heart. Public Revelation (with a capital R) ended with the death of the last apostle; it includes Sacred Scripture, Sacred Tradition, and the teachings of the Magisterium of the Catholic Church. It is a living Revelation, as the Holy Spirit continues to guide his Church through the Holy Father and the bishops of the world. But private revelation—the kind of revelation required for the discernment of one's vocation—is different. You cannot open the Gospel of Matthew and read directly from the lips of Christ, "Oh, and by the way, Thomas O'Malley of Arlington, Virginia, you are being called to diocesan priesthood." Though one's vocation certainly can be indicated in the Scriptures, it is first heard or experienced in the heart. I am using the words "heart" and "soul" to mean roughly the same thing: the deepest refuge of the human person where the Holy Spirit dwells. This is why your spiritual director will ask you from time to time, "What are you feeling and thinking deep down in your own soul?"

Be conscious that your own voice can sometimes speak out of disordered motives: selfishness, pride, or laziness. It can need correcting, especially when your own voice is self-deprecating: "You are not capable of doing that. You are a sinner. Nobody loves you. You are a failure. You have never succeeded in anything. You will never amount to anything." Thoughts like this can arise from low self-confidence, but Satan certainly can build upon this train of thought. Correct this voice by looking back at Christ and making an act of trust. Your previous failures and personal history of sin should not overshadow your discernment. Let your spiritual director and vocation director help you with this part of discernment. The essential question is still the same. Is God calling me to be a priest and is my heart peaceful about it?

Still, private revelations must be tested. What you think you hear God saying to you should always be verified by asking these questions:

~ Is my private revelation in conformity with Church teaching?

~ Does it agree with the Public Revelation of the Church?

~ Is it consistent with my God-given talents, desires, and life circumstances?

A lady once told me that God had spoken to her clearly, saying that she no longer needed to come to Mass or receive the sacraments. All she needed was the Holy Spirit and charismatic prayer. I informed her that she was not hearing the voice of God, but the voice of Satan. God will never command us to do the opposite of what he has already commanded us to do!

I am not suggesting that the voice of God never calls us to do scary things. His call is sometimes very frightening. This is why so many men run from the call to priesthood for so long. It is a call to trust him, even when asked to do something that you know will be difficult. This is the way our faith grows.

The Choice Between the Good and the Best

Often in vocation discernment, the conflict lies in having to choose between two good things, usually between marriage and priesthood. The voice you hear deep down might say, "I want both of these things." But this is not God's voice. He is calling you to only one of these two good things. The Greeks call this the "tragic exclusion." When you choose one vocation, which is a lifetime commitment, you must tragically give up another wonderful vocation, to which you are also very attracted. Discernment is not a choice between good and evil, but often a choice between the good and the best. What is best for you is your proper vocation. The voice of Satan, because he knows of your goodness and your desire to do God's will, will sometimes take a different tactic. He will tempt you not to do evil, but to accept only the good — not the best. Compromising the will of God is a very effective tactic of Satan.

"The biggest human temptation is to settle for too little."[42]

Thomas Merton

Don't accept anything less than God's perfect will for you. The voice of God will resonate with your own voice when you are thinking of your true vocation. In other words, if you are thinking with the mind of Christ, then the voice you hear will always be his.

One way to practice the discernment of voices is to become conscious of your thoughts when your mind is free. Where does your mind wander when you are otherwise unoccupied, when you are lying in your bed all alone at night, with no one to impress? Ask God, "Lord, why do I think about that so much? Whose voice is it? What are you saying to me through this voice or attraction?"

The word "discernment" means "to distinguish between." Learning to distinguish God's voice from all the others is an essential part of discerning a vocation to diocesan priesthood. "Speak Lord, your servant is listening."

CHAPTER 9

THE SEVEN STAGES OF A DILIGENT DISCERNMENT

Over the years, through my experience of working with men discerning diocesan priesthood, I have developed seven stages of discernment. I believe most men pass through these stages, to one degree or another. It will be helpful for you to examine these stages and to try to place yourself in a particular stage. By so doing, you will know what needs to happen next in order to keep moving forward. Please keep in mind that every vocation is a mystery, and thus every man passes through these stages differently on the way to priesthood. Some will pass through the first few stages only to discern that God is *not* calling them to priesthood. Others will keep going all the way to ordination.

Stage 1: The Initial Call

A man in stage 1 has recently experienced an attraction to priesthood for the first time. This initial stage of discernment often takes place during childhood, perhaps at Mass, in a Catholic school classroom, or when a priest invites a man to consider priesthood. It is usually a fascinating attraction that is not well understood, and it leaves one with a sense of wonder. Perhaps this is why many young Catholic boys "play Mass" when they are growing up.

However, for some men, this initial call happens as an adult, and it can be a jarring experience. It may happen after a good retreat, homily, or prayer time. It may happen after another person mentions the possibility of priesthood. It usually involves being drawn toward an especially holy or exemplary priest. I have seen this attraction triggered by attending an ordination Mass, by being personally invited by the bishop, by reading a book, seeing a movie, or enduring a tragedy. I have even read in the autobiographies of a few seminarians that they first thought about becoming a priest when they read about a scandal involving a priest. They reasoned, "The Church needs good priests. Maybe I should consider it."

In this stage, a man feels an initial, mysterious attraction to become a priest, made all the more mysterious since he has almost no information about priesthood, discernment, or seminary. The primary emotions are excitement and wonder. "Could God really be calling me to be a priest?"

Stage 2: Latency Period

A man in stage 2 has now been thinking about priesthood for some time, usually a few years, depending on when he entered stage 1. He is not thinking about it every day, however. Rather, more days pass when he does not think about it at all. The idea surfaces from time to time, usually at Mass, while praying at night, or when another person mentions it. He has not convinced that priesthood is a real possibility. Sometimes a man in stage 2 will prematurely "decide" that he is not being called to priesthood.

Nonetheless, he has gathered more information, through speaking with priests or seminarians, visiting vocation websites, or reading vocation materials. Usually he is a "cyber discerner," looking for information anonymously on the Internet. He may also be praying about his vocation and asking God to give him a sign, but the prayer is sporadic. Usually this man is hoping that the idea of priesthood is a passing fancy, and that he will be able to get married and forget all about it. If he is an adult, the man may be dating women and hoping to fall in love. He might pray, "God, please tell me that priesthood is not what you want from me." The primary emotions are a growing fear and denial. "Why am I still thinking about this?" A man in stage 2 is not very excited about priesthood.

Stage 3: Assessment Period

A man is stage 3 realizes that his attraction to priesthood will not go away, even though he has tried to avoid it. This man is now making a more serious effort to grow in his faith and prayer life. He may find a spiritual director because he realizes that he needs help discerning. He begins to fight the spiritual battle of surrendering to the will of God; some days he wins the battle, and other days he loses. This man's love for God is maturing and he begins to understand the joy of laying down his life for Jesus and his Church. His desire to serve others is growing, and he experiences happiness while serving.

A man in this stage is assessing specific fears now: the fear of celibacy, the fear of not being a holy priest, the fear of loneliness, and the fear of preaching in front of people. With the help of his spiritual director, he begins to assess his qualifications to see if he has the capacity to become a priest. He is now gathering much more specific information about priesthood and seminary life. A man in stage 3 might read a book like this one, whereas a man in stage 2 would probably not!

Though he is still discreet about whom he tells, he may contact his vocation director and disclose that he is discerning. He may go to a discernment retreat sponsored by the vocation office, but perhaps with the hope to "exclude priesthood" from his discernment. He wants to be able to look Jesus in the eyes and say, "I really discerned priesthood and you let me know this was not my call. I was generous. I was willing to sacrifice something very precious (marriage and family), and I am glad that you did not ask me to make this sacrifice."

This man is often still dating, hoping even more desperately to fall in love with his future wife, but also realizing this might not be in God's plan for him. He is trying hard to be sexually pure, with himself and the women he dates. He is trying to assess specifically whether he can live a chaste, celibate life. The primary emotion is still fear, though there is a growing love and trust in

God. Though he may still hope that God is not calling him to priesthood, a man in stage 3 begins to see that he could be happy and fulfilled as a priest. For the first time, he feels a small measure of excitement.

Stage 4: Discernment Shift

A man in stage 4 is moving quickly towards surrender and resignation to the will of God. He has been faithful to prayer, attended retreats, gathered information, and has come to the conclusion that God is *probably* calling him to be a priest. He feels a sense of peace should this be his God-determined vocation. His spiritual director and vocation director are telling him that he has the signs and qualifications. He still may be hoping that God is only calling him to seminary for a year or so, but not to priesthood.

A man in stage 4 has made the decision that he can no longer date women during this time. He realizes that this is not fair to the woman or to God. He must refrain from dating, at least until he discerns that God is not calling him to priesthood. He is talking earnestly with his spiritual director or confessor about celibacy and evaluating his ability to live chastely as a priest.

The essential element of stage 4 is the knowledge that discernment cannot proceed any further outside of seminary. He is just spinning his wheels. He knows that he must shift his discernment from the ordinary world to a seminary environment. He understands that going to seminary is not a final decision to become a priest, but only the next required step in the process. This man tells his family and close friends that he is thinking about giving seminary a try. He certainly has some anxieties and fears, but he also has a much stronger love and trust in God. He has seen the signs; he has felt the call; the call is persistent; he is growing in peace; and his spiritual director has recommended that he go to seminary. This man is thinking, "I can't believe it. I might actually become a priest. And I think I could even be happy as a priest!" Finally, he asks his vocation director if he may begin the application process.

Stage 5: Seminary Discernment

A man in stage 5 has been accepted as a seminarian by his bishop, and the bishop has assigned him to a specific seminary. I usually associate stage 5 with the first two years of seminary, either college seminary or pre-theology. This is a very important stage in discernment. He now has a developed spiritual plan of life: he is going to Mass every day, praying before the Blessed Sacrament, and seriously studying the faith. He is living in a seminary, surrounded by other men who are also discerning diocesan priesthood. This man is excited about his faith, but still not sure that he will be ordained a priest. He says to people, "Seminary is where God is calling me right now, but I am not sure that I will end up a priest."

In the first years of seminary, this man is falling in love with Jesus and the Catholic Faith. He is praying, going to spiritual direction, studying, and serving. He talks with his fellow seminarians about their vocational discernment. He asks God every day for more certainty that he should become a priest. He prays about whether to attend seminary for another year. This man is peaceful about the priesthood and has a growing belief that he will end up a priest, though he is keeping his options open. Friends, family, and acquaintances know that he is in the seminary and he is addressing their questions. His picture is on the diocesan poster of seminarians.

Stage 6: Consistent Peace

This man has been in seminary from two to four years and he has grown tremendously in faith, prayer, knowledge, and generosity. This man knows Jesus personally. He has spent countless hours in prayer and study and he is very capable of teaching others about Christ. The excitement of those early years in semi-

nary are over and he is now doing the hard work of priestly formation through daily prayer and study. This man is accustomed
to the idea that he is very likely going to become a priest.

He knows himself much better now, and knows that he can
fulfill the duties of a priest. He has had several summer assignments working in parishes and he finds that he really loves living
in a parish and doing parish work. He thinks and feels that God
wants him to be a priest, and he feels a residual peace and happiness. He is still talking with his spiritual director about celibacy
and chastity and praying that God will give him the gift of living
celibacy in tranquility of mind. He is receiving very positive af-
firmation from the seminary formation team, from his spiritual
director, from his vocation director, and his bishop. This man is
leaving the stages of discernment. He, and everyone else, as-
sumes that he will be a priest. He is excited about this and looks
forward to his ordination.

Stage 7: Moral Certitude

Stage 7 begins *at the very latest* when a man arrives back at
the seminary to begin third theology. This is not really a stage of
discernment so much as an end to discernment. A man in stage 7
is no longer asking God if he should become a priest or if he has
the gift of celibacy. He is preparing to be ordained a deacon at the
end of third theology and then, one year later, a priest. This man
has achieved moral certitude that this is God's will. He is not absolutely certain, because that is not possible, but he has received
every indication that he should become a priest. This man might
still be praying that God will stop him if he does not want him to
become a priest. But he says, "Lord, unless you send me a clear
sign that you want me to stop, I will keep moving forward."

A man in stage 7 is not asking God if he should become a
priest; he is asking God to help him become a good, holy priest.
This man does not have many fears left about becoming a priest.
He is confident, through the grace of Jesus Christ and his

extensive training, that he can do what a priest does and be what a priest is. The primary emotion associated with stage 7 is excitement.

E-mail your vocation director and tell him about your current stage of discernment. He will advise you on how to proceed.

Making a Diligent Discernment

In order to pass through these seven stages, you will need to make a *diligent discernment*. The word "diligent" comes from a Latin word *diligere*, which means to love and to choose, or to respond appropriately, after careful study. The word "discernment" comes from the Latin word *discernere* which means to separate by sifting; to distinguish between.

I would therefore define diligent discernment as a process of prayer and careful study that takes place over an appropriate period of time. It requires accurate information about priesthood, the guidance of the Holy Spirit, a good spiritual director, and the vocation director. Once a man has diligently discerned in this way, he can be confident that God loves him too much to let him make a mistake. A diligent discernment includes:

~ A daily, sustained spiritual plan of life which includes at least thirty minutes of private silent prayer. If you are not praying, you are not discerning!

~ Living a consistent Christian moral life and going to Confession regularly.

~ Attaining good, accurate information about diocesan priesthood and how to discern.

~ Seeing a wise, holy spiritual director at least monthly (or as often as possible) and being open and honest with him about everything.

~ Regular contact with your diocesan vocation director and bishop. You cannot discern diocesan priesthood without the Church!

~ Attending regular discernment groups, holy hours, and vocation retreats.

~ Serving others generously on a regular, continuous basis.

~ Doing all of the above consistently for a prolonged period of time (usually more than one year).

~ Having the courage to make a decision to move in one direction or another, once the diligent discernment has been made.

A diligent discernment leads to a generous decision to go to the next stage of discernment by going to seminary. Of course, it might also lead a man to make the correct decision that God is not calling him to diocesan priesthood. He can now exclude that possibility and continue discerning the will of God regarding his vocation.

I have known men who watched a single video about priesthood on a website, prayed a few days, and then pronounced to me definitely, "Father, God is not calling me to priesthood. I asked him and he told me no." This is premature, immature, and irresponsible. This is not being open to the will of God and it is not a diligent discernment. On the other hand, I have known men who have been going through the discernment process for twenty years and they are still "discerning" today! They still have not made a decision. But then again, they have made a decision—a decision to do nothing. Discernment is not a vocation! A diligent discernment means that a man discerns for a *sufficient amount of time* and then courageously makes a decision and acts on it.

CHAPTER 10

PRACTICAL IDEAS FOR DISCERNING DIOCESAN PRIESTHOOD

So far, I have covered some of the prerequisites for discerning a vocation to diocesan priesthood, which is sometimes called "remote preparation." In this chapter, I will offer some practical ideas for discernment, or what is sometimes called "proximate preparation." I have seen many of these practices bear fruit, but all of them will not be applicable to everyone. Do not think that you must do all of these things before you can go to seminary.

"Even if you are on the right track, you will get run over if you just sit there."[43]

Will Rogers

---

1. God Can't Drive a Parked Car. It's Time to Move!

If a man is moving — gathering information, praying, growing in holiness, checking out vocation websites, reading books, talking with his spiritual director — the Lord can guide his movements. He will close some doors, causing the man to turn and go a different way. He will open other doors for the man to pass through. Some men just sit in their rooms and pray, "Jesus, please tell me my vocation." And the Lord says, "I will. But God can't drive a parked car. Move!" Have you done everything that you need to do in order to know the will of God? If not, then maybe Jesus is waiting on *you*.

2. Leave the World of Secret Cyber-Discernment

A man cannot correctly discern diocesan priesthood by sitting alone in front of his computer all day, reading vocation web sites. Wonderful resources are available online, such as aptitude tests that measure if an individual has the characteristics to be a priest. While these sites provide helpful information, they also can lead to confusion if used alone without the guidance of a spiritual director and one's vocation director. Most men begin their discernment online because they can remain anonymous; they can "fly under the radar." But cyber-discernment is most useful in stages 1, 2 and 3 of discernment (as covered in Chapter 9). It can only take a man so far.

I recall e-mailing a man to ask if he had contacted his vocation director yet. He replied, "I have been corresponding with a vocation director in Australia." He had no desire to be a priest in Australia, but he was fearful of contacting his own vocation director. He was afraid the local vocation director might come to visit him and "blow his cover." Cyber-discernment is fine in the beginning, but eventually a man must discern face-to-face with those whom the Church has put in charge of this apostolate.

As a general rule, a man should let his local pastor know that he is considering priesthood, especially if he is already in contact with the vocation director of the diocese. The pastor will respect your request for confidentiality. He will not put your name in the bulletin next to a picture of a priest! Another reason to tell your pastor is to avoid embarrassment, to both you and him. It would be awkward if the vocation director mentioned to your pastor that one of his parishioners was discerning priesthood, but your pastor had no idea. Priesthood is about dealing with people and it must be discerned with people. Eventually you have to come out into the open and say, "Okay, I admit it. Priesthood is a possibility for me."

3. Contact Your Vocation Director

In whatever stage of discernment you might be, it is not too early to contact the vocation director of your diocese. Do not be afraid to take this step. You cannot make a diligent discernment without him! It is not possible to discern diocesan priesthood without the diocese, represented by the vocation director and your bishop. Go to the diocesan website, and send him an e-mail to begin correspondence. If you want to keep your discussions confidential, tell him. He will respect your desire for confidentiality. He won't send you mail addressed to your home with the diocese's vocation office logo stamped on the corner.

4. Attend Vocation Retreats and Discernment Groups

I have never seen the Holy Spirit work more powerfully in a candidate than on vocation retreats. I have organized many vocation retreats and I have preached many more. The axiom that "Jesus is never outdone in generosity" proves true about vocation retreats. When a man gives up several days to go on a vocation retreat, he will leave that retreat having received significant graces. He will be encouraged by hearing that other men have the same questions and fears as he does. Meeting other men in the diocese who are discerning priesthood is exciting.

Many vocation directors also sponsor discernment groups for the same purpose. These groups of young men meet with the vocation director once a month or so, perhaps pray a Holy Hour together, and then have pizza and a discussion. The vocation director basically guides the discussion around the different aspects of discernment of diocesan priesthood.

The vocation directors of most dioceses will normally sponsor these types of discernment events a few times per year and the bishop will often be present for some of them. If you are serious about doing the will of God and anxious about discovering your vocation, attend some of these events. Go to the web site, find out the dates for the next discernment events, sign up, and put them on your calendar. Do it now!

5. Say Three Hail Marys Every Day

It's an old practice, but very effective. Say three Hail Marys every day, asking the Blessed Virgin Mary to pray for you regarding your vocation. Add this to your spiritual plan of life and be faithful to it. This little exercise ensures that you think and pray about your vocation every single day. Finding your vocation is the most important discovery you will ever make in your life. It requires thought and prayer on a daily basis.

6. Find a Spiritually Nourishing Environment

Your old "drinking buddies" are probably not the best people to help you learn the will of God. Many men need to change environments in order to discern their vocations correctly. When I read the autobiographies of seminarians, I have noticed that many decided to start spending time with others who love the Lord Jesus. Some may have decided to attend a Catholic college or become active in their youth groups or campus ministries. Many seminarians once served in wonderful evangelization groups like NET (National Evangelization Teams) or FOCUS (Fellowship of Catholic University Students). If a man chooses to remain immersed in a secular and pagan culture, it will be difficult to live a holy life and to know and accept his vocation, because we are influenced powerfully — both for the good and the bad — by our culture and surroundings.

An old adage says, "If you always do what you always did, you will always get what you always got." Perhaps your old habits and lifestyle are not getting you anywhere. Maybe the Lord is waiting for you to become serious, to make a change, before he reveals to you your vocation. I am not suggesting that you should go off into the desert and become a hermit, but perhaps some changes in lifestyle are needed. Speak to your spiritual director about this.

God can't drive a parked car. Move!

7. Serve in Your Parish and Learn to Love the Sacred Liturgy

I once celebrated a funeral Mass for a small boy killed in a terrible farm accident. The church was packed and many non-Catholics had come to support the boy's family. After the Mass, a very distinguished-looking and articulate man introduced himself to me. He said, "Father, I am not a Catholic, but that was the most beautiful funeral I have ever attended. That's how I want to be buried." I told him, "Well, become a Catholic and we will bury you just like that!" He laughed and said he would consider it. In time, he did become a Catholic and he is a very prominent member of his parish to this day.

The Catholic liturgy is extraordinarily beautiful, and when it is reverently and authentically celebrated, it cultivates priestly vocations. Every priestly vocation is centered on the Holy Eucharist, so when young men are involved in the liturgical life of the Church, they experience a deeper appreciation for the gift of the Eucharist. Quite naturally, they begin to envision themselves actually celebrating the sacred liturgy.

Almost all of the seminarians I have known through the years were actively involved in their parishes prior to coming to seminary. They served as altar servers, lectors, Eucharistic ministers, sacristans, and youth directors. Some taught Sunday school or RCIA. and others visited the sick or the imprisoned. A man called to diocesan priesthood normally finds himself attracted to parish life. If you are not currently involved in your parish, the liturgy is a great place to start!

8. Pray Before the Blessed Sacrament

Most seminarians I know spent a lot of time in prayer before the Blessed Sacrament before they entered seminary. Praying before our Eucharistic Lord always draws a man's heart toward Jesus, and if he is called, toward priesthood. Go pray in an adoration chapel or during Holy Hour when the Eucharist is enthroned in the monstrance, or simply before the tabernacle in the church. The real presence of the Lord Jesus in the Holy Eucharist is the "source and summit" of the Catholic faith—and it is accessible only through the hands of a priest! This obvious point is not missed when a young man is kneeling before the Eucharistic Lord praying about his vocation. He might think "This is Jesus here. This is God. And priests exist to make him sacramentally present to the faithful!"

If there is an adoration chapel in your parish or vicinity, schedule yourself for at least one hour per week. If not, at least make it a part of your spiritual plan of life to pray regularly before the Blessed Sacrament.

9. Serve the Poor

I remember one man who had discerned for several years but never received a clear answer from the Lord. He finally quit his job and went to South America to serve the poor for one year, asking God to show him his vocation once and for all. He never came back. He found his vocation, serving there in generous single life. Many others have served in this way, then returned and went immediately to seminary. Jesus and the Kingdom of God can be seen and realized very powerfully in the very poor. Go search for him there. When you find Jesus there, you will know your vocation.

A man once told me about an amazing teacher he had in eighth grade in his Catholic school. One day, the teacher gave a homework assignment to his students to write one hundred times: "The only way to be happy in life is to serve other people, to lay down one's life for others." The man told me that he and the other students thought this was the stupidest assignment ever and a big waste of time. He did it begrudgingly and turned it in the next day, albeit very messy. As an adult, he said, "I cannot tell you how many times in my life, when I realized that I was not happy or fulfilled, I remembered that assignment. I then sought and found an opportunity to serve others and was lifted out of my dissatisfaction!"

Quitting school or your job to spend a year of your life serving the poor is a radical decision. Not all are called to do it. But the poor can be found everywhere. Perhaps you can serve the poor for a summer or for a week-long mission trip. Such a decision will bring you many graces and blessings—and perhaps clarity regarding your vocation. This path has worked for many others before you, even if they were not actively seeking their vocation. I recommend it highly, but ask your spiritual director and vocation director for their advice regarding where you should go and what you should do.

10. Visit a Seminary

Don't try to discern diocesan priesthood only by reading books, listening to vocation talks, and examining web sites. Go visit a seminary. Many seminaries have "Come and See" days during which you are invited to attend classes, morning prayer, Mass, and Eucharistic Adoration. You will eat meals with seminarians and ask them questions. You might even have the opportunity to meet with the rector, academic dean, and other seminary officials. I can assure you that you will leave the seminary with much better information for discernment. Most men think that a seminary is like a monastery, where everyone walks around in silence, with shaved heads, reading their Bibles. But you will discover something much different. You will kneel in the seminary chapel and ask yourself questions like: Can I see myself here? Do I belong here? Am I excited about this? What are my fears? What does my heart say? Is Jesus calling me to come and give seminary a try?

I recommend that you call your vocation director and ask him to schedule a seminary visit. Normally it is best to visit the seminary that is used by your respective diocese, because it likely will be the seminary you will attend, if that is your path.

God can't drive a parked car. Move!

11. Attend the Priesthood Ordination and Chrism Mass in your Diocese

The ordination of a priest is one of the most beautiful and powerful liturgies in the Catholic Church. If you have never attended one, put this on your to-do list immediately. I have read in the autobiographies of many seminarians that attending an ordination greatly enriched their discernment, or even triggered them to begin discerning in the first place.

One especially powerful moment occurs when the ordinandi (the man being ordained) prostrates himself face down on the floor of the cathedral while the people are singing the litany of saints. This man is laying down his life, literally, spiritually, and figuratively, for Jesus Christ and his Church! Everyone else in the cathedral, including the bishop, is kneeling, praying with the saints in heaven that this man will be a holy, faithful priest. Once the litany of saints is completed, the man comes to the bishop and kneels before him. The bishop lays his hands on the man's head in silence and then prays the required prayer of consecration. The choir often sings *Veni Creator Spiritus* (Come Creator Spirit). This man is now a priest forever.

Go to the next priesthood ordination in your diocese! They are usually held in May or June. The exact date will be listed on the diocesan web site. Your vocation director might need to secure a ticket for you, as space in many cathedrals is limited, so be sure to e-mail him in advance. And at the moment of ordination—when the bishop lays his hands on the man's head and the Holy Spirit rushes down—ask the Holy Spirit if he is calling you to be a priest.

Attending the Chrism Mass is another great discernment opportunity. This is the Mass during Holy Week when the bishop blesses the holy oils which will be used in all the parishes of the diocese for the administration of the sacraments. Every priest in the diocese (ideally) is present, and together they renew their priestly promises to the bishop. Seeing the unity and brotherhood of the priesthood can be very inspiring—and inviting.

12. Make a General Confession

Self-knowledge—an honest and total appraisal of who you are before God—is essential if you are to correctly discern your vocation. One helpful practice is to make a general Confession of your entire life. I recommend that you do this with your spiritual director, if he is a priest. If he is not, then find a good priest whom you trust. This is not the kind of Confession you make on Saturday afternoon before the vigil Mass! Instead, make an appointment for at least one hour.

To help remember your past, St. Ignatius Loyola recommends that you review your life in seven-year increments. For instance, at age seven, what sins had you committed or what sins were committed against you? What did you know of God, of sin, of goodness? What was your relationship with Jesus? Describe your vices and virtues during that time period. What happened to you that was formative or detrimental in your quest for holiness? What was your frame of mind regarding your vocation at the age of seven? Then review your life from the age of eight to fourteen. By this time, you will have emerged from the years of sexual latency, so your sins and struggles likely will include this process of sexual integration. The years of emancipation and individuation—fourteen to twenty-one—are the ones most people dread in this general Confession. Relax and tell it all. Continue to confess your sins, especially habitual sins, and describe your life in seven-year increments up to the present.

A general Confession is more than confessing the sins of your life. It is a complete appraisal of who you are before God. This is why it is important to include your virtues, your good deeds, and your good qualities. This is one thing that makes a general Confession different from an ordinary Confession. Talk about the good you did, what you learned, people whom you served, and virtues that you developed.

Please remember that you likely will have already confessed your sins in previous Confessions and they have already been forgiven. The purpose of the general Confession is not to make you feel bad about these past sins, but to help you review your whole life. You may discover there are people whom you still need to forgive. You may find that you need to ask someone's forgiveness. Once you see clearly where you have been, you will be able to see more clearly where to go.

I recommend a general Confession as an effective discernment technique, but please don't beat yourself up. As you remember and confess your sins, do it in a spirit of gratitude to God for his goodness, love, and mercy. Remember that even St. Paul persecuted the Church and had Christians killed before becoming one of the Church's greatest saints. This history caused St. Paul great pain. Like St. Paul, your personal history of sin is not an obstacle to your future greatness! Think of your past as the Old Testament of your life, and think of the years ahead as the New Testament—a time focused on Jesus.

Warning: some men approach their vocation director and express an interest in priesthood precisely because they have committed terrible sins and feel deeply guilty. They have the misguided idea that becoming a priest somehow will atone for their sins before God. I recall hearing of a young man who scheduled an appointment with his vocation director. The more the vocation director spoke to him, the more he realized that this young man did not really have the signs of a good candidate. He did not really have a desire to be a priest. He was not excited about it. He could not articulate why he was attracted to priesthood. Finally, the vocation director asked him outright, "You don't have to answer this if you don't want to, but have you committed some big sin that is really tormenting you?" The young man began to cry. He said that he had impregnated his girlfriend a year before and had taken her to have an abortion.

Since that time, he had not been able to forgive himself. Though he had gone to Confession, he could not sleep or eat. He was depressed. He had withdrawn from all of his friends. He was desperately seeking something to make himself feel better. He was hoping that by becoming a priest, all would be well. Of course, this is an inadequate reason for pursuing the priesthood.

"The last temptation is the greatest treason: to do the right deed for the wrong reason."[44]

T.S. Eliot

---

13. Write Down the Pros and Cons of Marriage and Priesthood

Most men who are discerning priesthood are trying to make a choice between the two "vocation sacraments" of marriage and priesthood. They are contemplating what the Greeks call "the tragic exclusion" — a decision to follow one good that necessarily means giving up another great good. A very helpful exercise is to go before Jesus in the Blessed Sacrament and write down the pros and cons of each of these vocations, as you see them. Detail the blessings and the sacrifices, then put them in order of importance to you. Pray over these lists and ask Jesus to show you what is most important. Show these two lists to your spiritual director and talk about them.

Perhaps you will need to go visit a holy Catholic family to learn more about holy marriage. Many men today did not grow up in stable, practicing Catholic families. They may have experienced divorce, fighting, alcoholism, and a general lack of stability. A man with this negative experience cannot rule out holy marriage in favor of priesthood because he does not know what holy marriage is! He has never seen one. Go and visit a good Catholic family recommended by your vocation director or pastor. It should be a family with several children, a family that

169

prays together daily, a family that attends Sunday Mass faithfully, a family that exemplifies an "intimate community of life and love."[45] Ask the husband and wife questions about the joys and sorrows of family life. Spend time with them and watch how they raise their children, with that wonderful grace-filled mixture of love, discipline, faith, kindness, work, and sacrifice. With this information, God can speak to you more clearly about holy marriage.

Do you have enough information to discern diocesan priesthood? Do you have enough information about both of these vocations? If not, you need more. Ask your spiritual director if your list is accurate and realistic. You cannot make a good decision without good information. If you have bad information, you likely will make a bad decision.

14. The "What Can I Live Without?" Meditation

One exercise in particular was very helpful in my own discernment of a priestly vocation. Though I had all the signs that I was called to diocesan priesthood, my heart was very attracted to marriage and family. I was continually going back and forth between the two and found myself at a standstill. Finally, my spiritual director, a holy Trappist monk, suggested a very creative exercise. He told me to go before Jesus in the Blessed Sacrament for two consecutive days, each time for one continuous hour. The first day I was to have a "holy fantasy" about marriage and family life. The second day I was to have a "holy fantasy" about being a priest.

On the first day, after asking for the Holy Spirit's inspiration, I spent the hour thinking and imagining my life dating the holy Catholic woman I would marry. I then imagined the marriage preparation program with the local priest and the day of the wedding. I spent time thinking about the honeymoon and returning home to ordinary married life. I imagined my profession and working to support my family. I spent time thinking about the joys and sorrows of married life. During this holy fantasy, my six children were born and they began to grow up. We had our children baptized and we took them to Mass every Sunday. We prayed daily as a family and read the Bible. We taught our children about Jesus and I brought them with me to the church to make a visit, going for ice cream afterward. I attended and coached their ballgames and sat through their piano recitals. We went on vacation in the summer and visited our in-laws at Thanksgiving and Christmas. I imagined disciplining the children, dealing with the bad decisions that they made, and loving them through it all. My wife and I had a few fights through the years but we made up afterward. There were a few sicknesses, accidents and injuries, and there were some crises in the family. I tried to imagine the good and the bad, the joys and the sorrows. I spent time imagining my wife and I growing old together. I attended the weddings (and ordinations) of my own children. That was especially interesting! The holy fantasy ended with my death, when I went before Jesus for my particular judgment. I died a happy death, surrounded by my wife and children and grandchildren, having received the sacraments of Confession, Anointing of the Sick and Viaticum. I went before the Lord and looked into his eyes earnestly and I asked, "Did I make the right decision? Was marriage my vocation?" The Lord did not answer as far as I could tell, but I was excited by the prayer. This was a powerful meditation and when I finished it, I thought "Marriage is the vocation for me."

The next day, I returned to the church to do the same exercise for priesthood. I asked the Holy Spirit to help me make this prayer well and I began a "holy fantasy" about being a priest. I imagined the application process and acceptance by the bishop (though I did not know much about it at the time). I tried to imagine what seminary was like, though it was difficult since I had never visited one. I imagined my ordination day and my first Mass. I looked intently at the Body and Blood of Jesus Christ in my hands, present because I had just said the words of consecration. "Jesus is God and he has come down here, for my sake and the sake of these people, because I am a priest." I began to hear Confessions and I preached mighty sermons. There were lots of conversions, too. (It was a fantasy, after all, so I made it a good one!) I imagined life in a rectory and working with other priests. I did baptisms and funerals. I celebrated Holy Mass at Christmas and Easter. I visited school children and had a great time teaching them about Christ and the Church. In my fantasy, they really listened and took to heart everything I said. I prayed a holy hour in the Church every day as a priest and became (in my imagination) more and more holy. I visited the sick and the suffering. I counseled those with heavy crosses and marriage problems. I began to preach retreats and to encourage young men to be priests, since I was so happy as a priest. I tried to be realistic, so I also imagined some lonely nights in the rectory when I greatly desired a wife and companion. People became angry with me for preaching about some of the tough moral teachings of the Church. I was transferred by my bishop several times and liked some assignments more than others. I celebrated ten years as a priest and then twenty-five. I had a few illnesses and had to carry those crosses. I tried to imagine what I looked like as a priest at the age of fifty and again at age seventy-five. I imagined what the people of God thought of me.

The holy fantasy ended with my death and I went before Jesus for my Particular Judgment. I died a happy death after being a faithful priest for over fifty years. I had baptized hundreds of babies and celebrated thousands of Masses. I had heard so many Confessions that I could not count them all. I was very peaceful on my deathbed, surrounded by my family, my brothers and sisters and my many nieces and nephews. They were all kneeling around the bed, praying the rosary. I had received all the sacraments and I had no regrets. I had spent my life working for God in a wonderful way. I was a priest of Jesus Christ and my treasure was in heaven! My parish was holding a vigil for me in the church. They had around-the-clock adoration of the Blessed Sacrament, praying for their pastor as I was dying. After I died, I went before the Lord and looked into his eyes earnestly and asked, "Did I make the right decision? Was priesthood my vocation?" Once again, the answer was not clear. If it was yes, it was not a resounding yes, but it was more than I had gotten after the marriage meditation.

At the end of the second day, I thought "This is not really helping me. It's just making me want both marriage and priesthood even more." Then I remembered the advice of the holy Trappist, who told me, "See which one you can live without." I began to reason that if I became a priest, I would never have my own wife and my own children. I would never have all of those wonderful moments that God gives a person in the married vocation. I would miss that very much. I greatly desired those experiences.

Then I began to reason that if I got married and had a family, I would never be a priest. I would never celebrate Mass and feed people with the Eucharist. I would never hear a Confession and wash away sins with the words of absolution. People would never call me "Father." With that thought, I felt a sword go through my soul. It was a great moment of grace. It was the day I realized that I *could* live without marriage and family, but I could *not* live without priesthood. It was a tragic exclusion, but it was the moment of truth.

15. Make the Spiritual Exercises of St. Ignatius Loyola

To make a retreat using the Spiritual Exercises of St. Ignatius Loyola is one of the best ways to discern your vocation. While I highly recommend the Spiritual Exercises, they fit some people's spirituality better than others. They are quite demanding and may not be for everyone.

The Spiritual Exercises were written by St. Ignatius Loyola, the founder of the Society of Jesus (the Jesuits), over a period of twelve years, from 1521 to 1533. In his own words, the Spiritual

Exercises are "a carefully planned method of examination of conscience, of meditation, of vocal and mental prayer and other spiritual activities."[46] Their purpose is very clear: to help a person remove his sinful addictions, to dispose him to learn what God expects of him, and then to discover it and do it. In other words, to help a person become a saint.

Historically, there is a tremendous saint-making power in the Spiritual Exercises: over four hundred fifty canonized saints have attributed great spiritual progress to them. Over forty Popes have formally approved and praised the Spiritual Exercises and strongly recommended them for use by the faithful. Blessed Mother Teresa of Calcutta first made them when she was sixteen years old and they changed her life. I once heard a priest say that the Spiritual Exercises of St. Ignatius Loyola are so powerful that they almost could be considered a sacrament—and he was not even a Jesuit!

How do the Spiritual Exercises work? They were written to be observed over a period of thirty days of silence. Typically, a person does not attend conferences or talks, as may be expected at a typical retreat. Rather, on an Ignatian retreat, the retreatant meets for one hour each day with the retreat master, who assigns certain prayers or meditations. The retreatant then meets again the next day and reports on his prayer experiences. Based on this report, he is given the next meditations or asked to repeat one of the previous ones. If the plan of St. Ignatius is followed correctly, the retreatant will be asked to make four or five one-hour meditations per day.

Thirty days of silence with long periods of prayer is very intense. It is not for everyone. But don't let this frighten you too quickly. Most retreat masters recommend that you begin with a weekend version of the Ignatian retreat. Then, if that goes well, you might want to sign up for an eight-day retreat. Most retreat masters will not even allow a person to attempt the thirty-day retreat until he has experienced the eight-day retreat. If this is something you think the Lord wants you to do, check with your spiritual director or vocation director. He can make a recommendation on how to proceed. Choosing the right retreat center and the right retreat master is very important to having the best experience.

God can't drive a parked car. Move!

16. The Agony of Uncertainty- Pray for a Different Sign

I remember hearing a priest give a vocation talk many years ago. He said, "If it looks like a duck, walks like a duck, and quacks like a duck, and upon further investigation, you discover that it has webbed feet, why do you keep asking if it is a duck?" He was making the point that some men have all the signs that they are called to become priests, but they don't want it to be true. They are struggling to surrender their will to God. They have not yet trusted that "in his will is our peace."[47]

Discernment is an agony. The word *agony* has its origins in the ancient Greek Olympic games when wrestling matches sometimes lasted for hours, exhausting the combatants to the point of collapse. The state of the two men during this match was described as *agony*. It is this same Greek word that is used in the gospels to describe the agony in the garden, the night before Jesus' death when he struggled to do the will of God: "My Father, if it is possible, let this cup pass away from me; yet, not as I will, but as you will" (Matthew 26:39).

Many men have prayed this agonizing prayer of Jesus many times while discerning their vocation. "Father, let this cup pass away from me. I would rather not become a priest. Yet, not as I will, but as you will." I think that most men desire certainty about their vocation precisely because discernment is such agony. In other words, a man reasons, "If I am going to do something for God as heroic as becoming a priest, I want to be sure it is really God's will." So he wants a clear sign—what I call an idiot-proof sign.

But sometimes when God sends signs, men still have trouble seeing them. A man I know, who is now a priest, told me about a conversation with his vocation director:

> It was about the hundredth time we were having this discussion, and he was understandably losing his patience with me. I said, "If God would only send me a sign, then I would go to the seminary and become a priest. I need a clear sign." And he replied in exasperation, "God has already sent you a sign. He has sent you a thousand signs! You just don't want to accept the truth."

It was a moment of grace. He knew that his vocation director was right. He had all the signs. So he changed the way he was praying that day. He was still asking for a sign but he prayed for it in a different way: "Lord, you have given me so many indications that you want me to be a priest and you have been so patient with me. Please send me an idiot-proof sign if you *don't* want me to be a priest. Otherwise, I am moving in that direction."

God never sent him any more signs, except that every door opened. He was accepted by his bishop to study for his diocese. He was accepted by the seminary. He completed his studies and he reached the day of ordination. He said, "On that day, I was finally certain that God wanted me to be a priest. God called me and the Church confirmed that call. Every year of my life since ordination, I am more certain that God wants me to be a priest. I have been happy and fulfilled. I have flourished in this vocation."

I recommend to you a very practical consideration. If you have all the signs—if you look like a duck in every way; if your spiritual director thinks you are a duck; if your vocation director and bishop both think you are a duck—you would be a quack not to go to the seminary!

17. Embrace the vocation that you perceive to be the most generous

Most men with whom I have worked are trying to discern between Holy Marriage and Holy Orders. As you have studied and prayed and tried to learn about both vocations, which of the two do you perceive to be the most generous thing you can do for God? Embrace that one and you likely will make the correct decision.

I knew of a man who asked himself in college, "What is the most generous thing I can do for God?" In his perception at that time, he decided priesthood was the most generous thing he could do for God. And he did become a priest. Interestingly, at his twenty-fifth anniversary of priesthood, he said that he had changed his understanding. He was more certain than ever that he was called to become a priest, but had changed his perception of which vocation was most generous. After being a part of so many wonderful Catholic families for twenty-five years and witnessing the sacrifices made by husbands and wives, he had come to believe that marriage was more generous.

Both marriage and priesthood require great generosity to live them as God intends. But try the exercise that worked for that priest. I recommend it to you because it has worked for others.

God can't drive a parked car. Move!

18. Pray a Novena to St. Therese, the Little Flower of Jesus

St. Therese, the Little Flower of Jesus, is one of the most popular saints for men desperate to know their vocations. St. Therese promised as she was dying that she would spend her time in heaven doing good for people on earth, and she has done so. Many seminarians and priests have related to me that they discovered their vocation through her intercession.

A novena is a spiritual devotion undertaken for nine consecutive days, usually asking the intercession of a particular saint for a special intention. A variety of different novenas to the Little Flower haven proven to be very efficacious. A person prays this novena, sometimes asking that God send him a rose through the intercession of St. Therese, if God wants him to go to the seminary.

One seminarian told me that he was out fishing with his father on a huge lake in Florida the day his novena ended. He was thinking, "There is no way I'm going to see a rose out here in the middle of this lake. I should be safe!" They were a very great distance from shore, enjoying a calm day of fishing. He suddenly looked down in the water and saw floating next to the boat a beautiful, perfectly formed, long-stemmed red rose! He said out loud, "I can't believe it. I can't believe it!" His father, who was unaware that he was discerning priesthood said, "What can't you believe?" He replied, "Oh, nothing Dad."

Now I would call that an idiot-proof sign, and he saw it that way, too. He entered seminary. This is only one of thousands of stories from people who have prayed a novena to St. Therese for different intentions.

St. Therese is a great saint and a doctor of the Church, but receiving a rose after a novena should not be seen as an infallible sign. Whether or not you get a rose, or whether you ask for a rose at all, St. Therese will pray for you and assist you in discerning the will of God. I do recommend that you ask her intercession, but I do not recommend that you make a life decision contingent upon receiving a sign of this kind. This is not consistent with the principles of a diligent discernment. But if a man has been discerning diligently and doing everything else correctly, a novena to St. Therese is a great way to cap it off. Ask St. Therese to pray for you that you may be docile and humble, obedient to the will of God. This would be a much greater gift than a rose!

19. Learn About Your Respective Diocese

You cannot discern a vocation to diocesan priesthood unless you have some basic information about your diocese. Most men have grown up in a particular "local church," a certain diocese through which they received their religious instruction, the sacraments, and spiritual support. First of all, I always recommend that a man give the benefit of the doubt to the diocese in which he was raised. If you have a strong connection to a certain diocese — especially the one in which you were raised — contact the vocation director and talk to him first, even if you also feel attracted to another diocese.

However, because some men moved around so much in childhood, no one single diocese feels like home. A prime example is a man who grew up in a military family, moving from state to state and country to country with great frequency. Or, in other instances, though a man grew up in a certain diocese, he found his faith and his vocation while attending school or living in another diocese, so he feels a connection to it. This is where he knows the most priests. How does this man discover God's will regarding which diocese to join? This is another discernment ("to separate by sifting") that this man must undertake.

Whether a man has already discovered God's will regarding the diocese for which he should study, or if he is still discerning that question, it is still necessary to gather some information. He should learn the answers to the following questions, as they will be important.

~ How many Catholics are in the diocese?

~ How many priests?

~ What is the morale and *esprit de corps* of the priests?

~ How many priest-less parishes are there in the diocese?

~ Which religious orders have priests serving in the diocese?

~ How many Catholic grammar schools and high schools are there?

~ Are there any Catholic colleges or Catholic hospitals?

~ Do you know the name of the bishop and some basic biographical information about him?

~ Have you read a brief history of the diocese?

~ How many seminarians does the diocese have and which seminaries are being used at present?

~ Is there a strong vocation program or is it struggling?

Another important consideration is the number of priests and seminarians you know in a particular diocese. In which diocese do you feel closest to the priests who are similar in age? Your friendships with these priests and seminarians will be critical.

Don't make a decision to apply to a certain diocese based on the supposed "orthodoxy" of the bishop. Bishops come and go with some frequency. You likely will serve under at least three to four bishops during your life as a priest, so that should not be the crucial question. Besides, you are not competent at this stage to judge the orthodoxy of a bishop, and even if you were it is not appropriate. Still, you will want to look at the general direction in which he is leading the diocese.

I know of one non-native priest in my diocese who had discerned, for good reason, that he was not called to become a priest of the diocese in which he had been raised. So he started looking at the web sites of different dioceses. Looking at photos of various bishops, he noticed that many of the bishops looked rather stern, whereas the bishop of my diocese was smiling. So he e-mailed me, the vocation director, and received an immediate response. A few years later he was ordained a priest and has been working happily ever since! While I am glad that he is happy and that he is in my home diocese, this is not necessarily the discernment method I would recommend!

In my opinion, the Catholic people in every diocese are wonderful. I have never been in a parish I did not love. Catholic people love their priests and they will be very grateful for your care and service. However, there are some general differences in the people of different dioceses and you should understand these differences. Some dioceses will be primarily composed of people of Irish, Italian, or German descent. You should be familiar with the customs of this ethnicity, especially if one particular group is predominant. Some dioceses will have large Hispanic immigrant populations and this will affect your priesthood should you decide to study for that diocese. You likely will be required to learn Spanish and to work, at least in some of your assignments, with these poor, often marginalized people. Some dioceses will have significant Native American populations and they might have reservations within the diocese. Some dioceses are primarily rural and the people would be employed in farming and mostly agrarian professions. Other dioceses are completely urban. This is all information you need as you prayerfully discern which diocese to approach.

Even if you are interested in a particular diocese, you should not automatically assume that you will accepted by the bishop to study for his diocese. You must not only select a diocese to approach, but they must select you! Discernment of diocesan priesthood always involves the diocese. I think some young men these days have the idea that every bishop is so desperate for priests, they can just shop around for the best deal. While it is true that most bishops need more priests very badly, they need good, holy priests who come to priesthood for the right reasons. The right reasons are that Jesus Christ has called you to become a diocesan priest and that he has called you to present yourself to a particular diocese.

Be careful not to choose a diocese solely because you feel at ease there. I mentioned that the friendships of other priests are important, as is familiarity with the diocese, but you also should consider where the Church needs you to serve. Discernment is other-focused, not self-serving. Be careful about a sense of entitlement. It can be Satan's way of suggesting, "I will be a priest, but only on my own terms." Don't go to a diocese just because you feel comfortable there. Go where God sends you. Perhaps God wants to use you powerfully in a diocese where priests are not so numerous? Talk to your spiritual director about these things and share with him the information you have gathered. He can help you sort it out and make a diligent discernment regarding which diocese to approach.

20. Envision Happiness in Priesthood

Most people, and especially men discerning priesthood, struggle to believe deep down in their hearts that they will be truly happy if they do the will of God. They may say that they believe it. They may tell themselves constantly that they believe it, and they even tell God in prayer that they believe it. But deep down, they worry and fret. Some days, they are convinced that they will be happy priests and other days, they worry. I see men leave priestly formation every year—and perhaps some never come to the seminary in the first place—precisely because of this lack of faith and trust. God has placed the desire for happiness deep within us, since happiness is our eternal destiny, and in this deepest part of our soul, we long for it and worry that it will not come. Every day in your prayer time, beg the Holy Spirit for the gift of truly believing in your heart (not just in your mind) that you will be happy—the happiest you can possibly be—in your correct vocation, even if it is priesthood. Envision yourself as a happy priest.

21. Become as Free as Possible to Discern

If a man is in serious debt, if he owns a home, or if he is in a serious relationship with a woman, his freedom to discern diocesan priesthood is limited. He may reason, "Well, I can't go to seminary anyway because I owe a lot of money, and I can't quit my job. How will I pay my mortgage? While I think God might be calling me to be a priest, I can't break up with my girlfriend."

Get out of debt and stay out. If you own a home, don't sell it, but neither should you buy one during this time of discernment. Go on a dating fast for a year to discern. The Lord will help you put your affairs in order if he is calling you to become a priest. If you are sincerely asking God if he wants this for you, then you should be sincerely ready to answer God by making a move. Become as free as possible to discern, and then to go to seminary, should he call you to go.

God can't drive a parked car. Move!

22. Read the Vocation Stories of Priests or Seminarians

Many seminarians have told me that they first felt an attraction to priesthood while hearing a priest or seminarian tell his vocation story at Mass. These stories are very interesting and they illustrate how God calls different men to priesthood in very different ways. They can be effective aids for your discernment.

In many dioceses, the Vocation Office requests that priests or seminarians tell their vocation stories at Mass on designated Sundays like World Day of Prayer for Vocations or Priesthood Sunday. Some vocation directors post articles, videos, and podcasts of these stories on their web sites. Others have the vocation story of one seminarian each week or month in their diocesan newspaper. I have also seen some excellent booklets that tell the vocation stories of priests and seminarians of a certain diocese. Your vocation director can help you gain access to this useful information.

23. Submit It to the Church

Every bishop in the world visits Rome once every five years to meet with the Pope and give a report on the state of his diocese. While he is in Eternal City, the bishop prays *ad limina*, which means *on the threshold* of the apostles in St. Peter's Basilica, asking God to bless the Catholic Church in his diocese. One particular bishop went to Rome very troubled in his spirit, for this would be his final visit. He was a sick man and had been suffering tremendous pain for many years. After a long, careful discernment, he had made the decision to retire for medical reasons, though he was not yet at the retirement age. He was anxious about whether he had made the right decision, even though his retirement had been accepted. He was sitting in a certain area of the Vatican palace, waiting to be called for his final private audience with Pope John Paul II. A certain Cardinal who was familiar with the case walked into the room and he could see the anxiety on this bishop's face. He walked up to him, put his hand on the bishop's shoulder and said, "Peter has spoken. You submitted it to the Church and the Pope has accepted your resignation. It is the will of God. Be at peace." The bishop said that at that exact moment, a great weight was lifted from his shoulders. He felt a great peace and he knew that he had made the right decision.

A man sometimes reaches a point of discernment where he simply does not know what to do next. He is between stage 3 and stage 4 and seems to have reached a stalemate. "Father, I feel paralyzed. I don't know what else to do to discern but I am still not sure where to go." I would say to this man, "I will tell you what to do. Submit it to the Church. Go to the bishop and tell him everything. Then do what he says." A bishop has a special charism from the Holy Spirit to make decisions like this. He can truly help a man make a final decision whether to go to seminary.

God also speaks clearly through the rector of the seminary when a man is accepted to begin his studies, and again when he is approved to be promoted to the next year of studies. So if a seminarian finishes his first year of theology and he is approved unanimously by the formation team, and the rector advances him to second theology—and his bishop and vocation director agree—the Church has spoken once again. If the man has peace, and his spiritual director encourages him to continue, the Church is speaking! All of these are very significant signs, leading to the ultimate sign which comes on ordination day.

If you have made a diligent discernment, but you are still confused and frustrated and don't know what to do next, I recommend this to you: submit it to the Church! Let the bishop decide. You can't go wrong this way.

God can't drive a parked car. Move!

CHAPTER 11

THE BLESSED VIRGIN MARY AND DISCERNMENT FEARS

A priest friend learned that he had cancer just a few years after he was ordained and required surgery. He told me this story.

> I remember waking up in the recovery room from the anesthesia after the surgery. As soon as I opened my eyes, I felt the presence of a great evil. It felt like Satan was all over me. He was on top of me, suffocating me, trying to take me away. I have never felt more fear in my entire life. Terrified, I cried out, "Mary, help me!" Satan immediately departed and I felt great peace and security. I began to pray, "Thank you Mary. Thank you Blessed Mother. Thank you." And then I fell back into sleep, but I will never forget that experience.

I asked him, "Why did you cry out to the Blessed Mother instead of to Jesus? Jesus is the Son of God, with infinite power. Why did you cry out to Mary?" He replied, "I don't know. I suppose because of my great devotion to her. I just know it worked."

The Mother of Priests

I have heard many vocation stories in my time. I have heard amazing accounts of how God gave a man certain powerful graces, sent him strong signs, and brought him back from a life of profligacy to a life of holiness. I always marvel at how God calls each man differently. Yet there always seems to be one thread that consistently runs through all of the stories: the Blessed Virgin Mary was a powerful influence in their call to become priests, and often the greatest influencing factor in getting them into seminary.

This is true in my own vocation story. In my last two years of college, I was struggling with my discernment. I was clearly between stage 3 and stage 4 (see chapter 9 for the seven stages of discernment). I had been praying very intently for two years and I had come to the conclusion that God did want me to become a priest. But I did not know what kind of priest I should become. I couldn't decide which religious order to join. I was certain I was not called to become a diocesan priest. That did not excite me at all. I had to trust my heart about that. So I had been to visit many different religious orders and I had been in correspondence with many others and received information in the mail. There was no e-mail or Internet in those days. But I was simply not attracted to any of these orders. Every time I went for a "Come and See" weekend, I came back having seen little that I liked. I came back discouraged and depressed. I prayed, "God, I'm trying to give my life to you here. Please show me where to go. I'm ready to become a priest!" But I was not getting any answers.

Jesus finally answered that prayer in my last year of college. He answered it by directing me to his mother. I remember praying the *Memorare* one day and the words struck me: "Remember, O most gracious Virgin Mary, that never was it known that anyone who fled to thy protection, implored thy help, or sought thy intercession was left unaided." I realized that I had not asked the Blessed Virgin to pray for me as I discerned. I did not have a very strong devotion to Mary at all. I thought to myself, "Well, I have tried everything else to no avail. I might as well try this." So I went down to the church that day and I knelt in front of a statue of the Blessed Virgin Mary. I told Mary, "I really want to do the will of God. I think he wants me to become a priest, but I don't know my next step. Please pray for me and ask Jesus what he wants me to do. Whatever he says, I'll do it. I promise."

In the meantime, I started praying a daily rosary. Yes, I had a rosary hanging on my bedpost but I had not prayed it in a long time. I had to go find a pamphlet to remind myself of the mysteries! And I started. I was really hoping that she would come through for me and tell me which religious order God wanted me to join. I was sure of only one thing—that I was not being called to become a diocesan priest.

I remember what happened as clearly as if it had happened yesterday. Two weeks later, my alarm went off at six o'clock one morning. I sat up on the side of the bed and I knew my vocation! I knew that God loved me and that he had been calling me from all eternity to be a priest—to be a diocesan priest in my own diocese of Savannah. And I was excited about it, though previously it had not been at all attractive to me. I still had to trust my heart, but I realized that *my heart had been changed*. Jesus had answered my prayer by changing my heart, through the intercession of his Blessed Mother. I applied and was accepted by the diocese to go to seminary. From that day, I have always trusted the Blessed Virgin innately; I pray the rosary daily and go to her especially when I need an answer.

The Blessed Mother Mary should be a part of your discernment of diocesan priesthood. She is the mother of the Church and you can't discern diocesan priesthood without the Church.

Children Learn Trust from Their Mothers

Sociological studies confirm again and again the importance of the mother-child relationship in learning to trust. Discerning a vocation to diocesan priesthood requires a great deal of trust. To overcome fear and anxiety, trust in God is essential—trust that he loves you, that he knows what is best for you, and that his plan will always bring you happiness and fulfillment. So many people in our culture grow up in families where a father was absent, physically or emotionally. The breakdown of the traditional family is a great spiritual problem, and many of future priests come from such families. I believe that a tender love and devotion to the Blessed Mother is the key to gaining trust in God our Father and his plan for us. She must be a part of our daily prayers. This is why, in every vocation story, her name always comes up.

The Fear Factor: The Most Effective Tool of Satan

"There is no fear in love, but perfect love drives out fear because fear has to do with punishment, and so one who fears is not yet perfect in love."

1 John 4:18

I once received a call from a newly ordained priest. He told me that he was extremely happy and he was amazed at how the grace of God worked in people's lives through his priestly ministry. I asked him what he liked best. His response shocked me: "Father, I love to preach. My homilies are going well and people seem to enjoy them." I reminded him that when he first came to seminary, he was terrified of preaching. He had feared that his shyness would prevent him from standing up in front of hundreds of people. But now he said, "Yes, I remember that, but the grace of Holy Orders is so powerful. That must be why I love preaching now." While I agreed with him that Holy Orders is a powerful sacrament, I reminded him that grace builds on nature: "You spent many hours in public speaking and homiletics classes. You studied preaching, prayed about your homilies, and practiced repeatedly—and now God's grace in the sacrament of Holy Orders has taken over where you left off!"

"Father, I am afraid..." I certainly wish I had a dollar bill for every time I heard a young man begin a sentence with those four words. Any book about discerning a vocation to diocesan priesthood must address the most effective tools of Satan: fear and anxiety. He uses these constantly and very effectively because he does not want you, or any other man, to become a priest. Satan knows and realizes the power of the Catholic priesthood much more clearly than we do. He is an archangel with a superior intelligence. As I mentioned earlier, it is the priesthood, not the men who are priests, that worries him. Jesus Christ, the Son of God and the High Priest, has given every priest tremendous power to forgive sins and to work for the salvation of souls. The priesthood is a great threat to the kingdom of Satan, and he knows it well. So Satan uses fear as his primary weapon against this great threat.

A basic principle of discernment is that one should never make any decision based on fear. All decisions should be made based on faith, love, and trust in God. In the rest of this chapter, I will list some of the most common fears, beginning with the ones most often mentioned. Many of these fears are similar or interrelated. Remember that no man will have all of these fears but almost every man will have some of them. See which ones resonate with you.

"To he who is in fear, everything rustles."[48]

Sophocles

Common Fears of Men Discerning the Priesthood

1. **Celibacy Fear.** Always number one on the charts! "I can't give up women. I could never be happy without sex. I fear that I will be miserable without a wife, children, and the sexual intimacy of marriage."

2. **Fear of loneliness.** "I fear living in a rectory all alone, without people that I love. I already feel lonely and I want that to change with my vocation. I fear that I will be lonely for the rest of my life if I become a priest."

3. **Family fear.** "I don't know what my parents will say when they discover I am thinking about priesthood. My dad may get mad and forbid it. Then what will I do? My brothers

will tease me. I need my family's support. I am afraid to tell them."

4. **Fear of disappointing others.** "I fear that if I go to the seminary, and then decide to leave and not become a priest, I will greatly disappoint my parents or my parish priest. Even worse, what if I left the priesthood? It is better that I not go in the first place."

5. **Lack of faith fear.** "I don't have enough faith to be a priest. I still question things and I struggle with doubts about God, heaven, hell—everything. A priest without faith is not a good thing."

6. **Overwork fear.** "I see how hard priests work and the lack of priests means that they will have to do even more. I fear that I cannot work that hard. Maybe I am too lazy. I am afraid I won't be able to do it and be happy."

7. **Scandal fear.** "I fear that if I become a priest, I might do something scandalous. Maybe I will have an affair with a woman, or some deep secret from my past will become known. I am a sinner with so many weaknesses. I love the Church. I don't want to damage her reputation by causing a scandal. It is better that I not become a priest in the first place."

8. **Poverty and obedience fear.** "I like my freedom too much. I am afraid that I will not be obedient to the bishop when he gives me an undesirable assignment. I fear living a life without all my toys. I like to buy nice things, make a lot of money, and travel. Priests have to live too simply. I am afraid that I will not be happy."

9. **Poster fear.** "I fear that when my picture goes up on the diocesan poster, people will look at me differently and ex-

pect me to act differently. I don't want anyone to know that I am thinking about the priesthood. It could damage my social life. My friends will think I am crazy. Girls won't go out with me."

10. **Vocation director fear.** "I fear that if the vocation director knows I am discerning the priesthood, he is going to harass me with phone calls, e-mails, and letters. I don't want a letter in my mailbox with the return address of the vocation office! I don't want that kind of pressure right now."

11. **Adventure-boredom fear.** "I am young and can do anything with my life that I want. I desire to travel, see the world, and have adventures. I fear that I might be called to become a priest and I will miss all of that. Diocesan priesthood does not look exciting. I don't want to be bored with my life. I want an exciting life. I fear closing off my options."

12. **Preaching fear.** "I could never stand up and preach in front of a huge crowd of people. I am not a good speaker and I get very nervous when I have to stand in front of others. I fear I will never be able to preach well, and there's nothing worse than a terrible preacher on Sunday. Everyone complains about him."

13. **Hypocrisy fear.** "I have lived a sinful life and a lot of people have seen me partying hard. What will they think or say when they see me preaching to them and teaching them about Jesus Christ? That will never work! They will call me a hypocrite."

14. **Discernment fear.** "I fear that I might choose the wrong vocation. I fear that I might not be called to priesthood and therefore, I will not be a good priest. I have had some fail-

ures in my life and I don't want to fail in something as public as priesthood. Everyone will know that I failed."

15. **Fear of prayer.** "Priests make a promise to pray the Liturgy of the Hours five times per day for God's people, they make a Holy Hour before the Blessed Sacrament, pray the rosary, celebrate Mass, and who knows what else! I am afraid that I can't pray that much."

16. **Lack of courage fear.** "I fear that I am too timid to challenge people to obey the commandments and the teachings of the Church. I do not like confrontation and conflict. I am a peaceful person. I could never endure persecution or torture for the Lord, and this may be coming in the Church."

17. **Fear of power over other people's lives.** "I have seen the power my priest has. People really listen to him and they do what he says. I am terrified of this power. What if I tell someone to do the wrong thing?"

18. **Fear of not enough solitude.** "People are always clinging to the priest and trying to speak with him after Mass. He has constant appointments and people need him twenty-four hours a day. I fear that I will need more silence and solitude than that."

19. **Fear of unpopularity.** "I fear that I will be a priest who is not popular with the people, like my pastor now. People do not like him at all and he is not very kind or charismatic. I also fear sometimes having to say no to people, as priests must do."

20. **Administration-leadership fear.** "I fear becoming a pastor of a parish and making financial decisions. I don't have the best leadership skills, my self-confidence is low, and I do

not think I would be a good administrator. I would be embarrassed if I could not run the parish well."

21. **Fear of being a priest in one's home diocese.** "I feel called to become a priest, but I fear belonging to my home diocese. The priests are not especially inspiring, they often do not follow the liturgical norms, and there are almost no seminarians. The bishop does not seem to lead strongly, especially regarding certain Church teachings. I am afraid that I would not be happy in this diocese."

22. **Fear of teaching or lack of intelligence.** "Priests have to teach RCIA and other classes, and I am not a good teacher. I fear that I will not be intelligent enough to answer the people's questions. I see so many well-educated people in my parish and I am not that smart. I struggle so much with school that I even worry that I would not be able to get through seminary!"

23. **Fear of dealing with suffering and death.** "I am terrified at the prospect of having to comfort people in the midst of their suffering or the death of a loved one. I would not know what to say. I don't like being around the sick and suffering and it makes me very uncomfortable."

24. **Fear of counseling others.** "I fear that I would not be effective in counseling people who are getting a divorce or having problems with addiction. I am not confident that I would be a good counselor."

25. **Fear of sacrifice.** "Priests have to make so many sacrifices for God. While I want to do this, I am afraid I will unable. I am not a very generous person."

26. **Fear of going back to school.** "I have been out of school for a long time and I wasn't a great student when I was there. I

am afraid I won't be able to do the academic work required to become a priest."

27. **Fear of the awesome duty of caring for souls.** "A priest is a doctor of souls. God has entrusted so much to a priest and I am terrified of that responsibility. What if I lose some people? Will God make me answer for their souls?"

28. **Unworthiness fear.** "I am not worthy to be a priest. I am a weak man. I have a long history of sin and I keep on sinning. I don't feel strong enough to be a priest and to help other people live a holy life, when I am not living a very holy life myself."

29. **Fear of being a public person.** "Thousands of people in the parish know the name of the priest. Everywhere he goes, people speak to him. They repeat what he says and they notice what he is doing. I don't like living in a fishbowl. I am a private person. I fear that this will cause me great stress."

30. **Fear of my lack of love for God.** "I simply don't love God enough and that is one of the reasons why I have so many fears! Priests should have a great love for God, and I don't. I am trying, but I feel inadequate."

31. **Fear of my lack of love for others.** "I get tired of people quickly and I don't often feel love and compassion for them. Priests have to love a lot of people, with a lot of love! I am afraid that I don't have that in me."

32. **Fear of working with children.** "I am not good with small children and I fear having to visit them in their classes. I am also afraid of hearing their Confessions; I would not know how to speak on their level."

33. **Homosexual or Pedophile Fear.** "If I were a celibate priest, I am afraid that people would think that I was homosexual. I have heard comments of that sort, and I don't want that said about me. I also fear that people would think that I was a child sexual abuser. I think pedophilia is horrible and I would never want anyone to think that I was a pedophile. I fear that people will judge me because of bad priests."

34. **Sexual Orientation Fear.** "I have some same-sex attraction and I fear that it might become known if I became a priest. It is a secret that I live with and I don't tell anyone about it. I would be horrified if I were a priest and somehow it became known."

35. **Fear of God (the disordered kind).** "I fear that God will punish me if I don't become a priest but I don't really want to be a priest. I also fear that I will never be happy if I am a priest, and I will never be happy if I run from my vocation. I fear saying yes and I fear saying no."

36. **Unhappiness fear.** This is the umbrella fear that overshadows and incorporates all the others: "I don't trust God enough to believe that I will be happy and fulfilled if I am called to become a priest."

Some of you may be thinking, "Thanks a lot, Father. I didn't have many discernment fears before, but now I can think of quite a few!" But it is much better to deal with fears directly, to take the bull by the horns and deal with them once and for all. Perhaps you can think of more fears that I did not mention. You might want to write them down and discuss them with your spiritual director. It is important to name all of your fears in order to overcome them.

Overcoming Discernment Fears

Every vocation director has encountered men who use fear as an excuse not to move toward seminary. They might say, "Father, I would certainly like to become a priest, but since I am terribly afraid of speaking in public, God will understand if I do not go." No, what God understands is that this man is using fear as an excuse not to answer his call.

I will not address individually the discernment fears listed above, as most of them can be overcome in the same way. I will discuss the celibacy and family fears in detail in later chapters, since they are especially prevalent. But I do want to comment on a few of the other fears.

Overcoming Adventure-Boredom Fear

I have never met a bored priest. Priests are extraordinarily busy doing many wonderful things for God's people. They live fulfilling lives. As in any vocation, aspects of being a parish priest can be monotonous at times, but the tremendous value of priestly work compensates for any monotony. Fear of boredom, like all fears, is simply not based on the facts. Diocesan priests have the opportunity to travel, and they have many friends and various hobbies. In my experience, priests have much more opportunity for recreation than Catholic husbands and fathers!

Remember that the greatest boredom possible is in hell. This is the place where people do not do the will of God. To do anything less than the will of God for your life will bore you!

Overcoming Fears of Prayer, Preaching, and Administration

The seminary is designed to prepare men to become priests. When the rector of a seminary recommends to the bishop that a man is ready to be ordained a priest, the rector is indicating that the man has at least the minimum qualifications and training to become not just a priest, but the pastor of a parish. He is capable of leading a Christian community. This is the goal of priestly formation—to provide not just priests, but pastors for the Church.

When a newly arrived seminarian says to me, "Father, I am afraid that I will not be able to give good homilies," I reply, "God is not asking you to preach well today. If he had wanted you to preach well today, he would have had you begin seminary six years ago. But since you are just arriving now, relax and trust the formation process. Your efforts to cooperate with the seminary program of priestly formation, together with God's grace, will transform you in more ways than you can imagine. This is what we do. We form priests. Trust us." By the time this man leaves the seminary, he will be capable of praying, preaching, and administering a parish, as well as many other things. Priestly formation is a transformative process!

Overcoming Fear of Loneliness

Most diocesan priests do live alone and they will be lonely from time to time, but most priests are not *chronically* lonely. All people in all vocations (including marriage) are lonely from time to time. A seminarian will be given the opportunity to work in several parishes over his time of formation. Having these experiences, praying through them, discussing them with his spiritual director and then listening to his heart, will help a man discern if he will be able to live diocesan priesthood without chronic loneliness. This fear or concern can be a sign from God about priesthood, but it can also be a sign that a man needs to understand *why* he is always lonely. If a man is chronically lonely and he never learns the reason, he might attempt marriage and find that he is still chronically lonely. Most diocesan priests report tremendous satisfaction and fulfillment in their vocation.

Transforming Fears into Concerns

Marie Curie once said, "Nothing in life is to be feared; it is only to be understood."[49] Knowledge and love always alleviate fear. If a man follows the principles of a diligent discernment, then he will be doing everything necessary to overcome his fears.

"Humility is the true appreciation of one's gifts."[50]

St. Teresa of Avila

Men are often concerned about their own inadequacy. For example, a certain man may have many gifts, but he simply does not have the gift of teaching. Because he is discerning priesthood, this is a legitimate concern. But being concerned is not the same as being afraid! Fear causes physiological changes that are harmful to the body. Fear paralyzes a man from moving forward. But a *concern* should motivate a man to seek more information, to discuss the issue with his spiritual director and vocation director, and to ascertain if this concern is a "game stopper." In this case, it is not. The seminary will help him develop teaching skills through classes, workshops, and field assignments. He also will grow in teaching confidence during his summer assignments. He may even participate in a special program where he teaches the faith all summer, going from parish to parish. In other words, his concern will be addressed in the program of priestly formation.

Satan is the origin of many fears, but not all. Some fears are caused by our own disordered souls — our lack of faith, hope, and love. Or they are triggered by earlier events in our lives. We can't blame everything on Satan.

I know a man whose father abandoned the family when he was five years old. It caused this young man great distress and he grew up struggling with depression and low self-esteem. The father came in and out of this young boy's life, always making the child very excited and making promises—promises that he would never keep. The boy was deeply wounded. Then, when he was in high school, his mother died tragically in a car accident. This young man was trying to discern priesthood but he found that he could never trust God. He thought, "All those who love me abandon me. Will God be any different? Can I trust that I will be safe?" His fear paralyzed him from moving towards seminary. This hesitance was certainly understandable, given his life history, but that did not make the fear rational. One of the most important tools in dealing with fear is to understand that the fear is irrational. Be aware that each individual man will be more prone to certain fears than others, because of his life history. As St. Ignatius of Loyola pointed out centuries ago, Satan always attacks his enemies at the weakest place.

The Theological Virtues

All fears can be overcome by increasing one's faith, hope, and love. In fact, it is not overly simplistic to state that every problem known to man can be fixed by these three theological virtues. A man who is filled with these virtues would reason in this way:

> God is infinite in power and he loves me infinitely. There is no snatching out of his hand. God will never send me where his grace cannot sustain me. If he asks me to do something difficult, like become a priest, he will give me the grace to do it. I will not fail because he is with me. And I will be happy because I am doing his will. Even if I lack some of the needed qualities, God will help me develop them. In his will lies my peace.

Wouldn't it be wonderful to think this way and to sincerely believe it all the time! Faith, hope, and love are the keys to this kind of peace. These virtues were infused into your soul at Baptism, but pray that the Lord will increase them.

201

Don't Stop Praying!

If a man is not praying faithfully, his fears will multiply quickly and run wild. I have seen this many times through the years as a vocation director. A man with signs of a vocation to priesthood would be making a diligent discernment, moving along well, then suddenly disappear from the radar screen. He would not return my phone calls or e-mails, other than to say that he is no longer interested. I would e-mail the man back and ask, "Have you have stopped praying? This always happens when a man stops praying. But I cannot force you to pray or to do anything else. That must be your free decision." This is an example of a man who has violated a primary rule of discernment: he stopped praying and then made a decision based on his fears.

A Penance to Trust

When I am hearing Confessions or doing spiritual direction and a man is really struggling from fear and anxiety, I will often give a special penance. I tell him to write his own Act of Trust. I say, "Write it in your own words, short and to the point. Then commit it to memory by saying it one hundred times over the next few days. This will end the official penance." Then I recommend to the man that, in the future, every time he experiences a feeling of fear, he say that prayer over and over again. The prayer might be something like this: "Jesus, I love you and I know you will take care of me. I trust you. Please increase my trust." People have told me that this penance has worked amazingly well in helping them to overcome their fears.

"Behold, I am the handmaid of the Lord. May it be done to me according to your word."

Luke 1:38

You're Not in the Boat Alone!

Being with others who are in the same situation as you can bring peace. This is true for small children when they deal with fears for the first time; the presence of parents or siblings is a consolation. Even as an adult man trying to discern your vocation and dealing with fear, it is consoling to remember that you are not alone. The Church provides a vocation director, a spiritual director, seminary formators, as well as other candidates and seminarians. Many candidates have the idea that they are the only ones with certain thoughts or fears. Attending discernment retreats, visiting a seminary, or simply having a good conversation with another seminarian can allay these fears. Don't keep everything to yourself. If you rely on the help of others, I think you will find that many of your fears will dissipate quickly.

Most importantly, don't forget that Jesus is in the boat with you. If he is calling you to become a priest, he will see to it that you have the grace to overcome your fears.

Can't Fear and Anxiety Be Signs that I Am *Not* Called to Become a Priest?

I do not think so. Fear and anxiety most often discourage us from doing God's will. But because the primary locus of revelation is the human heart, God sometimes does speak through *a lack of peace*. For example, if a man is feeling a consistent lack of peace deep in his heart about becoming a priest, even though he is praying regularly and consulting with his spiritual director, then this is likely a sign from the Lord. Lack of peace is not the same thing as fear or anxiety. It is a gentle word from the Holy Spirit saying that this man is not called to be a priest.

Devotion to the Blessed Mother Mary always helps decrease fear and increase trust in God. I recommend that you make a daily consecration to the Blessed Mother, pray a daily rosary, and read a good Marian book. Mothers teach their children to trust. I believe that the Blessed Mother is a key component in overcoming discernment fears. She is the greatest patron saint of discernment! She is the mother of priests. This is the reason when priests tell their vocation stories, her name always comes up.

Perfect love casts out all fear.

CHAPTER 12

HOW DO I TELL MY PARENTS THAT I WANT
TO BE A PRIEST?

"As they traveled along, they met a man on the road who said to him,
'I will follow you wherever you go.' Jesus answered, 'Foxes have holes
and the birds of the air have nests, but the Son of Man has nowhere to
lay his head.' Another to whom he said, 'Follow me,' replied, 'Let me
go and bury my father first.' But he answered, 'Leave the dead to bury
their dead; your duty is to go and spread the news of the kingdom of
God.' Another said, 'I will follow you sir, but first let me go and say
goodbye to my people at home.' Jesus said to him, 'Once the hand is on
the plough, no one who looks back is fit for the kingdom of God.'"

Luke 9:57-62

I have known men who felt called to become priests, but
they knew that either one or both of their parents would be op-
posed. So they did not go to the seminary. Or they did not go for
a long time.

Parents often misunderstand their son's vocation to priesthood. This may be because they are not Catholic. Or they may be
nominally Catholic and barely practice their faith. It is difficult
for a person whose faith is strong to understand this call from
God, and it is next to impossible for those whose faith is weak. If
the parents are believing and practicing Catholics, they may have
a better reaction, but not always. And this is understandable. It
is hard enough for the man himself to understand what is
happening.

"For those who believe, no explanation is necessary. For those who do not believe, no explanation is possible."[51]

St. Augustine

According to a study of the ordination class of 2009, commissioned by the United States Conference of Catholic Bishops, almost sixty percent of newly ordained priests said that a parent or family member tried to talk them out of becoming a priest. Parents, siblings, and extended family can be a very influential in discernment. Many young men have told me that their greatest fear is the day they will have to tell their family that they are going to the seminary.

Specific fears include these:

~ "What if my parents do not want me to become a priest? They are going to say that they want me to provide them with grandchildren. Should I disobey my earthly father in order to obey my heavenly father? I need my family's support."

~ "I fear that I might disappoint my mother. She has been hoping and praying that I would become a priest ever since I was little. She used to leave pamphlets about priesthood in obvious places in my room. I am afraid that if I tell her I am going to the seminary to give it a try, she will be ecstatic, but if I leave the seminary, she will be devastated."

~ "My family is so dysfunctional that I have no idea what they will say. As it is, I will have a long way to go because of family problems. I love my family and I forgive them, but I suspect that they will be more of a burden to me than a support if I become a priest."

Nearly very young man who is discerning priesthood has asked himself how his parents will react. I actually had one candidate ask me if he could go to seminary secretly and not let his parents know that he was there! He wanted to be sure he was going to stay before he bothered them with this big news. I told him, "No. You must tell your parents. Go ahead and get it over with." We all love our family and we want them to be pleased with our decisions. But the reality is that, in some cases, they will not be pleased. Discerning priesthood and doing well in seminary is much easier with family support, but it is not essential. We have to choose Jesus Christ over everything and everyone.

This is illustrated in the lives of many of the saints. St. Alphonsus Liguori disappointed his father and his entire family when he left the practice of law to become a priest.[52] But he realized that his heavenly father had a lot more important things to say to him than his earthly father. This might have been true, but his earthly father said a great deal! In fact, he was furious. St. Francis of Assisi's father felt the same when St. Francis gave to the poor the goods of his father's clothing business, and then went off to serve Jesus and rebuild his Church on a full-time basis.

St. Bernard of Clairvaux initially had a difficult time with his family. His mother died when he was seventeen and he became very depressed. He felt the call to become a Cistercian monk but he just could not make a move. He wavered and wavered. Finally, in desperation, one day he stopped in a church by the road and begged God to tell him what to do. He left that church resolved to go to the monastery. His family and friends tried to dissuade him. But not only did he remain firm, he enlisted four of his brothers and an uncle to go with him! Thirty-one men in all followed St. Bernard into the monastery.

Jesus warned us clearly that there could be problems.

Do not think that I have come to bring peace upon the earth. I have come to bring not peace but the sword. For I have come to set a man against his father, a daughter against her mother, and a daughter-in-law against her mother-in-law; and one's enemies will be those of his household. Whoever loves father or mother more than me is not worthy of me, and whoever loves son or daughter more than me is not worthy of me; and whoever does not take up his cross and follow after me is not worthy of me.

Matthew 10:34-37

The fourth commandment tells us that we must honor our father and our mother. When we are children, we must honor them by our love, respect, and obedience. The Catechism of the Catholic Church (#2217) tells us that, once we reach the age of emancipation, we are no longer obliged to obey our parents. We must always love, honor, and respect them, and we must be ready and willing to help them should they need our help as they grow old. But once a person reaches the age of emancipation, he is an adult and he must make his own decisions about his life. In U.S. culture, this age of emancipation is usually around eighteen years old, when a man leaves home for college or goes out on his own. If an adult man feels called by God to become a priest and he has made a diligent discernment, he must go to the seminary and give it a try, whether or not his parents are supportive.

I have met with many concerned parents through the years and discussed their son's desire to become a priest. Like all good parents, they want to be sure that this really is a call from God and not a passing whim. They want to be sure that someone (like the pastor or the vocation director) is not pressuring them to go to the seminary. They don't want their son to be brainwashed! They worry about their son's happiness and they question the prudence of his going to the seminary so young. (One mother told me that exact thing. Her son was thirty years old!) They especially worry about celibacy and whether their son will be happy and fulfilled without a wife and children. In other words, parents share many of the same fears as the candidate himself. And like him, they need good information to alleviate those fears.

It is interesting that most priests come from families of multiple children. Rarely have I met a seminarian or a priest who was an only child. If a man is an only child, he is the parents' only hope for grandchildren and he might expect that there will be more resistance to the idea of priesthood.

Good parents love their sons and it is their God-given duty to protect them and to guard them against making imprudent or rash decisions. After I met with the parents of candidates and answered their questions, they were usually more peaceful. They understood that going to seminary is not a final decision to become a priest. They understood that seminary is not a prison and the man is free to leave anytime he chooses, most often without even incurring debt.

Of course, there is a big difference in going to a college seminary right after high school and going to a major seminary once a man has finished college. We will talk about the different tracks a man can take in a later chapter, but it is understandable why a parent would be more concerned about the college seminary.

Parental Advice

"Father, wouldn't it be wiser for my son to get a couple of years of college under his belt first, to date a few girls, and have some normal college life experiences? Then if he still wants to go to seminary, I will support him."

While this may seem like good advice in most cases, sometimes the suggestion to live a "normal college life" is really an invitation to live a life of grave sin. This will not help anyone discover the call of God. I am not saying that the parents desire that for their son, but that is the reality on many campuses today.

I am convinced that God calls some men to go to seminary earlier than others. One high school senior asked me point blank if he should disobey his parents, sign up for the diocese, and go to the seminary. I told him, "No, obey your parents for now. They love you very much and they are giving you prudent advice. The seminary will still be there after you finish two or four years of college. But find a way to grow in faith while you are there."

While I would almost never recommend to an eighteen-year-old senior in high school that he disobey his parents and go to the seminary, I have at times had to recommend to a twenty-three-year-old senior in college that he obey God's call, despite his parent's wishes — and then trust God to help his parents understand in time. In my experience, given enough time, parents usually do become more comfortable with their son's decision to become a priest. My father is a Baptist and he was definitely not excited when I told him that I was going to seminary. However, now that I have been a priest for many years, and he sees that I am happy, fulfilled, and doing good work for the Kingdom of God, he is proud of me and very supportive. Parents can see when their son is happy and fulfilled doing the work of a priest. In my experience, these parents become very proud of their sons, even if they still have some lack of understanding and discomfort with the whole idea.

A Common Mistake: Too Much Support

Some parents can be too supportive, actually placing undue pressure on their son to go to seminary and become a priest. This is a grave mistake. I certainly understand the pride that parents feel to have one of their sons become a priest, but parents must be careful not to be overly exuberant.

Here are the mistakes that some parents make. They call all their relatives and friends immediately and tell everyone that their son is going to become a priest. They start buying chalices and vestments when their son begins first college or pre-theology — still six or eight years away from priesthood ordination. They constantly say things like, "When you are ordained a priest, you will…"

This is undue pressure. It must be explained to parents that—to use a marriage analogy—going to the seminary is like beginning to date someone exclusively. It is still a long way from buying a ring and getting engaged. Much can happen. It might not work out. Parents should be supportive but not overly exuberant.

I have known men who went to seminary primarily because they wanted to please their mothers. This is not a good reason to become a priest and it will often end badly. I have known others who went to seminary, discerned God telling them to leave seminary, but they did not leave because they feared disappointing their families. These ended badly as well. If God tells you clearly that you are not called to become a priest, no matter how far along you are in the seminary, please do yourself and the Church a favor: leave the seminary! Go home and find your true vocation. And do this even if your parents will be disappointed.

The Ideal Parent of a Seminarian

Many parents have asked me this question. "Father, I want to support my son, but I don't want to put too much pressure on him. What should I do?" I always advise parents to tell their son something like this: "I love you very much and I am proud of you for even considering priesthood. I will pray for you and support you as you go to the seminary. I will be very proud of you if you become a priest. But I will be equally proud of you if you discern that you must leave the seminary. I will welcome you home and help you in any way I can to find your true vocation. I am just proud that you love Jesus this much and that your faith is this strong."

Parental Formation

> Each year his parents went to Jerusalem for the feast of Passover, and when he was twelve years old, they went up according to festival custom. After they had completed its days, as they were returning, the boy Jesus remained behind in Jerusalem, but his parents did not know it. Thinking that he was in the caravan, they journeyed for a day and looked for him among their relatives and acquaintances, but not finding him, they returned to Jerusalem to look for him. After three days they found him in the temple, sitting in the midst of the teachers, listening to them and asking them questions, and all who heard him were astounded at his understanding and his answers. When his parents saw him, they were astonished, and his mother said to him, "Son, why have you done this to us? Your father and I have been looking for you with great anxiety." And he said to them, "Why were you looking for me? Did you not know that I must be in my Father's house?"
>
> Luke 2:41-49

Many parents experience great fear and anxiety when they first learn that their son might want to become a priest. They fear losing their son, even as Mary and Joseph feared losing Jesus. They fear he might not be happy. Since parents have many of the same concerns as the candidate, it is important to give them good, accurate information. One idea is to invite your pastor or vocation director to dinner. Over a meal, the entire family can ask questions and listen to the vocation director respond. The evening usually ends with parents feeling much more at peace about their son giving seminary a try. Vocation directors love to do this, not only to give the parents more peace, but also because meeting the family of a candidate can tell him a lot more about the candidate himself. As a vocation director, I always wanted to meet the man's family and spend some time with them prior to accepting the man as a seminarian.

Many diocesan vocation offices have an annual event for seminarians and their families. This enables the parents of the seminarians to meet one another and to exchange contact information. Some vocation directors actually provide parents a list of the names, phone numbers, and e-mail addresses of other seminarians' parents, in order to facilitate communication.

Besides what happens in the diocese, some seminaries have Family Weekends where parents and siblings can come to visit. They see their son's seminary room and classrooms, learn about the formation program, meet other seminarians and their parents, and receive answers to many of their questions. Parents are consoled to meet the rector and professors of the seminary who are in charge of their son's priestly formation. I have seen mothers of seminarians become good friends through events like these. Many mothers talk frequently to one another about their sons as they pass through the different stages of priestly formation. Bringing parents with you to attend an ordination Mass is also a great idea to accustom them to what might be coming in the future. In a sense, parents are in formation also, learning to be the parents of a seminarian and eventually, of a priest.

A Final Word of Advice

Let me give one final word of advice to you when the time comes to tell your family that you are going to seminary. Please give your parents a break! This is not an easy thing for them to hear. They likely will have mixed emotions about this news. They need some time to process all of this and to get answers to their many questions. You are their child! They brought you into this world and sacrificed themselves to raise you and to teach you about Jesus Christ. Be patient with them no matter how they react. Parents are not the enemy here! On the contrary, in most cases, God used them to nurture your vocation in the first place.

Once you have made a diligent discernment and reached stage 4—the time you know you must continue discernment in a seminary—you must sit down with your family and let them know. No, you cannot go to the seminary in secret! You must tell them. Go ahead and get it over with. You might be pleasantly surprised by their reaction.

But even if it does not go well, trust that God will take care of both you and your family. As time passes, as they get more information and as they see that you are happy and fulfilled as a priest, they will come around.

CHAPTER 13

CELIBACY, CHASTITY, CHARITY, AND CHEERFULNESS

"Some are incapable of marriage because they were born so; some, because they were made so by others; some, because they have renounced marriage for the sake of the kingdom of heaven. Whoever can accept this ought to accept it."

Matthew 19:12

I have heard many young men through the years say things like these:

~ "I can never become a priest because I like girls too much."

~ "I am afraid that I will be lonely and not happy without a wife."

~ "I really struggle with masturbation. I am not holy enough to become a priest."

~ "I have a history of sexual activity; I am not a virgin. Can I still become a priest?"

~ "I have some degree of same-sex attraction and this worries me greatly. Can I be accepted to go to seminary with this problem?"

~ "It is not so much giving up sex that worries me, but not having a companion. I don't know if I can live my life happily without the intimacy of a wife and having my own children."

215

The requirement of celibacy is certainly one of the greatest sources of anxiety and fear in a man who is discerning priesthood. This is especially true because we live in a sex-saturated society and culture. Sex or sensuality is on our televisions, computers, billboards, magazines, and newspapers. And the sex that is displayed is not at all the holy, beautiful vision of human sexuality that is taught by Jesus Christ and his Church. The message we receive from the media and culture is very clear: no person can be happy and fulfilled unless they are having a lot of sex. But this is simply not true.

The purpose of this chapter is to give some guidelines for discerning if a man has received the gift of celibacy from God. Many wonderful books have been written on the topic of chastity and celibacy, and I have listed some of them in an appendix. This chapter is not for the purpose of defending the celibate priesthood (though I would certainly do that) or even explaining the theological reasons for celibacy. It is for the purpose of helping a young man discern diocesan priesthood, with celibacy as an integral part of that discernment.

Celibacy goes with priesthood in the Latin Rite. If a man is called to become a priest, then he will receive the gift of celibacy from God along with the call to priesthood. Celibacy and priesthood must be discerned together. It is true that in the Eastern Rites of the Church, some priests are married, but the assumption I make in this book is that the reader is discerning priesthood in the Latin Rite.

As a vocation director, during the formal interview with a candidate, I would always ask the candidate if he had ever been sexually abused by another person in any way. I asked this question primarily because if this candidate was sexually abused, especially when he was a child, it often seriously affects his psychosexual development and maturity. If he was sexually abused, then he will usually need some additional assistance to heal from this wound and to gain the peace he desires through sexual integration. Sexual integration, or at least making great progress in that direction, is necessary in a man called to priesthood.

However, I would argue that, in a sense, *every* young person who has grown up in the U.S. since the 1960s has been sexually abused—visually and emotionally—simply by living in this sexually disordered culture. Many, if not most, young people have been robbed of their sexual latency period, that beautiful time of life when a little child is simply unaware that he or she is a sexual creature. They are most often robbed by seeing some explicit sexual act on television, the internet, or in print. I do not say that every young person has been sexually abused in this way to encourage a "victim mentality," but only to say that for a man trying to live a holy and pure life, it can be very challenging to reverse the sexual disintegration caused by the culture. This is true for all men, not just those called to become priests.

The requirement of celibacy is a source of fear and anxiety in part because of our sexually disordered society, but also simply because it is such a powerful drive in every young man. Sadly, most men today, even among those applying to become priests, have a sexual history of some kind or another. These men love the Lord Jesus and know the teaching of Christ and the Church in this regard, and thus many feel great shame about their sexual history. Some have had sexual intercourse with a girlfriend, or at least "gone too far." Others have struggled mightily with pornography on the internet and/or masturbation. But in my experience, the men who have suffered the most are those who have some degree of same-sex attraction. Many have lived in fear about this for years, especially if they have had homosexual experiences with another person. Other men discerning priesthood do not have a sexual history *per se*, but they worry greatly about celibacy. Since most men feel the sexual desire so intensely, especially during puberty and young adulthood, they certainly would be concerned whether they would be able to live peacefully and joyfully without sex.

Sometimes God uses celibacy to show a man that he is *not* called to become a priest. St. Thomas More was one of these. As a young man, already a successful attorney, St. Thomas More felt called to live the life of a Carthusian, a very strict monastic life. Much to his father's displeasure, he moved into the London Charterhouse for four years and strived to live a monastic life. He eventually abandoned this pursuit. When asked why, he replied that it was "better to be a chaste layman than a priest impure."[53] St. Thomas More had discerned, through intense prayer, spiritual direction, and mortification, over an extended period of time, that he did not have the gift of chaste celibacy. He returned home, married, fathered a number of children, rose quickly in the government, become Chancellor of all England, and eventually was martyred for his faith. St. Thomas More became a saint in his respective vocation, but he was not called to become a priest or a monk. And God showed him his vocation *through* his discernment of celibacy. Notice, though, that he had to go away and give it "the old college try" before he came to know God's will for him.

The good news is that God's grace can accomplish all things! With the power of Jesus' cross, a man can overcome sexual lust and live his life peacefully in his respective vocation, even in the celibate vocations of priesthood and religious life. It can be done. It is possible. There is much evidence. For example, there are approximately four hundred thousand Catholic priests worldwide. The huge majority of these men at one time said these or similar words: "I can never become a priest because I like girls too much." Well, all four hundred thousand of them are priests now, so obviously something must have happened between the time they first had that thought and the day of ordination. God will never send us where his grace cannot sustain us. Contrary to the message with which we are bombarded, people can be very happy and fulfilled in life without being married or engaging in sexual relations.

Change Your *Fear* of Celibacy into a *Concern*

"How do I know whether God has given me the gift of celibacy?" The answer is that you must make a diligent discernment of celibacy, just as you do for priesthood as a whole. By gathering good information, praying, talking about celibacy in spiritual direction, living chastely, and listening to your heart, you will be able to transform the fear of celibacy into a concern. In this way, the discernment of celibacy will not paralyze you or traumatize you; it will help you grow in sexual integration.

Definition of Terms

Celibacy. The state of being unmarried, specifically for the sake of giving oneself full time to build the Kingdom of God. This is a gift from God, to which a man must be called.

Chastity. "The successful integration of sexuality within the person and thus the inner unity of man in his bodily and spiritual being" (CCC #2337). Chastity is the virtue that moderates the desire for sexual pleasure according to the principles of faith and right reason. Priests, sisters, married persons, and single persons are all called by God to chastity, to use their sexuality according to God's plan in their specific state in life. Married persons live chastely by using the gift of sexuality exclusively with one another, according to the teachings of Christ. Priests live chastely by not having sexual activity with anyone, but loving people the way Jesus loves.

Charity. The supernatural virtue infused at Baptism by which a person loves God above all things for his own sake, and loves others for God's sake. Charity is to will good to another and to provide that good if one is able.

Cheerfulness (or gladness). A result of interior happiness, shown in one's external disposition and even facial expression. Cheerfulness is the emotional counterpart to a person's well-being. Cheerfulness comes from human flourishing.

I believe that these four Cs work together in a man who is called to become a priest: celibacy, chastity, charity, and cheerfulness. Studies have shown that priests have one of the highest ratings of fulfillment of all occupations. The vast majority of priests say that if they had to make the decision again, they would choose to become priests again, knowing what they know now. By and large, priests are very happy and fulfilled. This is a fact. Why is this so? How can this be, since priests do not have sex? Since they have no wife?

The Church teaches that God calls some men to celibacy as a stimulus to pastoral charity. Charity is the litmus test of holiness. And holiness means happiness. Celibacy is a particular way of living chastity, which is designed by God to lead a man to love the way Jesus loves (charity) and that leads to joy. It leads to cheerfulness! Celibate priests are happy because they are flourishing, living out their correct vocation. God did not make us only to survive this life. He made us to flourish!

Blessed Mother Teresa of Calcutta, in her simple yet profound way, describes only three steps in the spiritual life: loving trust, total surrender, and joy. This is also an accurate way to describe the vocation of priesthood.

"I have told you all this so that my joy may be in you and your joy may be complete."

John 15:11

To Which Marriage Are You Called?

When I was a vocation director, I would often ask men this question, "Do you think that you are called to marriage or to priesthood?" After I studied *The Theology of the Body* by Pope John Paul II, I no longer ask that question. Now I ask, "To which marriage are you called?" Every man in the world is called by God to marriage: to give himself and to sacrifice himself in a permanent way for his bride, for the sake of the Church. Then, with his bride, he is called to bear fruit for the Kingdom. A husband does this when he and his wife give themselves and sacrifice themselves for God and for one another in order to bring forth new life. A priest does this by his love and fidelity and care for his bride, the Church, which also bears fruit—a concept known as the *fecundity of virginity*. A priest bears great spiritual fruit for the Kingdom with his bride, by bringing forth thousands of spiritual children. The scriptures often speak of the joy of a bride who is espoused to a king. To be called in this way is a great honor and gift. So often the celibate life is portrayed as a dour, sad existence that priests simply endure. On the contrary, to be espoused to the Bride of Jesus Christ is a tremendous honor, gift, and privilege.

If a man decided to marry a certain woman primarily because he likes the idea of cutting the grass, changing the light bulbs, and putting out the garbage, we would question the man's sanity. One doesn't marry for these reasons. A man marries a woman because he is in love with her. The other responsibilities do come with marriage, but they are far down the hierarchy of importance and emphasis. They are not the motivation for the marriage. In a similar way, a man should become a priest, not primarily because he likes the idea of the work of a priest, but because he is in love with the Bride of Christ, the Church.

Working with Christ and his bride brings a priest a great feeling of joy, happiness, and fulfillment. As one of the former rectors of Mount St. Mary's Seminary used to say, "The greatest sign of a healthy seminary is to walk down the halls and constantly hear the men laughing." Cheerfulness is an important sign that a man is being called to celibacy and that he is living it out well. It is a privilege to work in a seminary and to see joy and cheerfulness in the men!

"While it is true that no one will ever call me daddy, thousands call me Father!"

I am not saying that celibacy is the only way to holiness and happiness. By no means is this true. It is God's will that all of his children be both holy and happy in their respective vocations. But I am trying to dispel the myth that celibate priests are not happy and fulfilled. The overwhelming evidence shows that they are.

Engagement and Marriage

I often use the analogy that coming to seminary and discerning priesthood is very much like a dating relationship with a young woman. Going to seminary is like an exclusive dating relationship with one woman; you are no longer dating others while you discern marriage with this one lady, the Bride of Christ! When a man returns to the seminary to begin third theology, this is analogous to an engagement. You are now engaged to be married and no longer discerning marriage to this woman. You are making plans for the wedding by preparing for diaconate ordination. And diaconate ordination and priesthood ordination are analogous to the actual wedding ceremony. Though all analogies are inadequate, this analogy works well in thinking about the years in priestly formation. Just as some couples in an exclusive dating relationship break it off before the engagement, having discerned it is not God's will, so some men discern out of seminary before the engagement and wedding.

To which marriage are you called?

What is Sexual Integration?

Pope John Paul II, in *The Theology of the Body*, teaches that union with God passes only through sexual integration. Another expression for sexual integration is "integration of body and soul." Since union with God is the goal of Christianity—most profoundly in heaven—sexual integration is essential. It is the goal for all people in all vocations. What exactly is sexual integration?

Sexual integration refers to a psychological, physical, and spiritual ability which enables a man to do the following:

~ To accept and love himself as a human being made in God's image, with a body and a soul.

~ To accept and love himself as a sexual being, made for union.

~ To understand the profound mystery and gift of God's plan for human sexuality and to be in awe of it.

~ To accept sexual tension peacefully and to vigilantly fight the battle against sexual impurity in mind, heart, and body.

~ To be able to look at a woman and not immediately see her as a sexual object, but to see her first and foremost as a child of God and a temple of the Holy Spirit.

~ To love people truly, the way God loves people, and to never desire or consent to use another person in any way.

Sexual integration and psychosexual maturity are evidenced in a man who can make good, mature friendships with both men and women and knows how to maintain and respect appropriate boundaries.

Sexual integration for a man called to priesthood is a slowly developing grace over the course of a man's life that only God can give. But it is also a grace that a man has gained through prayer and sacrifice, and this grace enables him to live celibacy in tranquility of mind.

The biggest indication that a man has not yet fully attained sexual integration is lust:

~ If a man masturbates

~ If he looks at women lustfully

~ If he fantasizes about sexual activity

~ If he looks at pornography

~ If he uses people sexually

It is also a sign of sexual disintegration if a man has some psychosexual dysfunction or disorientation. Examples are same-sex attraction and sexual fetishes (such as sexual attraction for a woman's feet).

St. Augustine understood sexual integration. In his writings he implies that virginity is lost through masturbation.[54] He meant that when a man masturbates, he is showing that he has not been fully integrated in body and soul the way God made a human to be. Pope John Paul II expounds on this concept in *The Theology of the Body* when he re-defines the term "virginity" as sexual integration. The usual definition of virginity describes a person who has never engaged in physical sexual intercourse, but these two giants of the faith see virginity as something much more profound. And this is great news. It means that a person with a sexual history can "reclaim his virginity," so to speak, by attaining sexual integration.

It is widely known that St. Augustine struggled mightily with his purity. Prior to his conversion, St. Augustine had a mistress with whom he fathered a child. He had a very difficult time giving up this relationship. Many men, especially those engaged in the battle for sexual integration while discerning priesthood, love to quote him when he said, "O God, give me chastity; but not yet!"[55]

This is why Pope John Paul II wrote in *The Theology of the Body* that "everyone in heaven is a virgin." Even if a woman was married and had ten children on earth, she is a virgin in heaven. Why? Because everyone in heaven has attained sexual integration, or they wouldn't be there. Union with God passes only through sexual integration.

The huge majority of men—yes, even holy men who really love the Lord Jesus, like you—have to fight a long, arduous battle to attain sexual integration. Jesus said, "Without me, you can do nothing" (John 15:5). I suspect the Lord was especially thinking about sexual integration when he said these words. Fighting the battle for sexual integration is one of the tasks God has given to us in this fallen world and it pleases God greatly when we fight it, even though we may fall at times.

Marriage is Not a Cure for Sexual Disintegration

Some men think that they will get married since they are not able to control their sexual desires. They reason that if they get married, they can have sexual intercourse with their wife every day, and the sexual tension they feel so strongly will be relieved. But when they get married, these men learn quickly that marriage is not a cure for sexual disintegration. And because they never fought the spiritual battle to achieve it in the first place, their sexual problems cause them difficulties in marriage. Sexual integration is essential for all people, whether they are called to marriage, priesthood or religious life. So when a man says, "I can never become a priest because I like women too much," I always suspect that he is not fighting the battle for chastity and is under the false illusion that marriage will fix his problem. It will not.

Can I Go to Seminary If I Have Not Yet Achieved Sexual Integration?

A certain amount of sexual self-mastery must be demonstrated before a man can begin seminary studies. It is true that during their seminary years, men grow tremendously in this area. They learn about celibacy and chastity. They develop the prayer life required to live celibately. They gain the ability to establish mature, deep friendships with both men and women. The seminary is a place where a man can make significant advancements in this area. And no man has ever been ordained a priest having already achieved perfect sexual integration. However, a man must be able to demonstrate that *he can live chastely for a significant period of time.*

But what exactly does this mean? I will answer this question by giving five examples.

Example 1

A man comes to his vocation director and says that he was sexually active with his girlfriend up until six months ago. But they have broken up now, and he has been to Confession and begun seriously discerning priesthood again. He had been thinking about priesthood since eighth grade but it was put on the back burner when he began dating in college. He wants to know if he can go to the seminary this fall.

This man needs to demonstrate that he can live his life chastely for about two years before he goes to seminary. He needs to get a spiritual director and develop a good prayer life. He needs to go to Confession regularly. If he dates, he should date chastely. He is not ready for seminary this fall. He has not done a diligent discernment of celibacy. He may even be rebounding from his breakup.

Example 2

A man who is a senior in college comes to his bishop and asks about seminary. He is heterosexual, but has never been sexually active with a woman. He has viewed pornography off and on since high school and masturbated. In his first two years of college, he did this fairly regularly but he has not viewed pornography in the last two years. He has been meeting with his spiritual director monthly, attending daily Mass, and serving in his parish. He has significantly cut down on the occasions of masturbation.

This man would likely be permitted to begin seminary studies after graduation. He has demonstrated that through prayer, study, and spiritual direction, he is both fighting and winning the battle for sexual integration. He likely will make much greater progress once he begins seminary.

Example 3

A man tells his spiritual director that he has some occasional same-sex attraction, but he also has heterosexual attractions for adult women. His attraction for women is actually much stronger and it bothers him immensely whenever he experiences a homosexual attraction. He has never been homosexually active, but several years ago he did have a few heterosexual experiences, short of sexual intercourse. He is now attending daily Mass, adoration, praying his rosary, seeing a spiritual director regularly, and his prayer life and moral life are really improving.

This man's bishop and vocation director would have to make a prudential judgment, once they have gathered all the information, whether to accept this man to begin seminary. Since this man has a strong prayer life, a good spiritual director, and completely embraces the Church's teaching on sexuality, he likely would be accepted at least to college seminary or pre-theology.

He has demonstrated that he is both fighting and winning the battle for sexual integration.

Example 4

This man has been discerning priesthood all through high school and college. He has attended discernment retreats and is active in his parish. He is approaching his last year of college, the obvious time to apply to seminary. When his vocation director asks him why he is delaying, he finally admits that he is struggling with chastity. This man's spiritual director has been working with him on this for four years and yet he still habitually views heterosexual pornography online and masturbates. This happens four or five times per week. Upon further questioning, he also reveals to his vocation director that he was sexually abused by an uncle four or five times when he was seven years old and "things have not been right sexually" as a result. It has also contributed to low self-esteem and depression. Even worse, this man has never been able to tell his parents or his spiritual director about this abuse, because he is afraid of what it will do to his family, and also because his spiritual director is a priest he greatly admires and he does not want to disappoint him.

This man is clearly not ready to go to seminary. Because of the sexual abuse and his lack of full disclosure about it, he has some serious psychosexual dysfunction, which is manifesting itself in addiction to pornography and masturbation. This man has some deep internal pain and he likely will need Christian-based psychotherapy to experience healing. Had he been able to disclose four years ago to his spiritual director the fact that he was sexually abused, he would be much further along toward healing and sexual integration today. Still, it is possible that this man could one day become a priest, but he is not ready to go to seminary now.

Example 5

A man applies to go to the seminary for his diocese and he is very humble and fully disclosing about every area of his life. He is an excellent student, has good social skills, prays very faithfully and serves in his parish. Every area of his life seems to be in pretty good order—except chastity. He still commits the sin of self-abuse (masturbation) about three or four times per month, even though he is trying very hard to overcome it. It does not happen every week but when it does happen, it usually happens more than once. This man prays and attends Mass daily, goes to Confession regularly and discusses this with his spiritual director. He is constantly saying to his spiritual director, "Why can I not stop committing this sin? I don't want to do this. I want to be holy. Perhaps I am not called to become a priest? Maybe this is a sign?"

His spiritual director assures him that he *should* go to seminary and that eventually, with the grace of God, he will overcome this sin. The man is not so sure; but his spiritual director is correct. All things considered, this man is fighting the good fight for sexual integration and he is winning many of the battles. When he loses a few of these battles, because he is a righteous man, he feels great shame and disappointment. He beats himself up about it and it causes him to doubt his vocation. This scenario is very common for men entering seminary today.

Dealing with Masturbation

Fr. John Hardon, S.J. spoke of the "providential purpose of sin" in his retreats on the Spiritual Exercises. This expression does not mean that God *wants* a man to sin, but it means that sometimes God *permits* a man to keep falling in a particular sin, precisely because he is trying to prevent him from committing a greater sin. And God is also preparing him to be a compassionate confessor for other sinners when he is a priest. If the particular man in example 5 had prayed to overcome his impurity and God had immediately answered his prayer (which God is very capable of doing), and he had never committed self-abuse again, this man would likely have become extremely proud of his purity. And pride, in the long run, is a much more serious sin than a sin of passion like masturbation. A proud priest is an unmerciful priest. He treats God's people and his brother priests poorly and he is harsh in the confessional.

God will sometimes use a man's struggle with sin to keep him humble, to keep him on his knees praying for help—to help him be merciful to other sinners. St. Augustine wrote, "We learn to do good by having done bad."[56] God is orchestrating all things to make us into the saints he is calling us to be within the vocation he is calling us to embrace. And God is so awesome, so good, and so powerful, he can even use our sins to accomplish this.

In this ongoing, arduous battle for sexual integration, your spiritual director or confessor is the one who can guide you. With regard to masturbation, the Catechism of the Catholic Church says:

> To form an equitable judgment about the subject's moral responsibility and to guide pastoral action, one must take into account the affective immaturity, force of acquired habit, conditions of anxiety, or other psychological or social factors that lessen or even extenuate moral culpability.
>
> CCC #2352

In other words, even though masturbation is always a grave matter, every occurrence of masturbation in a young man's life is not necessarily a mortal sin. With this in mind, some spiritual directors recommend the following to some of their directees, if they fall by masturbating:

~ Immediately try to make a perfect Act of Contrition: "Jesus, I am sorry for this sin and for all of my sins precisely because I love You and you deserve all of my love. This is the greatest motivation for my sorrow. I am sorry because I love you."

~ *Believe* that God has truly forgiven the sin of self-abuse as a result of your perfect Act of Contrition, and that you are restored to a state of grace, if the sin was mortal.

~ Receive Holy Communion with love when attending Mass (hopefully, on a daily basis), even if you have not been able to get to Confession since your sin.

~ Understand that, even though God has forgiven your sin, you will still have to go to Confession in order to be reconciled with the Church. Going to weekly Confession should be part of your spiritual plan of life. Confess this sin with your other sins weekly whenever it is committed.

With regard to receiving Holy Communion after the sin of masturbation, your spiritual director or confessor will need to be consulted. Canon 916 of the Code of Canon Law indicates that Holy Communion should not be received when conscious of grave sin without prior sacramental Confession unless a grave reason is present and there is no opportunity of confessing. In this case, the canon says that a person can make a perfect act of contrition with the intention of confessing as soon as possible. Your spiritual director or regular confessor knows your soul and is the best person to help judge if the grave matter of masturbation is in fact a mortal sin in your case. He is also aware of the conditions mentioned above that can lessen the culpability of a man with regard to this sin, and he will guide you in this matter.

Beware that Satan uses shame to attack men in this area. He suggests, "Well, you have done it now. You are in a state of mortal sin and you can't go to Communion. You might as well masturbate again and enjoy it. Why not go look at some pornography to help you?" This temptation leads to binges of impurity, and the establishment of sexual addictions.

By following the plan outlined above, a man realizes that God can immediately and completely forgive him because of his effort to make a perfect Act of Contrition and therefore, the next temptation is a new opportunity to show his love for God, even though he may have failed the last temptation. I have seen this approach greatly help men to overcome their struggle with self-abuse, at times even more effectively than the man who will not receive Holy Communion until he has been to Confession. It helps prevent binges of sexual impurity.

Don't stop working for sexual integration. The sin of masturbation will one day be conquered through prayer, spiritual direction, mortification, the assistance of Our Blessed Mother, regular exercise, and good mature friendships. Eventually, a man's life of prayer will help him to love God more than he loves this particular sin. Only then will he stop. And when that day comes, this man's faith will be much stronger and more mature. He will not become proud or unmerciful. He will know both in his mind and in his heart that the words of Jesus are absolutely true: "Without me, you can do nothing" (John 15:5).

The Best Candidate for Priesthood

The best candidate will be a man who has normal, heterosexual attractions for adult women, who has not been sexually active with another person and who has been able to demonstrate sexual self-mastery with regard to lust (fantasy, masturbation, pornography, etc.). This is a man who has developed affective maturity and can have wholesome friendships and relationships with both men and women. In other words, the best candidate is a man who is clearly moving towards sexual integration.

Obviously, it is best never to have committed sexual sins with a woman. Why? Besides the fact that sin is a lack of love for the Lord Jesus, there is a practical reason. When it comes to living purity, *imagination* is one thing but *memory* is something else. If a man has X-rated sexual memories in his mind, these memories will come up again and again in times of temptation. They will make living purity more difficult, though still not impossible. With God, all things are possible, but this man may need to work and pray for the healing of some of these memories. The past is the past. We cannot undo our personal history of sin. But we can love and serve the Lord even more because of his love and mercy for us.

Should a Man Have Chaste Dating Experiences Before He Enters Seminary?

This is a question that is asked by many young men and there is no single answer that applies to every man. I know many excellent, well-balanced, holy priests who never once went out on a date. They never had a steady girlfriend and they never had any sexual experiences. They live their priesthood in celibacy, chastity, charity, and cheerfulness. They live celibacy in tranquility of mind. Yet I know other priests, also very holy and well-balanced, who dated quite a bit, who had steady girlfriends and who (at least some of them) had sexual experiences. They also live their priesthood in celibacy, chastity, charity, and cheerfulness.

Should a man date? Many spiritual directors answer, "Why hold a candle in the wind? Why risk losing something so precious as a vocation to priesthood by forcing yourself to have some dating experiences?" While I certainly see their point and agree that a call to priesthood is a precious gift, I also believe that some men will not be able to live celibacy chastely, in tranquility of mind, without having dated. Every man has to discern this question with his spiritual director and approach it carefully. Some men will discern that they need to have some dating experiences before they will feel peaceful giving seminary a try. Others do not need this.

Here are some caveats to the question of dating. First of all, it is important that dating be chaste. So many young men and women who have grown up in this culture have not been properly formed with regard to purity. Even if a man has the best intentions for purity, sometimes the woman has not been properly formed in this area. She too has grown up in a culture that encourages "hooking up." Sexuality is a powerful drive; any man who thinks he is strong enough not to fall sexually with a certain woman under the right circumstances is wrong — and he is a fool. If it happens that he becomes sexually active, it becomes much more difficult to discern priesthood and celibacy properly. The prophet Jeremiah said, "More tortuous than all else is the human heart" (Jeremiah 17:9). Sexual union makes the heart attach strongly, which makes breaking off an unhealthy relationship even more difficult.

I have heard people say (including some priests) that a man should "know what he is giving up" before he goes to seminary. It sounds almost as if they are encouraging men to go out and commit sexual sin! We should never encourage anyone to sin nor should we say something that even gives that impression. One may never do evil that good will come of it.

However, *healthy* Christian dating can be beneficial. Consider the alternative. In the old system of priestly formation, let's say in the year 1950, a man might go off to a high school seminary right after grade school. In those days, a seminary was very much like a strict monastery. There were no newspapers allowed, no televisions, and contact with the outside world was strictly curtailed. A man might not even see a woman for most months of the year, except for a religious sister in habit who ran the infirmary, or a secretary or two. He would certainly not spend any time speaking to a woman his age. When this seminarian went home for the summer, he was usually required to "check in" with his pastor immediately upon arrival and he was expected to spend most of his time at the parish. This seminarian never had the opportunity to develop good, mature friendships with adult women. Then the man would be ordained a priest at the age of twenty-five, after having been in this very secluded seminary system for eight or even twelve years (if he attended a high school seminary). He would then be sent to work in a parish. In his first year as a priest, a young, attractive, and very distraught woman would come in to see him because of marriage problems. Her husband is cheating on her; he is physically and emotionally absent and she does not know what to do. The priest listens kindly, offers some good Christian advice, prays with her and ends the appointment. The woman is truly grateful. She puts her hand on the priest's hand and squeezes it to show her appreciation. She means nothing sexual by the gesture, but he has never even held the hand of a woman! Sexual and emotional feelings are aroused in the priest, and the story goes on. Often there is not a good ending to this kind of story.

Women constitute more than 50 percent of the Church. And women do most of the work in the Church. Look at the daily Mass crowd in your parish. You will see it is mostly women. A priest must be able to love and minister to these children of God without sexual feelings getting in the way. A priest must be able to develop and maintain mature friendships with both men and women of all ages. This is why a seminarian should be moving steadily towards sexual integration. For all of these reasons, some healthy Christian dating before seminary can be beneficial — though it is not absolutely necessary.

Is It Ethically Permissible for a Man Who Is Seriously Discerning Priesthood to Date?

If a man is seriously discerning priesthood, then he should, in conscience, tell a woman this before he begins to date her. He cannot use a woman in a dating relationship, just so that later he will be able to go to seminary in peace. I have seen candidates use women in this way and it is not acceptable. Pope John Paul II explains in *The Theology of the Body* that, "the opposite of love is really not hate. The opposite of love is to use another person as a means to an end." People are to be loved. They are not to be used.

If this man is discerning both marriage and priesthood, and he honestly tells the woman this from the beginning, and she agrees to begin the dating relationship anyway, on the grounds that marriage is still a possibility, then it is ethically permissible. I have had many spiritual directees who were dating women and discerning priesthood during their college years. But there will come a time for every man who is discerning priesthood to enter a "dating fast." His spiritual director will eventually tell him that he cannot seriously discern priesthood (and expect to advance in his discernment) while dating a particular woman. Why? Because there is a great difference between giving up women in general and giving up a specific woman, whom you happen to love. I know many men in the seminary who had to make the decision to break up with their girlfriends specifically so that they could discern priesthood.

Remember that giving up "women in general" is required of every man in every vocation. A man who is married must give up all women, because he has been called to give himself completely to one particular woman—his wife. A priest also gives up women so as to give himself completely to one particular woman— an extremely beautiful woman, the Bride of Christ.

Can I Go to Seminary if I Have Been Sexually Active in My Past?

Once a man has demonstrated that he can live chastely for an extended period of time, he likely will be accepted for seminary even if he has a sexual history. But in this case, the time of sexual sobriety will need to be extended. The bishop and vocation director will have to make this prudential judgment. In order to help them make the right decision, it is of supreme importance that the candidate be completely honest about everything in his sexual past. St. Thomas Aquinas said that long-practiced chastity is comparable to virginity.[57] If a man has an extensive sexual history, then he needs an extended period of chastity to show himself and his bishop that he is in fact moving towards sexual integration. Most vocation directors require a candidate to demonstrate at least two years of sexual sobriety. He needs to demonstrate by long-practiced chastity that, by all indications, God is giving him the gift of celibacy. This man needs to reclaim his sexual integrity. If he cannot demonstrate this — if he keeps falling sexually with women or if he is not making progress with regard to self-abuse — then this should be seen as a sign that he is likely not called to become a priest.

I know a priest who told me that he had been sexually active prior to going to seminary. He had sexual intercourse with three different women during his college years. Eventually he did go to seminary after college, having lived chastely for more than two years, and he grew even more sexually integrated in seminary. As his day of ordination approached, this man felt the Holy Spirit encouraging him to contact those three women to ask their forgiveness. He called each of them, told them he was about to be ordained a priest, and asked their forgiveness for his sexual past. All three of these women were very moved by this gesture and immediately reciprocated, asking for his forgiveness for their part. One of the women even started practicing her faith again! God can bring good even from our sins. I tell that story not to recommend this particular practice, but to stress the fact that sexual integration is possible, even for men who have a sexual history.

Sexual Impediments to Priesthood

Pedophilia and ephebophilia are much more serious disorders in the whole spectrum of sexual dis-integration. <u>If a man has one of these disorders, he ought never to become a priest or be permitted to become a priest</u>. Pedophilia is a psychological disorder characterized by an adult experiencing sexual preference for prepubescent children. Ephebophilia is a psychological disorder indicating sexual preference for mid-to-late adolescents.

The Sexual Abuse Crisis

The Catholic Church has suffered horribly since 2002 from what become known as the Sexual Abuse Crisis. It became known that Catholic priests had sexually abused young people and children in many dioceses and that some bishops, knowing that these priests had abused minors, nonetheless re-assigned them to other parishes. This is the greatest scandal that the U.S. Catholic Church has ever faced. People have suffered greatly. Above all, the children who were abused and their families have certainly suffered and many continue to suffer the effects of sexual abuse. Catholics in general have suffered and been embarrassed that such a terrible thing occurred in their Church. The rest of the good, faithful, healthy priests have suffered by being maligned along with the relatively small number of unhealthy, very sick priests who committed this evil. It has cost the Catholic Church over two billion dollars in settlements and caused inestimable damage to the Church's reputation.

Pedophilia and ephebophilia are extremely serious forms of sexual disintegration, usually combined with other psychological or emotional problems. Having one of these conditions permanently excludes a man from pursuing priesthood. The great majority of U.S. sexual abuse cases involving priests since 2002 have actually been cases of ephebophilia, not pedophilia, and the cases usually involved homosexual men with this serious illness acting out on post-pubescent boys.

Can a Man with Same-Sex Attraction Go to Seminary to Become a Priest?

The answer is… it depends.

In 2005, the Vatican issued a document called "Instruction Concerning the Criteria for the Discernment of Vocations with Regard to Persons with Homosexual Tendencies in View of Their Admission to the Seminary and to Holy Orders." One key passage reads as follows.

> Deep-seated homosexual tendencies, which are found in a number of men and women, are also objectively disordered and, for those same people, often constitute a trial. Such persons must be accepted with respect and sensitivity. Every sign of unjust discrimination in their regard should be avoided…. [However] it is necessary to state clearly that the Church, while profoundly respecting the persons in question, cannot admit to the seminary or to holy orders those who practice homosexuality, present deep-seated homosexual tendencies or support the so-called "gay culture."
>
> Different, however, would be the case in which one were dealing with homosexual tendencies that were only the expression of a transitory problem — for example, that of an adolescence not yet superseded. Nevertheless, such tendencies must be clearly overcome at least three years before ordination to the diaconate.

This document says that the Church cannot allow ordination of men who are active homosexuals or who have "deep-seated homosexual tendencies." These norms do not rule out ordination for men who have experienced transitory homosexual tendencies or episodes, as long as they have been clearly overcome "at least three years before ordination to the diaconate." The wording of this document, when it came out, re-sparked an ongoing conversation about the nature of homosexuality and why some men have same-sex attraction in the first place. Those questions, while important, are not our purpose here.

Some bishops, vocation directors, and seminary formators believe that if a man has *any* same-sex attraction, he should not move forward towards priesthood. They argue that it is an occasion of temptation to put the man in a seminary with hundreds of other men. If ordained a priest, he may live in a rectory with other priests. They say that we should never place a man in an occasion of sin like this. Others argue that it is impossible for a man with same-sex attraction to live and embrace celibacy. What they mean is that because the virtue of celibacy is a giving up of something precious and greatly desired (marriage and sexual intimacy with a woman), and a man does not even desire marriage because he is sexually attracted to men, it is not possible for him to embrace celibacy. They ask how a man who is not attracted to women can fall in love with and marry the Bride of Christ. Finally, they argue (quoting the facts) that the majority of sexual abuse cases that have harmed so many young people were actually homosexually active priests acting out on post-pubescent boys— what is called ephebophilia. For all of these reasons and others, they argue that men with same-sex attraction should not be admitted to seminary.

The problem with this approach is that there are many different degrees of same-sex attraction. Consider these scenarios.

~ If a young man has a single same sex experience when he is nine with another nine-year old boy, does that make him gay? No, of course not.

~ If a fourteen-year old boy, socially awkward, with an absent and abusive father, thinks for a year that he might be homosexual, but then he gets a

240

girlfriend at sixteen and forgets all about it—is he a homosexual? No. This is an example of a transitory homosexual tendency.

~ If a twenty-two year old man, who has dated several women and never been conscious of any same-sex attraction, has several dreams over the years about a homosexual encounter which results in a nocturnal emission, could he still be a candidate for priesthood? Yes.

~ But what about a man who has struggled with a degree of same-sex attraction all throughout high school and college? He has viewed some homosexual pornography and masturbated in the past, but has never had a homosexual encounter. He does have some attraction for women; he has dated a few girls and he sometimes fantasizes about marriage and family. Is he a candidate for priesthood? Does he have deep-seated homosexual tendencies? Now the answer is not so clear.

~ A man has had homosexual inclinations for as long as he can remember and he has been homosexually active with many different men. He has frequented the gay bar scene. All of his friends are practicing homosexuals and he can never remember being attracted to a woman. This man is clearly an active homosexual with deep-seated homosexual tendencies. He is not a candidate for priesthood.

These examples give you an idea of the possible ranges of men who have some same-sex attraction. They are clearly not all the same.

Defining Homosexual Tendencies

The 2005 Instruction from the Vatican states that: "The Church cannot admit to the seminary or to holy orders those who practice homosexuality, present deep-seated homosexual tendencies or support the so-called 'gay culture.'" How might *deep-seated homosexual tendencies* be differentiated from *homosexual tendencies that are only the expression of a transitory problem*?

A person with deep-seated homosexual tendencies would:

~ Identify himself as homosexual

~ Under severe stress may experience strong physical and sexual attractions to adult males and to adolescents of the same sex

~ Engage in homosexual behaviors

~ Harbor excessive anger toward the Church because of the teachings on sexual morality

~ Refuse to defend the sacrament of marriage

~ Have strong narcissistic conflicts

~ Refuse to try to understand their emotional conflicts which lead to same-sex attraction

~ Defend the use of homosexual pornography

~ Demonstrate excessive anger toward those who are faithful and loyal to the Church's teaching on sexual morality

In contrast, a person with some transitory same-sex attraction would:

~ Not identify himself as homosexual

~ Be motivated to understand and to overcome emotional conflicts

~ Seek psychotherapy and spiritual direction

~ Desire to live and teach the fullness of the Church's teaching on sexual morality

~ Not support the homosexual culture, but see it as antithetical to the universal call to holiness

~ Support the sacrament of marriage and the right of a child to a father and a mother

The document says that, "Nevertheless, such tendencies must be clearly overcome at least three years before ordination to the diaconate." A man who has some transitory same-sex attraction as described above, but who has been completely self-disclosing and who is working very hard with his spiritual director or counselor, might be able to begin seminary at the college or pre-theologate level. This means that the man would have a minimum of five to seven years of intense priestly formation before his ordination to the diaconate, which is usually at the end of third theology or the beginning of fourth theology. This would allow sufficient time for the essential growth in affective maturity required by the Church.

The 2005 Vatican instruction continues:

> The candidate for ordained ministry must attain affective maturity. Such maturity will allow him to relate properly to men and women, developing in him a true sense of spiritual fatherhood for the ecclesial community that will be entrusted to him.

I once attended an excellent conference on this topic given by James Cardinal Hickey, former Archbishop of Washington, D.C. One thing he said struck me: "In my experience as a rector of a seminary and as a bishop, I have learned that if a man has homosexual attractions and if he has been sexually active with another man before seminary, if ordained a priest, the likelihood that, in times of stress, this man will regress into some homosexual behavior is much higher than a man who had been heterosexually active before seminary and ordination" (my paraphrase).

Because having homosexual inclinations is a disordered attraction, and because homosexual activity is a disordered behavior, the stress that comes from priestly work can trigger a desire to "self-medicate" by returning to that disordered behavior. Cardinal Hickey was stressing that this likelihood is much higher in men who have been homosexually active than in men who have been heterosexually active. The point here is that having been *homosexually active* is a more serious issue than just having had or having same-sex attraction transitory tendencies. This is why the Vatican directive implies that if a man has experienced transitory homosexual tendencies, he could possibly be admitted to college seminary or pre-theology as long as they have been clearly overcome for at least three years before diaconate ordination. My opinion is that, should he ever be accepted at all, an even longer period of sexual sobriety is necessary for a man who has had homosexual episodes.

The issue of homosexuality and how it develops in individuals is still being studied and there are different opinions. What we do know for sure is that there are different degrees of same-sex attraction and many variables in those degrees. Every bishop and vocation director must evaluate every candidate carefully, thoroughly, and *individually*. Every man is an individual person with his own experiences, graces, gifts, successes, and failures. How each man handles sexual tension can vary greatly.

During the application process, it is imperative that the candidate be completely honest with his vocation director and bishop. The ordinarily required psychological testing also will target psycho-sexual development and maturity, and a complete sexual history is usually taken. In the end, the diocesan bishop must make a prudential judgment regarding acceptance. If a man has been forthright and honest about everything, this judgment will reflect the will of God.

In my personal experience working with seminarians for more than fifteen years, the majority say that they have only heterosexual attractions for adult females. A much smaller percentage would say that they have some residual same-sex attraction. Many of the men who do have some same-sex attraction I have found to be heroically holy men of great integrity. They are men who love the Lord Jesus greatly. They did not choose same-sex attraction and they do not want it, but they carry this cross with courage, praying faithfully for strength, and fully embracing the Church's teaching on human sexuality. These men can make very fine priests.

If a man has some same-sex attraction or aberrant sexual behavior, then I recommend he do one thing immediately: get a holy, wise spiritual director and talk about it. Stop living in the shadows of shame. Stop living in fear that someone is going to find out. Jesus Christ came to set us free! Talk about it, deal with it, pray about it—and the grace of Christ will come to you. Whether or not you become a priest, this approach will bring you blessings and peace.

The Vatican Instruction indicates that a *practicing* homosexual or a man with deep-seated homosexual tendencies ought never to be ordained a priest. The Church *cannot allow* ordination of men who are active homosexuals or who have deep-seated homosexual tendencies.

But a man can be accepted for study if he has a significantly lesser degree of same-sex attraction which he has completely disclosed. He should completely and enthusiastically embrace the Church's teaching on marriage and sexuality. He should be growing in affective maturity and must have clearly overcome the transitory same-sex attraction, living chastely for at least three years before his diaconate ordination. Still, the bishop must make the prudential judgment. Help your bishop make the decision that reflects God's will by being completely honest and self-disclosing.

The Permanent Deacon Compromise

Every young man discerning priesthood and celibacy will at some point try to resort to what I call "the permanent deacon compromise." He will say to himself, "Since I like girls so much, I will just become a permanent deacon. That way, I can still get married and have a family, yet work full time for the Church."

First of all, this idea is insulting to the permanent diaconate. The permanent diaconate is a call from God; it is a vocation. It is not a vocation of compromise. It is not something "less." Secondly, the permanent deacon compromise does not work. To do anything less than the will of God for your life will bore you! If you are called to become a priest, then nothing else will do. If God chose you for priesthood, becoming a permanent deacon means that you will not be in your correct God pre-determined vocation. God will have called you to something, and therefore given you the grace to live that vocation, but you compromised that call for something else.

Let me be clear. Some men like St. Thomas More discern that they are not called to celibacy and therefore are not called to priesthood. That is fine, as long as it has been a diligent discernment. But a man discerning priesthood should do just that—discern *priesthood*. Later on, after discerning marriage and finding one's wife (if called to marriage), would be the time for discerning permanent diaconate, should the Lord call you to that. Forget the permanent deacon compromise. I understand why you want to go there, but it does not work.

"I should like you to be free of anxieties. An unmarried man is anxious about the things of the Lord, how he may please the Lord. But a married man is anxious about the things of the world, how he may please his wife, and he is divided."

1 Corinthians 7:32-34

Discerning Celibacy in Seminary

I began this chapter by saying that a man must make a diligent discernment of celibacy, just as he does for priesthood as a whole. Celibacy must be discerned over an extended period of time. When the time comes for a decision, listen to your heart. If peace is present in your heart, then you should move forward.

Seminarians usually arrive at major seminary still unsure whether or not they have the gift of celibacy. This is normal. They have *indications* that celibacy is God's call for them, and they have already demonstrated that they are moving towards sexual integration. After the first year in seminary "practicing celibacy" so to speak, a seminarian will again evaluate if he is peaceful. Is he living the four Cs: celibacy and chastity leading to charity and cheerfulness? Is he living everyday with joy?

I usually ask seminarians to rate themselves monthly on a scale of 1-10, moving towards a peaceful celibacy or an ability to live celibacy in tranquility of mind. The 1 indicates a great lack of peace and a 10 indicates a readiness to be ordained a deacon immediately. Over a period of several years, I use this rating system to see if the man is making progress. If he averages 8 or 9 the last two years before ordination, that is a very good sign. If his scores vary erratically, from 2 to 7 to 3 to 2, this is not good.

Neither is it a good sign if a man finds that he is "white knuckling" chastity every day—barely hanging on trying to remain pure at great cost to himself, and not living with joy. "Better to be a chaste layman than a priest impure."

Men called to become priests, who are praying faithfully, ordinarily find that their peace regarding celibacy and their overall joy slowly increases year by year. There are of course the normal ups and downs involved in this battle, but peace and joy increase. The man realizes that, overall, he is not just surviving, but flourishing!

Loneliness and Longing for a Companion

A priest friend once told me this story:

It was Thanksgiving and I had celebrated the early Mass in the parish and then gone to my sister's home to spend the day. It was one of those wonderful, unforgettable days. There were many young children there, my nephews and nieces, laughing, playing, and just enjoying life. The meal and fellowship with my family was perfect and family life just seemed beautiful. Late in the evening, around nine o'clock, I drove back to the rectory, about half an hour away. When I pulled into the parking lot, everything was black. All the lights were off in the rectory and church. I had given my assistant the day off and he would not return until the next day. As I walked up the steps and put my key into the door, my mind was still on my family and the wonderful events of the day. Suddenly, I felt a pang of deep loneliness. It was much worse than I had ever experienced in my twenty-five years of priesthood and I was troubled by it. Immediately, as I was trained to do, I went through the rectory and into the attached church. I knelt down in the darkness before Jesus, the tabernacle barely visible from the light of the red sanctuary candle. I said, "Jesus, I feel lonely." I knelt there for about twenty minutes, just looking at the Lord and waiting. Suddenly, I heard Jesus speak to me very clearly in my heart. He said, "You belong completely to me." I know it was Jesus because immediately I was filled with joy and tears came to my eyes. I prayed, "Thank you Jesus. Thank you. I want to belong completely to you. Thank you for calling me to be a priest."

The older a man gets, generally speaking, the less intense the battle for sexual purity. However, the battle for sexual integration is life-long. Older priests will sometimes say that although their sexual tension is less, the desire for intimacy is always present. God made us for intimacy and the Church would never ask her priests to give that up. The purpose of celibacy is to learn to love the way the saints love in heaven. Celibacy is about intimacy with Jesus, the only one who can fill the void that is within us all. This is why prayer is so essential in the life of a priest. Intimacy with Jesus leads to love and intimacy with his people. Therefore priests who pray faithfully generally are not lonely. But when a priest is not praying and when he isolates himself from people, this can lead to loneliness and the desire to self-medicate to take the edge off.

Yes, there will always be some nights in the life of a priest when he lies in bed and aches for a companion. God made us this way. He made us for union. But the priest raises his mind and heart to Jesus in these times and says, "Yes Lord, I ache tonight for a female companion. But my life is an eschatological sign to the world that you alone can fill the human heart. And I am glad to ache for you, to bring that truth to the world. I am glad you called me to be a priest! Now I am going to sleep."

Married Catholic Priests and the Pastoral Provision

Aren't there some married priests in the Latin Rite of the Catholic Church? Is that an option for me?

In 1980, the Holy See, in response from priests and laity of the Episcopal Church who were seeking full communion with the Catholic Church, created a special pastoral provision. Under the provision, the ordination to the Catholic priesthood of married

Episcopal priests was made possible. The pastoral provision is a service rendered to the bishops of the United States by which former Episcopal ministers who have been accepted as candidates for priestly ordination in the Latin rite of the Catholic Church receive theological, spiritual, and pastoral preparation for ministry.

Since 1983, over seventy married men have been ordained for priestly ministry in Catholic dioceses of the United States through the pastoral provision. These married men are ordained Catholic priests, but they understand that should their wife predecease them, they will not be permitted to remarry. The pastoral provision has also been used for other formerly Protestant clergy such as Lutheran ministers.

Unless you are already an ordained Episcopal priest or Lutheran minister, married, and you have become a Catholic, this is not an option for you.

Will Priests Ever Be Allowed to Marry in the Roman Rite?

Priesthood and marriage are not mutually exclusive, theologically speaking, as is indicated in the last section. Celibacy is a law of the Church. It is not Divine law. This means that the Church has the authority to change this law and to allow *future priests* to marry, should the Holy Spirit direct our Holy Father, the Pope towards this course. Interestingly, this would not affect the promise of celibacy made by priests already ordained, but only those to be ordained in the future.

It would be a grave error to enter seminary and to be ordained a priest anticipating that this law of the Church will be changed in the future. Many seminarians around the time of the Second Vatican Council did just that. They went forward with ordination fully expecting that they would be allowed to marry within a few years. While the post-Vatican II days were a time of great speculation in the Church, and many were suggesting this change, it did not occur. Many of these priests later left the priesthood, saying that they felt betrayed.

It is my strong opinion that the law of celibacy for priests is healthy for the Church, and I am not at all suggesting that I want it to change. The world desperately needs authentic eschatological witnesses—men who witness by their lives that Jesus is the only thing that can fill that deep void in all of our souls.

The Importance of Honest Self-disclosure

In my fifteen years as a vocation director and seminary formator, I have known men who discerned priesthood and eventually went off to seminary while hiding some important fact about their sexual identity or history. Some lied to me or their own vocation director about having same-sex attraction. Others lied about a problem with pornography and addictive masturbation. Some lied about previous sexual encounters, usually of a deviant nature. Some lied or withheld information about having been sexually abused when they were children. Still others had a clandestine relationship with a woman during their seminary years, usually a former girlfriend with whom they were not able to make a final break. In every case, these men and their aspirations for priesthood ended badly. None of them are priests today, nor are they still in seminary. Almost all of these men said to me, after the truth had come out, "Father, I'm sorry I lied. I just hoped that going off to the seminary would solve my problem."

No! I cannot over-emphasize that going to the seminary will not solve a serious problem with sexual disintegration. Just as marriage is not a cure for sexual disintegration, neither is seminary. Yes, a seminary is a holy place with a structured life of prayer and regular spiritual direction. It is a good environment living with other men who really love the Lord Jesus. It is a great place to grow! No question about it. That is why it is called a seminary (from the Latin *seminarium*, which means a seed plot or garden). But it is also a very intense formation program and it is stressful. Stress can actually exacerbate sexual disintegration if it has not been disclosed and is not addressed in the open. By "in the open," I mean by being honest about everything with your vocation director and spiritual director. Most men are terrified and embarrassed by their sexual struggles and that makes it very difficult to reveal them. They are afraid that revealing something sexual that is not quite normal will result in their not being accepted. But hiding one's sexual struggles and lying about it causes even more problems.

The first problem is a matter of conscience. A man is studying to become a priest, yet he knows that he lied about something very important. Perhaps he did not overtly lie but he withheld information he knows he should have provided. This will certainly weigh on his conscience and give him a heaviness of heart: "I am studying to be a priest yet I am not a man of integrity. I am dishonest." The second problem is that the man lives in fear that his big secret will be revealed in some way. He will not have peace in the seminary. In my experience, the sexual problem or secret almost always comes out eventually. Sometimes, another person alerts the seminary that they know this man had sexual problems in a previous life. Usually, the man's spiritual director (if the man is even revealing this problem in Confession) strongly encourages the man to bring this issue into the external forum. Of course, the seal of Confession is inviolable, but the spiritual director can strongly encourage the man to go to his vocation director or the rector of the seminary. Why? Because he needs help to overcome this difficulty. Just as little children are afraid of the dark, adults are afraid of the light. Bringing these issues to the light of Christ from the beginning will help a man grow and heal. If he keeps his secrets in the dark, the problem only will grow worse.

"But Father, I fear that I will not be accepted if I reveal everything about my sexual life." God is the one who calls men to priesthood and God already knows the details of your sexuality.

If you are not accepted to become a priest because of some sexual dysfunction or problem, then that means God does not want you to become a priest. And if God does not want you to be a priest, you should not want to become a priest. If you pursue priesthood anyway, it will end badly.

Your problem may not be nearly as bad as you feared. I have interviewed many men who were considering priesthood. On a number of occasions, a man would say something like, "Father, I am going to be completely honest, though I am scared and embarrassed. Once or twice, I have had a dream of a sexual encounter with another man. This dream resulted in a nocturnal emission. I don't think I am homosexual and I was horrified by the dream. Does this mean that I cannot be a priest?" These men were so happy to learn that many men, totally heterosexual men, will admit anonymously to having had a dream of this kind. It does not mean that you are homosexual and it does not mean that you cannot be a priest. "Father, thank you for telling me that. That has bothered me all my life. I feel so much better." I can remember others telling me that, when they were five or six years old, they once improperly touched their younger sister or another small girl. Actually, this "playing doctor" is common among small children. It is a childhood exploration of the human body.

Jesus said, "The truth will set you free" (John 8:32). Tell your vocation director and spiritual director everything. Tell them and they will help you understand if your particular sexual concern is serious. And if it is serious, they will guide you to get the professional help you need to overcome it. They will not just kick you out the door. Your vocation director and spiritual director are first of all *priests*. And priests love and care for all of God's people, not only those who are able to become priests themselves.

Caution: if any person, even a priest, tells you that you should not mention something about your sexual life to your vocation director, do not listen to that person! Tell your vocation director everything. As I think back, most of the above-referenced cases of men who lied to me about their sexual disintegration were men whose vocation to priesthood might have been salvaged. Their sexual dysfunction needed to be dealt with, but it was not fatal for priesthood. Had they only told their vocation director the whole truth from the beginning, they might be priests today.

To Live Fully an Effective Life of Celibate Chastity

The Program of Priestly Formation says in #93:

> To live fully an effective life of celibate chastity requires: a) a knowledge of one's sexuality and sexual desires; b) an acceptance and valuing of one's sexuality as a good to be directed to God's service; c) a lifelong commitment to growth, which means continuously integrating one's sexuality into a life and ministry shaped and expressed by celibate chastity. Certain habits or skills are necessary instruments... Among these habits and skills are: appropriate self-disclosure, a cultivated capacity for self-reflection, an ability to enter into peaceful solitude, ascetical practices that foster self mastery over one's impulses and drives, and a habit of modesty. An especially important practice is holding all persons in the mystery of God... This practice means viewing all persons in God, interceding for them before God, and claiming responsibility to direct them to God.

Meeting the Stage 4 Woman of Your Dreams

This is a great mystery to me. Many, many times, when a man realizes that he can no longer discern priesthood outside of seminary, and he begins the application process to join his diocese, he meets the woman of his dreams! The fourth stage of discernment, as described in chapter 9, is when a man makes the decision to try seminary. He has already made a decision not to date, as it would not be fair to the woman he was dating. And then the man will come to his vocation director and say, "Father, I have just met the most wonderful Catholic woman. She is beautiful, holy, smart, sweet — and she likes me! I have been looking for this woman all of my life. Why does she come along now, when I am signed up to go to the seminary in two months? Is this a sign from God that I should not go to seminary? Should I stop my application?"

No, it is not a sign from God. It happens all the time, though I don't know why. Does God orchestrate this, just to test the man's resolve? Does Satan try to make it happen, to stop the man from going to seminary? I don't know, but I know it is not a sign from God to stop the application. It is one of the questions I want to ask God when I get to heaven!

When I was a vocation director, I had some men pursue the dating relationship with this *perfect woman* anyway. They stopped their application, in spite of my protests, in order to go and date the woman of their dreams. It never worked out. They never married. Eventually, they would come back and begin the application process again. But they had usually missed the date to begin seminary that year.

One vocation director I know always tells his candidates when they pick up the application, "Oh, by the way, your romantic life is about to improve!" They reply, "Father, if you had told me that before, I would have applied sooner!"

Celibacy, Chastity, Charity and Cheerfulness

Men who are called to become priests flourish in their vocation. They do not just survive. They flourish. They are called to be celibate as an eschatological sign to the world. Like all men, priests are called to attain sexual integration, and this leads to the charity of Jesus Christ. Celibate chastity helps men to love and care for others more generously. And this selfless charity in the image of Jesus leads to joy. Contrary to the message of the media, priests are some of the happiest men in the world.

Is God calling you to celibacy for the sake of the Kingdom? Is he calling you to become a diocesan priest?

CHAPTER 14

MY PATH TO PRIESTHOOD: WHEN DO I START?

"Before I formed you in the womb I knew you, before you were born I dedicated you, a prophet to the nations I appointed you. 'Ah, Lord God!' I said, 'I know not how to speak; I am too young.' But the Lord answered me, 'Say not, "I am too young." To whomever I send you, you shall go; whatever I command you, you shall speak. Have no fear before them, because I am with you to deliver you, says the Lord.' Then the Lord extended his hand and touched my mouth, saying, 'See, I place my words in your mouth!'"

Jeremiah 1:5-9

When should I go to seminary to discern priesthood?

Should I attend a college seminary or pre-theology program?

Should I finish college before I go to seminary?

How do I know when I am ready to take a more formal step like this?

What is the maximum age at which I can be accepted to begin seminary?

We have a saying in vocation work: A vocation is like fruit on a tree. If you pick it too soon, it is not ready; but if it stays on too long, it rots. The decisions a man makes during discernment—and when he makes them—are critical parts of the process. This chapter covers the most common ways that men move toward priesthood. As you may imagine, there are a number different tracks or paths to ordination.

Today's seminaries are filled with men of many different ages. Some men in college seminary are only eighteen years old, right out of high school, whereas other men in major seminaries are in their sixties. (There are even seminaries that specialize in older candidates.) How does one navigate this spectrum and decide when it is the right time to begin seminary formation? The first rule is one already covered: Do not try to make this decision alone! Contact your vocation director for guidance and options, and then discuss these options with your spiritual director.

Timing will depend on many factors which are specific to the individual: How long have you been discerning diligently? How much formation have you already had? What is your level of maturity? What is your level of education? Are there any serious formation issues which need to be addressed before beginning seminary? Do you have any unpaid debts (other than student loans which can be deferred)? Are your parents supportive? Do you simply feel ready and anxious to begin? These are the kinds of questions which will help you and your spiritual director discern God's will in this regard.

I once knew a saintly young woman who eventually joined a wonderful religious community. She had been a missionary for FOCUS (Fellowship of Catholic University Students) for one year and was considering two very fine religious orders, one in the U.S. and one in Italy. She had been to several Come and See retreats with both orders. She explained to me what it felt like when she had pondered joining the Italian order, "Father, I felt like I was about to jump off of a cliff." She was very attracted to the order and wanted to join, but she could not understand why it was so difficult to jump. Was it supposed to be this hard? I advised her not to jump—yet. The timing was not right, but the right timing eventually directed her to the right place. One year later, toward the end of her two-year FOCUS commitment, after much prayer and spiritual direction, she decided to join the religious community located in the U.S. This time, she told me, it was much easier to make the move. It did not feel at all like she was jumping off of a cliff, but rather like taking a simple, albeit large, step. She was still understandably nervous about taking such a big step, which is a normal feeling. One of the sisters had given her this wise advice: "When the time is right, a vocation is like picking a ripe apple off of a tree. It is ready. Picking it does no harm to the apple or to the tree. It picks easily." The time had now come for this young woman; the fruit was easily and peacefully picked.

Don't Be a Jumper or a Fence-Sitter

Virtus in medio stat (virtue is always in the middle). When it comes to timing, don't be either a jumper or a fence-sitter. A jumper is someone who goes off to a retreat one weekend and has a powerful Jesus Experience. The Lord really touches this man and he understands God's infinite, unconditional love for the first time. The thought of priesthood comes to him and he is very excited. The man comes back from the retreat, picks up the phone and calls his vocation director, "I want to go to the seminary. Can I start in the fall?" This man has never before contacted his vocation director. He has never been to a discernment retreat with the diocese. He has not even had a stable prayer life or spiritual director, and he had not been thinking about priesthood at all before this past weekend. No, he is not ready to *jump* into seminary. He has not made a diligent discernment. He is only in stage 1 or 2 of the discernment stages (see chapter 9).

On the other extreme, we find the fence-sitter, the man who cannot make a decision to go to seminary. Often this man has done a lot of reading and praying about his vocation. He has attended a number of discernment events. He has many of the requisite signs and qualities. His vocation director has encouraged him by saying (often in frustration), "The time has come. You are spinning your wheels. You cannot know if you are called to priesthood unless you go to seminary." But this man is a fence-sitter. He simply can't make the decision to give seminary a try.

Sometimes I will encounter a man who is fifty years old and has been considering priesthood for twenty-five years, but has done nothing about it. At age fifty, he is still unsure. I say to this man, "Listen, had you gone to seminary twenty-five years ago, when your vocation director and spiritual director encouraged you to do so, God would have shown you clearly whether or not you were called. You would either be a priest right now or you would have moved on with your life, having permanently ex-cluded the possibility. As it is, you are fifty years old and still wondering." This is not always completely the man's fault, as circumstances of life can contribute to his inability to make a de-cision. Still, I have seen some of these men eventually get off the fence, go to seminary, and become priests.

"If the Almighty's compassion is deeper than the chasms and higher than the mountains, and his omnipotence and richness exceeds all imaginable boundaries, we only need to do one thing: jump."[58]

St. Francis of Assisi

The Launch Window

The vocation director in Savannah, Georgia, Fr. Tim McKeown, likes to use this image:

> NASA is in the business of launching space shuttles and they have to monitor things very carefully when they are trying to launch. The conditions have to be just right and they monitor many things like the rotation of the earth, ba-rometric pressure, and incoming storms. Often they have a very specific launch window, a window of opportunity, and if they miss it, it might not be possible to launch that shuttle again for some time. There is a launch window in

vocation discernment also. God orchestrates many things in a man's life leading to the day of launch. That day is usually the day when a man moves boldly towards his vocation to priesthood, by filling out the application or arriving at the seminary.

I think the engineers at NASA are both excited and nervous on any day they launch a shuttle. It is a massive endeavor fraught with many possible dangers. But they know when the launch window appears, they must pull the trigger. It is the same with your vocation, but with a vocation it is much less dangerous. Why? Because God will never send you where his grace cannot sustain you. If God orchestrates your life such that an obvious launch window has opened — move. Discernment itself is not a vocation! Pull the trigger. Do not be afraid. God will take care of you.

Rumination Time

The word "ruminate" means "to chew cud; to meditate at length; to muse; to reflect on." Just as a flower or a piece of fruit begins developing on the tree long before it is ready to pick, so a vocation has to go through a time of maturation in the mind and heart of a man. Most priests can remember clearly the time they first thought about becoming a priest. Yet in most cases, it was several years before they officially began the process of applying to the diocese. In most cases, the idea comes to a man as a special grace, through the invitation of an individual, by reading a book, or hearing an inspiring homily. The man thinks about it and wonders why he feels some attraction and excitement. Then he begins to think of the fears (I can't get married!) and he quickly pushes it to the back of his mind. As I said earlier, one of the signs of a true vocation to priesthood is that the idea will not go away, even when you try to make it go away. It keeps coming back from time to time. The submarine keeps resurfacing! The man thinks a bit more about it, prays some more. This time, he might actually read a bit about priesthood. Then he once again pushes it to the back of his mind. God orchestrates this process, gently reminding the man of his calling. The man usually needs a rumination time to come to terms with this radical call from God.

When I was a vocation director, I clearly remember giving a presentation at a Catholic high school about vocations. I can remember the exact class and still see some of the students' faces. They were very polite students. They were respectful and interested; they listened and they asked good questions. Before I left, I gave them some pamphlets about vocations, along with my contact information. Three years later, I received an e-mail from a young man, now a sophomore in college, expressing an interest in priesthood! In the e-mail he told me that he first seriously thought of priesthood that day in his high school class when I visited, but he was afraid to say anything or to contact me then. He had to go through the rumination time. And God walked with him through that time, always respecting his freedom, helping him to grow in faith and trust. After his second year of college, he knew he had to pull the trigger. He began corresponding with me and I helped him complete a full, diligent discernment. Today he is a happy priest.

Give Your Youth to Jesus

"To have beautiful and holy thoughts, to write books on the lives of the saints, all of this does not count so much as answering as soon as you are called."[59]

St. Therese of Lisieux

If a man feels a call to become a priest at a young age, and he is confident in that call, then there are definite advantages to going to seminary early. A man who begins his freshman year in a college seminary will have more opportunity to learn and to be formed in Catholic spirituality, philosophy, liturgy, languages, and culture than a man who goes to a secular university. The man who begins early, if he perseveres in going straight through the seminary system, will have eight continuous years of priestly formation: four years of college seminary and four years of major seminary. In seminary parlance, we call these "lifers." During this time he will have been "protected," so to speak, from many of the de-forming influences one might find in a secular university.

More and more men are coming to seminary these days while still very young. Every man is different and some are more ready than others to enter seminary at a young age. But there is something beautiful and generous about giving one's youth to Jesus. It is inspiring when a high school senior says, "I think Jesus might be calling me to become a priest, and I love him so much that I am ready to do whatever he asks!"

Some men are ready to go to college seminary as freshmen. Others are ready as juniors. Others are simply not ready to begin seminary until after college or even after some work experiences. I hear many people in the Church say things like: "Men need to have more life experience before they become priests. They need to finish college, date, have a job, and experience how most people in the world live. These are the men who make the best priests." While I certainly agree that God makes use of all previous life experiences in priesthood, such a blanket statement is neither appropriate nor true. I know many wonderful priests who are "lifers," who went to seminary right out of high school and continued straight through for eight years to ordination. And I know many other wonderful priests who arrived at ordination by a very different route. Every vocation is different; it is not accurate to assert that the ones who arrive by the latter route are superior. Nor is it accurate to say that the "lifers" are always superior.

Some men will say to their vocation director, "Well, I think that I will end up a priest, but I want to live life a while first. Let me get a job and make some money for a couple of years. Then I will come back." While this can sometimes be valid, I still say, "Give Jesus the first shot. Give him the very best years of your life. I promise that you will not be disappointed."

At What Age Can a Man Enter Seminary?

Once again, it really depends on the man. God can certainly call a person to their respective vocation from a very young age. St. Therese of Lisieux greatly desired to follow her sister into the Carmelite monastery at the age of nine and again at the age of fourteen. On a pilgrimage to Rome, she actually asked the Holy Father himself for permission to join the Carmel at the age of fourteen. In the case of a man pursuing priesthood, Canon Law stipulates that a man cannot be ordained a priest prior to the age of twenty-five, no matter how early he begins priestly formation. I have noticed a trend in the last five years towards younger men coming to seminary. As I write this book, college seminary enrollments are rising every year and many are having great success. The Holy Spirit works differently in the Church in different seasons.

Different Paths or Tracks Leading to Diocesan Priesthood

There are many different paths to ordination. Your parents, your spiritual director and your vocation director will all be important resources as you make the decision regarding *when* to go to seminary and *by which track*. The rest of this chapter describes the most common tracks to seminary and ordination.

Track 1 - College Seminary (8 years)
Men who begin seminary formation immediately after high school

This man has been thinking about priesthood since he was seven years old and it has been a persistent interest. He was very involved in his parish all through high school, serving Mass, working in the sacristy, and participating in the youth group. His attraction to priesthood increased during his final two years of high school, during which he began seeing his pastor for occasional spiritual direction. He has been corresponding with his vocation director during these last two years and has been on a couple of discernment retreats. He has not dated much, but still feels like God is calling him to become a priest. His vocation director is encouraging him, as he has many of the signs and qualities needed to become a good priest. His parents are cautiously supportive. So he applies to his diocese, is accepted by the bishop during his senior year of high school, and is sent to a college seminary.

At college seminary, the young man is introduced to the four pillars of priestly formation: human, spiritual, pastoral, and academic. College seminary provides a well-balanced liberal arts education including the core courses found in almost all university curriculums. It also provides the thirty hours of philosophy and some credits in undergraduate theology which are required by the Program of Priestly Formation (PPF). Normally this man would major in philosophy, though there are exceptions. Then, if he still feels confident and peaceful that he is called to become a priest, and the diocese and seminary recommend him to go forward, he goes on to a major seminary for four years to study theology at the master's level. The major seminary is sometimes in a different place than the college seminary, but there are some programs which have both minor and major seminary together. This man does not date during this eight-year period of formation.

265

The college seminary track is a very good path to priesthood when a man is ready to begin the process early. It gives a man a very thorough priestly formation over eight years.

Track 2 - College Seminary Transfer (8 - 9 years)
Men who begin seminary formation after a few years of college

This man is not ready for college seminary out of high school so he goes on to a regular college, either Catholic or secular. He is seeing his spiritual director, living a serious spiritual plan of life, and making a diligent discernment. He dates and lives the life of an ordinary college student, but he is striving for holiness. After one, two, or even three years of college, he is ready to make a move so he applies and is accepted by his diocese as a seminarian. He is sent by his bishop to a college seminary for his final years of college, during which he studies the requisite philosophy and pre-theology courses and receives the required two years of PPF formation in the other three pillars. Depending on the number of transferable credits into the college seminary, he graduates with his degree in philosophy in two or three years. After graduation, he goes on to major seminary for four years of theology and is ordained a priest. Track 2 is very common these days.

Track 3 - Discernment Program in College (8 - 10 years)
Men who complete some of the pre-theology prerequisites at a
Catholic college

This man has been thinking and praying about priesthood for some time but he has many fears and unanswered questions. He has had some casual contact with his vocation director and he has spoken with his pastor about priesthood. He has a girlfriend from the youth group and he has been dating her for two years. After high school, he decides to attend a Catholic college, primarily because some of his friends are going there, and because his youth director told him it was a good school. After arriving there, he notices that there is a certain group of young men who are always hanging out together, always at Mass together, and some-times wear distinctive shirts. They seem to be joyful and friendly. Upon inquiry, he learns that they are part of a "pre-theologate group" — a group of men who are publicly discerning priesthood. Eventually he joins them. He signs the required "covenant," making certain promises on a semester-by-semester basis. This usual-ly includes the promise to attend Mass daily, see a spiritual direc-tor, go to Eucharistic adoration, serve others in some designated way, and pray some parts of the Liturgy of the Hours. It often includes some restrictions on dating. The man's spiritual life grows tremendously in this program. He gets very excited about holiness and discerning the will of God. He is encouraged both by his brothers in the program and by the priests who serve as facilitators. He establishes regular contact with his vocation direc-tor during these college years and applies to his diocese during his senior year. After graduation, he becomes an official semina-rian for his diocese.

After graduation from this Catholic college, during which he was in the discernment program, will this man continue directly into a major seminary? Maybe. The vocation director and semi-nary academic dean will have to evaluate not only his academic transcripts but also his formation in the other three pillars: hu-man, spiritual and pastoral.

Be careful with non-seminary discernment programs. Though many of them are excellent places of Christian formation, if the particular discernment program is not in conformity with the pre-theology requirements of the PPF, then you might still have to complete two years of pre-theology *in a seminary* after college before beginning major seminary. As the PPF says: "Pre-theology programs are designed to address all four pillars of formation (academic, human, spiritual, pastoral), not simply to meet academic requirements" (#62).

You also will need to know which tracks your diocese will permit. Some dioceses, for example, do not permit a seminarian to attend a pre-theology program, outside of a college seminary or major seminary, so Track 3 is not an option. The most popular discernment programs like this on the eastern side of the U.S. are at The Franciscan University of Steubenville in Ohio and Ave Maria University in Florida.

Track 4 – Catholic or Secular College (10 years)
Men who begin seminary formation immediately after obtaining a college degree

This man has been thinking about priesthood during his high school years but does not feel ready to go to a college seminary right after graduation. He has been active in his parish and suspects that he is being called to become a priest, but he is not sure of this, and his parents are encouraging him to go to college first. He has been speaking with his vocation director and has been to a couple of events sponsored by the vocation office. So he makes the decision, with his pastor's guidance, to attend a local Catholic college which has a very good reputation (or a secular college with a great Campus Ministry program). He wants to go to an environment of formation and not de-formation. He becomes active in campus ministry, starts seeing a priest for spiritual direction, lives a spiritual plan of life, and attends some retreats. He also dates a couple of different women, goes on some service trips, and studies very hard in his selected major, biology. Towards the end of his four years of college, during which he has grown tremendously in his spiritual life, he comes to the realization that God is indeed likely calling him to priesthood and his vocation director agrees that he should apply. He goes through the application process during his senior year of college. After graduation from college and acceptance by his bishop, this man is sent to complete two years of pre-theology studies, which is required before beginning the study of theology in a major seminary.

Keep in mind that attending a pre-theology program generally indicates that a man already has a four-year college degree. Normally the diocese decides which seminary a man will attend for these two years of study. It may be in a college seminary. It may be in a major seminary. Or it may be in a diocesan-sponsored house of formation where the seminarians live together under the direction of a priest, but take their philosophy and other PPF prerequisites at a local Catholic college.

After this man completes the two years of pre-theology, then he goes on to a major seminary to study the four years of theology. You will notice that this man has a total of ten years of study leading to priesthood: four years of college, two years of pre-theology, and four years of theology. This is probably the most common track for men entering major seminary.

If you are thinking of attending a Catholic college, be careful. Sadly, just because a college is Catholic does not automatically mean that the environment will be positive and formative. Ask your vocation director which Catholic colleges he recommends.

Track 5 – College Graduate (6 years, after college)
Men who begin seminary formation a few years after obtaining a college degree

A man finishes college normally and gets a job in the world. He is active in his parish and has a serious spiritual plan of life. Feeling drawn to serve, this man might become a lay missionary for a few years, join the Peace Corps, or serve the poor in some way. Or he may simply serve generously in his parish while working at his profession. After making a diligent discernment, this man applies and is accepted by his diocese and he is sent to an approved pre-theology program, which he completes in two years. This is followed by four years of theology in a major seminary.

Track 6 – Non-College Graduate (6 - 8 years)
Older men interested in beginning priestly formation but who do not have a college degree

This man does not yet have a college degree, though he is past the traditional college age. His program of formation will have to be worked out with his vocation director and bishop, as there are many factors including age, life experience, and job experience. If he has some college credits, he likely will be sent to complete his college degree and pre-theology simultaneously. Most dioceses will require him to get this college degree first, even if it takes him the entire four years, but there are some creative ways to go about this, especially if the man is older. Having a college degree and the pre-theology formation is very important before going on to theology and required by the PPF, so the number of years this takes can vary greatly.

Track 7 - Convert or Revert
Men who have recently become Catholic or returned to the Church

Every vocation director will get some calls from new converts to the Catholic faith. "Father, I just joined the Church at Easter and I want to be a priest. When can I start?" We call this "new convert enthusiasm," and it is refreshing and exciting to see. But this enthusiasm must be tested over the course of time, to make sure that the desire for priesthood is an authentic call from God and not just an emotional high from first receiving the sacraments and being a member of the holy Catholic Church. Vocation directors have an expression for men like this: "We want you to breathe Catholic air for a while before you breathe seminary air."

The Program of Priestly Formation advises vocation directors not to admit new converts to go to seminary until they have been practicing their faith for at least two years. It is best for the convert to live as a Catholic and experience the liturgical cycle of the Church: Advent, Christmas, Ordinary time, Lent, and Easter. He should have sufficient time to read Catholic literature, learn

270

about the saints, go on a pilgrimage or a retreat, and deepen his post-baptismal period of mystagogy.

The PPF (#67) mentions three classes of candidates: recent converts to the Catholic faith, recent reverts to the Catholic faith, and Catholics who never left the Church but have recently experienced significant spiritual conversions. In all of these cases, a diligent discernment is required, which entails the test of time. In other words, these men will not be permitted to be *jumpers*. Experience shows that they jump out of seminary as quickly as they jump in.

Nonetheless, I have seen many priestly vocations originate through the three classes of candidates mentioned above. Our seminaries are full of converts, reverts, and Catholic men who had powerful conversion experiences. So if you fit into one of these classes, I congratulate and encourage you. And I recommend that you contact your vocation director so as to begin a diligent discernment of priesthood. He will help you choose which track to seminary is right for you.

The general and prudential rule is to discern in stability. It is unwise to make major life decisions in time of transition or change. If a man has just become a Catholic, if he has been changing jobs frequently, if he is dropping in and out of school, if he is not showing stability and consistency in his life, his vocation director likely will require that he establish and maintain stability for a period of at least two years before he will be permitted to begin seminary. The vocation of priesthood is a very stable vocation; it is a lifetime commitment. One should not begin this process coming from a life of instability.

Track 8 - High School Seminary
Boys who begin discernment in high school

Would I ever recommend that a man attend a high school seminary? Not very readily. First of all, very few exist today, at least in the United States. Fifty years ago, high school seminaries were more prevalent, but almost all have closed except some run by religious communities to promote vocations within their communities. In the 1967-68 academic year, there were sixteen thousand men in high school seminaries in the U.S. Enrollment is down to just over one thousand men today. These high school seminaries are places of good, solid Christian and human formation for these very young men, but a man who is only a freshman in high school cannot have made a diligent discernment of priesthood. High school seminaries are more like good Catholic boarding schools with increased emphasis on spirituality, catechism, Latin, and Christian formation. The PPF does briefly cover high school seminaries in #142-145 and #165-174.

I believe that a man should stay with his parents and family at least throughout high school, as the family is the primordial Christian community. I am sure that there are some exceptions, especially with the terrible dysfunction in some families. But as a general rule, I don't recommend high school seminaries.

I do know some wonderful, elderly priests who followed track 8 and began in a high school seminary. They continued in college seminary for four years and then major seminary for four years; in total, they remained in seminary for twelve consecutive years. These priests are the real lifers!

High school seminaries are uncommon today, at least in the United States, though it might be the right track for some young men.

What is a Pastoral Year?

Some dioceses and some seminaries require that every seminarian complete a pastoral year at some point during their formation. This is a year-long period—often after second theology—when a man lives and works in a parish so as to experience parish life firsthand. Studies show that the pastoral year is a very effective means of increasing the vocational confidence of a seminarian. Seminarians who complete a pastoral year and return to seminary often report an extremely high rate of satisfaction and peace regarding their vocation. And once they are ordained, they almost never leave priesthood.

This sounds like a great idea. Why is it not required in every case? Because adding a pastoral year to the above mentioned tracks adds yet another year to the already lengthy process of formation. Some bishops, needing priests very badly to staff their parishes, and realizing that the pastoral year, while it is helpful, is not always necessary, do not require it as a matter of course for their seminarians. Sometimes, though, a vocation director will decide that a certain man needs to complete a pastoral year in order to work on a specific formation issue. Other times, the seminarian himself will request a pastoral year specifically to experience priesthood in the parish and increase his vocational confidence. When a seminarian asks for this, it is almost always granted him.

Most seminaries and dioceses do not mandate a pastoral year for all seminarians as a required part of their formation program. Nonetheless, it is an option, and is frequently a very effective means of clarifying discernment, evaluating one's pastoral skills, and developing more vocational confidence.

Why Hold a Candle in the Wind?

If your vocation is the most important discovery you will ever make, and if priesthood is an extraordinary privilege, and if your vocation can be so easily poisoned or lost altogether — why go to a secular university? Why hold a candle in the wind? I think the answer is that some men are simply not ready to go to a college seminary and they want (and *need*) to live the life of a "normal college student" first. Each man is different and God calls each one differently. But the life of a "normal college student" should not be a life of debauchery and sin that weakens faith. My strong advice: *Go to a place of formation and not de-formation.*

The general principle of discernment in this regard is to go to a place where you will receive good, solid, Christian formation. I have seen men discerning a vocation to priesthood go to a secular university and lose their vocation. I have even seen them lose their faith. On the other hand, I have seen others who went to a secular university and had their faith strengthened as a result.

Miraculously, God used my own experience in a secular university to strengthen my vocation. I grew up Catholic in a largely Protestant environment in a small South Georgia town, where almost everyone I knew was a conservative Christian. That changed in college. In the university I attended, I witnessed atheism and paganism for the first time. I also encountered very enthusiastic evangelical Christians for the first time, who challenged me regarding Catholic teaching. This motivated me to study and learn the teachings of the Church so that I could explain them clearly to these devout Evangelicals. I wanted to win arguments! This was certainly not the best motivation, but I did learn to teach and defend the Catholic faith — and this knowledge strengthened my own belief. The Lord used these experiences to strengthen my faith and my vocation, though I do not necessarily recommend this path to others.

If a man who suspects he could be called to priesthood makes the decision to go to a secular college first, he should make a *very thorough investigation* of the Catholic opportunities available, before he arrives on campus. He should know for a fact that there is a solid, active Catholic campus ministry. It should be an orthodox program that offers opportunities for growth in faith. It should offer service opportunities and good Catholic fellowship. A man should not leave college without having studied Sacred Scripture and without knowing the teachings of the Catholic Church. Most of all, this man should know the Lord Jesus, personally and intimately, experienced through many hours of prayer, study, and service of others. Ideally, the man should have a good priest spiritual director, with whom he will meet regularly and to whom he will be accountable with regard to prayer, moral living, and character formation.

The men who arrive each year to begin studies at any seminary have widely varying degrees of Christian formation. Some have natural gifts from God that make them well-suited for priesthood. Some have had much better Christian formation than others, beginning in their own families. You don't choose your own family. Some families are significantly better than others with regard to overall human and Christian formation. Some families are simply not very healthy in this regard. We have an expression in seminary to describe this situation: "The family into which you were born was not your decision or your fault, but it is your problem." On the other hand, regardless of the remote formation received in the family, some men simply made better choices, seeking out healthy environments and with people who encouraged them to grow in holiness. Seminary for some men is more difficult precisely because they have not done the remote Christian formation, either growing up in their respective families or through their own decisions. Grace builds on nature, but it always respects our free decisions! The point is that if a man did not grow up in a stable, Christian family where he received solid formation, it is even more important that he attend a college where he will receive good formation.

Don't hold a candle in the wind. Even if you are not ready for seminary, go to a place of formation and not de-formation.

When Should I Contact my Vocation Director?

The short answer is *now*. Even if you are much too young to go to a seminary or if you are just beginning your discernment, make contact now. Send him an e-mail and tell him who you are and where you are in the stages of discernment. He will help you begin the process of making a diligent discernment of diocesan priesthood. He can also explain the formation requirements for your specific diocese.

Your vocation director will know the reputations of the local colleges and their campus ministries. He can recommend a good spiritual director in that area. He will guide you to go to a place of formation and not de-formation. Whether or not you are called to become a priest, your choice of college is important to your life as a Catholic Christian. Don't make the decision alone! It will still ultimately be your decision, but get advice from wise and holy people.

Your peers are generally not the ones to trust in this regard. They are not formators. They need formation just like you. Don't make your next decision thinking only of where all your friends are going. As one former spiritual director of mine used to say, "They may be going to hell and you don't want to go there!"

Track 9 - Older Men
Men who enter seminary past the traditional age, often after other careers

This chapter on timing and tracks would not be complete without a discussion of older men entering seminary—men in their 40s, 50s, 60s, or beyond. This phenomenon has become much more common since the 1990s. Often these men felt called to priesthood when they were younger, but were not encouraged—or even actively discouraged—from moving forward, either by a priest, a family member, or by the troubled and confused culture that followed the Second Vatican Council. Often these men have been married, raised their children, and then been pre-deceased by their wives. In other cases, men were married, divorced, and received a declaration of nullity from the Church. Many of these older men have had very successful and lucrative careers prior to seminary.

Older candidates are sometimes referred to as "belated vocations," though some people have protested that this phrase is inaccurate. After all, God has his own timing for each of us. In the same vein, some vocation directors stress that it is improper to refer to "second-career vocations," since priesthood is not a job or a career. It is a life that requires total giving of self; it is not a nine-to-five job.

What is the maximum age at which a man can be ordained a priest? The policy differs among dioceses. When I was vocation director in Savannah, the general rule was that a man had to be ordained a priest by the age of fifty-five. Therefore, depending on which seminary program he attended, he would need to begin his seminary studies by the age of fifty or so. The rationale was that the man would serve the diocese as a priest for at least twenty years (if he worked until the age of seventy-five, the usual retirement age in most U.S. dioceses), which was worth the substantial investment to send him through seminary. This was a general rule and it was not binding in every case.

Don't assume. Ask your vocation director! "Father, I have been thinking about priesthood for the last several years, since my wife died, but I guess I am too old. I am fifty now but I do feel an attraction to priesthood." Do not assume that you are too old. Talk to your vocation director and ask him to help you evaluate your situation. Even if you are too old for your own diocese, another diocese might have a different age policy—and a great need for priests. God can't drive a parked car. Move!

If a man is divorced and has children, can he go to seminary? Any man who was married and divorced (and his wife is still living) must receive a declaration of nullity for his marriage before he can apply to go to seminary. If the man has children, then those children must be grown and on their own, having reached the age of emancipation and no longer in need of their father's regular presence, and his emotional and financial support. This requirement in regard to children also applies, of course, in the case of a widower. If the children are small, this man must wait until they are appropriately emancipated. Some bishops might ask that the divorced man find a different diocese, outside of the diocese in which he was married and divorced.

Special Seminaries for Older Men

In the United States, there are several seminaries designed specifically to train older candidates. The most popular of these are Blessed John XXIII Seminary in Weston, Massachusetts, Holy Apostles Seminary in Cromwell, Connecticut, and Sacred Heart School of Theology in Hales Corner, Wisconsin. These seminaries are aware that time is of the essence with these candidates. They are aware that many of these men already have extensive knowledge and experience in many different areas. These seminaries have specially-designed curricula to condense the number of years of study. Often these older candidates, as long as they already have a college degree, study a minimal amount of philosophy during the same four years that they study theology. It is a shortened course of study leading to priestly ordination.

Pros and Cons of Older Candidates

There are both pros and cons with older candidates for priesthood. They often do have a wealth of knowledge and business experience, and many have achieved great holiness through many years of prayer, service, and suffering. Some of these men, as priests, are very capable administrators and they use their skills to serve the diocese in other areas as well. I know many excellent priests who were older men by the time they went to seminary and they have been great assets to the Church.

Some older men have accumulated significant wealth and offer to pay their own way through seminary. This is rarely permitted because paying one's own way might give the idea of *having one's own way* in other areas as well. Sometimes older candidates can be set in their ways and not very open to formation in the seminary. The vocation director will look carefully to see if a particular man has the gifts of humility and docility; otherwise he will not be formable.

If you are an older man who is discerning a vocation to diocesan priesthood, then time is of the essence. Contact your vocation director immediately and find out the next step.

Losing Your Job to Go to Seminary

Any man discerning priesthood who has an established career — no matter what his age — will have to face the possibility of
losing his job in order to give seminary a try. "Father, I am making a lot of money and have great benefits. If I go to seminary for
a year and then discern that I am not called to become a priest, I
will not be able to get my position back. What will I do then?"

I always reply to this question: "Jesus is never outdone in
generosity. Once you have carefully discerned that seminary is
where Jesus wants you to go, then go and be at peace. Trust him.
He is quite capable of taking care of you, whether or not you end
up becoming a priest." Maybe the Lord does not want this man to
become a priest, but to do some other important work in the
Church, and so he is trying to get this man out of his present job
so as to steer him in a different direction via the seminary. I have
seen this happen more than once.

Track 10 - The Mystery Track

What if you don't fit into any of the tracks mentioned in this
chapter? Every vocation is a mystery. God calls men at different
times, in different ways, and under different circumstances. God
can arrange other ways for a man to receive the necessary philosophical and theological education and formation, though I have
described the most common paths in this chapter. Your bishop
alone must decide if and when you are ready to be ordained. I
have seen some very creative tracks through the years.

It's really very simple: obey God and all will be well. But
obey God by doing *what* he tells you to do and *when* he tells you
to do it! One must discern in space and time.

279

A vocation is like fruit on a tree: if you pick it too soon, it is not ready; but if it stays on too long, it rots.

CHAPTER 15

THE APPLICATION AND ADMISSIONS PROCESS

Once a man has made a diligent discernment and decided that he must enter the seminary to further discern his vocation, he must apply to a diocese to be accepted by the bishop as a seminarian.

When you request an application, it should not come as a surprise to the vocation director, because a diligent discernment implies that you have *already* been in touch with the vocation director. If you do nothing but private cyber-discernment – sitting in front of the computer and talking in the internal forum with your spiritual director – do not expect your vocation director to simply hand you an application the moment you walk in the door and tell him that you want to go to seminary.

Your vocation director needs to get to know you. He must be convinced both that you are a good candidate and that you are ready to take the step of going to seminary to continue your discernment. This is his job. Once both you and he agree that seminary is the next step, he will guide you through the application process.

There is no standard application process in the United States. Every diocese has its own system, but most dioceses have similar requirements. This chapter provides an overview of the most common elements of the application process.

Remember: never begin to fill out the diocesan application or start any part of the application process until your vocation director has invited you to do so and you have carefully read the diocesan instructions for applying.

The Formal Comprehensive Life Interview

A comprehensive interview was always the first and most important aspect of the application process for me when I was a vocation director. I would always conduct the interview *before* giving a man an application. It lasted as long as two or three hours because I asked questions about every area of the man's life and took detailed notes on the computer as the candidate talked. I asked the candidate to tell me about his life almost year by year. I asked him about all aspects of his life: family, school, friends, sports, dating, physical and emotional health, work history, moral life, faith development, vocational discernment, and more. Much of this information is required elsewhere in the application also, but I always got a more complete overall picture of the man by asking the same questions through several different mediums. Once this interview was over, I would usually know if there was something about this man that was a "game stopper." If there was not, and he wanted to continue, I would give him the application. Your vocation director might handle this interview differently, but every vocation director does something similar to get to know you well.

Diocesan Application

The diocesan application is a form that asks questions about every major area of your life, including biographical items such as contact information, place and date of birth, family details, education, work experience, and health. It is usually a fill-in-the-blank questionnaire. It must be filled out carefully and thoughtfully. While some diocesan applications can be found online, many vocation directors do not make it available online precisely because they want to give it to you only when they are convinced you are ready for it. Many dioceses have a PDF version of the application that can be filled out and returned electronically, or printed out and filled in by hand. If you can, I recommend typing your answers. If you do complete it by hand, be sure to write legibly. I have had to insist that some candidates fill out the application again due to sloppiness. Remember that everything you do — and how you do it — tells your vocation director and bishop about you. You want to make a good impression! Finally, be sure to return your completed application in a reasonable time.

Photographs

Most dioceses require two or three color photographs of the candidate to accompany the application. These photos should be head shots and they should look distinguished. I have received many "action shots" during the years; these are not appropriate or acceptable. Dress up nicely and have the photos taken professionally. Sometimes these photos are even used on the diocesan poster or in the diocesan newspaper so ask your vocation director before you have the photos taken. Depending on your level of philosophical or theological studies, your vocation director might want you to wear clerical clothing (a Roman collar), a cassock, a coat and tie, or some other specific dress code.

Autobiography

The autobiography that every candidate must write is one of the most important documents in the application file. Each diocese will have guidelines for length, formatting, and content. Follow the guidelines carefully. Most autobiographies are seven to ten pages typed; if the guideline sets a maximum of ten pages, don't write twenty! It should give a detailed description of your life from birth to present. Like the formal interview, it should cover your family life growing up, education, faith development, vocation discernment, social life, extracurricular activities, dating, sexual history, and work history. Make sure that there are no "holes" in your autobiography — certain periods of time which are unaccounted for. Mention your strengths and weaknesses, and your spiritual plan of life at the current time (such as daily

Mass, holy hour, rosary, Confession once per week, etc.) Be sure to explain any incident which could be a red flag for your vocation director. For example, describe in detail incidents such as dropping out of school, getting fired from a job, getting in trouble with the law, or applying to another diocese or religious order. Besides your vocation director and bishop, the seminary admissions committee also will read this document carefully, and use it to help evaluate your writing ability and to help you set goals once you arrive in seminary. It is important that this document be thoughtful and well-written. I have read autobiographies of candidates with atrocious grammar and spelling, giving the impression that the man never even reviewed what he wrote. That is not a good first impression.

Several Short Essays on Designated Topics Regarding Priesthood

Most dioceses have a candidate write several short essays on various topics about priesthood and celibacy. These essays are designed to show the vocation director and bishop what you already know and believe about priesthood, which helps them determine whether you are pursuing priesthood for the right reasons. They are not meant to be research papers with footnotes and quotes from Church documents. Your vocation director and bishop already know what the Church teaches about priesthood! They want to know your own understanding before you begin priestly formation. Think carefully about the essays, make an outline, and write them well. But it is not necessary or recommended to do research.

Letters of Recommendation

Every diocese requires a number of recommendation letters from people who know you well. Usually they will want the perspectives of people who know you in different capacities. For example, they might want one letter from your pastor, one from a friend, one from a teacher or co-worker, and one from your parents or siblings. Do not personally request these letters until you have read carefully the application instructions. Most dioceses simply want you to give them the names and addresses of the people whom you want to write your recommendations. The vocation director will send them a letter directly, giving them clear instructions on what information is being sought. If you were to request the letters directly and they were insufficient, they would have to be re-written. Also, the vocation director often will want these letters sent directly from the writer to the vocation office in a sealed envelope. They should not be given to the candidate and personally delivered. However, it is appropriate for the candidate to ask each of these persons if they would be willing to write the letter, before giving their contact information to the vocation director.

Sacramental Records

Your application dossier will need at least two copies of your personal sacramental records: Baptism, Confession, First Communion, Confirmation, and (in some dioceses) parent's marriage. These are required even if you were baptized in another church and converted to Catholicism later. Both the diocese and seminary will need these records.

The Baptism certificate is especially important. It is not acceptable to make a copy of the original Baptism certificate that you have in your records. You must contact the church of Baptism and ask them to send two newly-issued Baptism certificates will all notations directly to the vocation director and seminary in unopened envelopes, sealed with the parish seal. The Baptism certificate, if it is from a Catholic parish, will usually have notations of the other sacraments on the back.

The church of your Baptism, if it is Catholic, is the church where all of your sacramental records are permanently kept. If you were baptized at St. Luke's parish in San Diego, for example, but immediately moved to Mississippi and received Confession and First Communion there, that information will have been sent back to St. Luke's and recorded in their records in San Diego. If you then moved to New York and received Confirmation there, that information will have been sent back to St. Luke's. Therefore, by just contacting the church of your Baptism, you can usually attain all of your sacramental records and receive newly issued documentation of those records.

If you were married and your wife is deceased, you will need to attain the sacramental marriage record and your wife's certificate of death. If you are divorced with a decree of nullity, you will need to supply the marriage record, the divorce decree, and the decree of nullity. Some vocation directors will want more information about the civil grounds for the divorce. If you joined the Church as an adult, but were earlier baptized in another church, you also will need a certificate of Profession of Faith.

Two Copies of All Academic Transcripts

The registrars of your high school(s), college(s), college seminary, or other graduate programs will need to send originally-issued copies of your academic transcripts to your diocese and seminary. These transcripts must arrive in sealed envelopes directly from the issuing institution. This means that the envelope must arrive unopened and it must have the institution's seal imprinted on the envelope and the transcript.

Any man who was in formation previously for another diocese or religious order will need transcripts of academic work and copies of all of the yearly evaluations received during the time in that formation program. The reasons the man left that formation program must be crystal clear and documented in writing from the rector or novice master.

Recent Physical Examination

The diocese must know that a man is physically capable of doing what a priest does and that he does not have any serious or congenital illnesses. Most dioceses give a health form questionnaire to the candidate which he must complete and then bring with him to the doctor for the physical exam. The doctor then completes the form and mails it to the vocation director. This exam includes standard blood work, tests for tuberculosis and AIDS, chest X-rays, and other tests. Usually the man is to go to his own family doctor for this exam, but in some cases there is a diocesan doctor selected who already knows exactly what the vocation director wants done. Ideally, this exam should be done within one year of beginning seminary. Most seminaries require their own health paperwork, though the diocesan-required tests need not be repeated. The seminary will usually accept copies of this paperwork.

Every seminarian is required to have health insurance and to supply proof of this insurance. Most dioceses provide this for their seminarians, though some require their college-level seminarians to purchase the college's health insurance plan.

Psychological Evaluation Report

The purpose of the psychological exam is first to rule out psychosis in a candidate and then to determine if the candidate has the emotional and psychological stability to care for others in diocesan priesthood. Your vocation director will give you the contact information to make this appointment, or his office will make the appointment for you.

Each diocese has selected certain psychologists, psychiatrists, or licensed clinical professionals to conduct a psychological exam for priesthood candidates. This person will have already done many of these exams and he knows exactly what information is being sought. The exam can be long and tedious, but it is not unpleasant. Depending on the doctor and the specific requirements of the diocese, it may last three to six hours in a single day, or consist of several sessions over several days. The psychological exam may include tests such as the MMPI, Rorshach inkblot, an IQ test, addiction prone scale, sexual addiction screening exam, and many others. The examining practitioner often has already read your autobiography and application, so he or she will already know a lot about your life, including some of your strengths and weaknesses. Still, there is usually a brief life interview as part of the exam.

Important: please request from your vocation director (and the examining psychologist) the opportunity to meet again with the psychologist to receive feedback from the exam after it is complete. Most seminarians come to seminary never having seen the results of their psychological exam and never having had those results explained. It is true that the psychological report is the property of the vocation office, not the seminarian candidate. The seminarian will usually not receive a copy of the final report. But it is important, in my opinion, that the results be explained to the seminarian by the psychologist, because the discussion of his strengths and weaknesses can help him set goals once he begins seminary. It is not a good idea for the seminarian to receive only a written copy of the report, as these reports are not easy to interpret and they can be upsetting without the accompanying explanation.

Sometimes the psychologist will recommend counseling or therapy for the man with the seminary counselor for some issue or another. It is good for the seminarian to know that counseling has been recommended for him (or mandated by his vocation director) before he arrives at the seminary.

F.B.I. Fingerprinting and Criminal Background Check

As part of the due diligence requirements in thoroughly checking out seminary candidates, most dioceses require F.B.I.

fingerprinting, sex offender background checks, and criminal background checks. Your vocation director will tell you how this is to be done and how to arrange it. If a man has a criminal record of any kind, this will need to be explained in great detail to the vocation director at the very beginning.

Diocesan Requirements Regarding Prevention of Sexual Misconduct and Child Abuse

Every diocese in this day and age will have requirements for seminarians to comply with the Charter for the Protection of Children and Young People, the official document of the U.S. Catholic bishops to prevent child sexual abuse. This usually involves a short instructional course in addition to some reading and the above-mentioned background checks.

Credit Check

Some dioceses also require a credit check, though it is not as commonly required as the criminal background check. If a man has ever declared bankruptcy or otherwise defaulted on monies owed, this will need to be explained in detail. Financial mismanagement can be an obstacle to acceptance: inability to balance his account, excessive credit card debts, a history of gambling, or compulsive spending. Though many dioceses provide a small stipend for incidental expenses, there are miscellaneous expenses involved with seminary that the diocese does not pay and a man must have the resources to pay those expenses. If a seminarian is in a position of financial hardship, it is important to talk about this with the vocation director early on. It is not possible and not permitted to have a part time job while in seminary. Priestly formation is a full-time job.

Can a man be accepted to go to seminary if he has unpaid debts? The Church will be very careful not to give the impression of accepting candidates into seminary who are running away from their financial responsibilities. If a man has unpaid debts, these must be resolved, or a plan must be made to resolve these debts which is accepted in writing from his creditors. Likewise, if a man has children, he is financially responsible to care for those children until they reach the age of emancipation. Many candidates in our seminaries today have unpaid student loans and these loans can be deferred as long as a man is in school. Once the man is ordained a priest, then he makes regular payments on these loans. But if the debts are non-deferrable loans or monies owed, the man cannot begin seminary until they are resolved.

Interview with Priests or Lay People on the Vocation Screening Board

Some dioceses ask their candidates to interview privately with several priests or other members of the vocation board. These are usually one-hour informal meetings and they are normally very pleasant. These board members write the vocation director their impressions and sometimes vote on the man's candidacy. (While vocation screening boards can be helpful and are found in some diocesan programs, most dioceses in my experience still do not utilize them.)

Interview with the Bishop

In many dioceses, the final step in the admissions process is a private interview with the bishop. Once the entire application dossier is complete, with all the above-mentioned components, the bishop reviews the file and then interviews the candidate. In every diocese, the bishop bears the final responsibility for all decisions. Though he may depend heavily on his vocation director's judgment, the bishop will make the final decision whether to accept a candidate.

Dress formally, arrive early for your appointment, and try to make a good impression. Your bishop knows that "the paper is not the person." He has already read what you have written and what has been written about you. Now he wants to meet you. He wants to personally know the man that he will eventually ordain to priesthood. This may sound unbelievable, but I have heard of men arriving late for their appointment with the bishop, dressed in shorts and flip flops! You are meeting with a successor of the apostles; it would behoove you to act as if you understand that.

The above components make up the application process required by most dioceses. Once a candidate has completed these components, he will receive notification regarding acceptance. In some dioceses, the bishop accepts the candidate in his meeting with him. In other dioceses, he is informed by the vocation director and the decision is further communicated in a follow-up letter.

Deferral of Acceptance

The decision is sometimes made that a man is not ready to begin seminary formation. There can be many reasons for this deferral of acceptance. Perhaps the man has some serious internal turmoil and needs counseling and, in the opinion of the psychologist, this therapy would be too intense to undertake concomitant with seminary formation. Perhaps the dearth of social skills is so severe that the bishop needs to see more positive evidence that this man will be able to develop the minimal requirements. Maybe the man's intellectual abilities are in question and the diocese will want him to prove that he can do college level work by getting a year of college under his belt. Whatever the reasons, they will be communicated clearly to the applicant and help will be offered to resolve his issues. I have seen many cases where a man's acceptance was deferred by a year or two to work on some issue, and after this time, the man came to seminary and did extraordinarily well.

Non-Acceptance

There will be other cases where a man is not accepted because of a serious red flag that emerged during the application process. In this type of case, whatever the issue, the man will be told quite directly, though kindly, that he cannot be accepted. Most likely, he can never become a priest, though it depends on the issue. Again, most vocation directors continue to offer help and guidance to the man, so that he can work to become healthy in the area of concern and be an active member of the Church.

In my experience as a vocation director, I almost always knew if there was a game-stopping issue very early in the application process. I would never allow the man to undergo the full battery of tests if I knew he would not be accepted. However, sometimes the vocation director is simply not sure whether or not the man should be accepted, and he wants the vocation board and ultimately the bishop to help make that decision. Each diocese will have its own model with regard to this final decision.

Who Pays the Costs of the Application Process?

The various components of the application process can be expensive. The psychological exam alone may cost a thousand dollars or more, and the total cost of application may be several thousand dollars. Most dioceses pay the major expenses of the application process, cognizant that this would be quite a burden on the majority of candidates, but each diocese will have their own policies in this regard. When I was a vocation director, the diocese paid the cost of the psychological exam and the background checks, but we asked the candidate to pay for his own physical exam, as he usually went to his own family doctor. I also had several Catholic doctors in the diocese who would do free physical exams for seminarian candidates who did not have a family physician. Whatever the policies of your diocese, I can promise you that inability to pay will not prevent you from applying. If there is hardship, simply be honest about this with your vocation director and he will assist you.

Can I Apply to Several Dioceses at Once?

Absolutely not. This practice is common when applying to graduate schools, but it is not appropriate for priesthood. Your vocation director and bishop have extended to you an invitation to apply to study for priesthood in your diocese. This is a great honor and privilege. It would be an insult if they knew you were applying to other dioceses at the same time, hoping to take the best deal. A vocation to diocesan priesthood is not about finding the best deal. It is about discerning to which diocese the Lord is calling you and then applying to that diocese. Any man who applies to multiple dioceses likely will not be accepted by any of them.

How Do I Choose Which Seminary I Will Attend?

Normally, a seminarian candidate does not get to choose the seminary he will attend. Some dioceses permit the candidate to visit a few different seminaries which the diocese uses and to give his preference, but the bishop and vocation director will make the ultimate decision. If your diocese has its own diocesan seminary, then of course, you will most likely be sent there. Most dioceses do not have their own seminaries but they have chosen one or two seminaries which they primarily use for the priestly formation of their men.

In 1984, I was first accepted by my bishop to study for the Diocese of Savannah. In his interview with me, after he had given me the good news that I was accepted, he asked, "So where would you like to go to seminary?" My face became very red and there was an uncomfortable silence. The truth was that I had no knowledge of Catholic seminaries, much less the reputations of different schools. I was embarrassed that I had no answer to give him. So I finally said, "Bishop, I'm sorry, I don't even know any

Catholic seminaries. Would you please recommend one?" He laughed out loud and said, "I think I could make a recommendation." I left that interview knowing where I would spend the next five years.

How Long Does the Application Process Take?

Depending on how quickly a candidate completes the required paperwork and gathers the required documents, the process can take from two to six months. Scheduling an appointment with a psychologist and physician and receiving their reports may take two or three months, so beginning the process early is important. Most seminaries begin orientation in early August, so counting backwards you can see that the process should begin in the spring at the latest. The process can be expedited, though, so ask your vocation director whether it is too late to begin seminary in the fall.

What If a Candidate Lies in the Application Process?

The Church is in need of mature, holy priests who are first and foremost men of integrity. When I would begin the formal interview of the application process with a man, I would make it very clear that the interview required complete honesty. I would begin in words like these:

> I expect already that you are not perfect, that you have a personal history of sin, that there are likely things in your past that are embarrassing to you and that you would rather not say. These may be things that you have done, things that were done to you, or simply things about yourself that you find painful. They may be sexual problems or difficulties in another area of your life. However, I will need to know everything about you in order to properly evaluate your application, and I will ask you some very direct questions. It is critical that you answer all questions,

verbal and written, completely and honestly. I promise you that I will treat you with great kindness and compassion regardless of what you say, and that I will help you to move forward, even if I am not able to accept you as a seminarian. But if you lie or withhold information about anything, no matter how small, and I discover it, you will not be accepted as a seminarian and if you had already been accepted, you will be dismissed. If I cannot trust that you are completely honest and open about something as important as priesthood, I will not be able to trust you with the souls of God's people. Do you understand this?

Once the man said that he understood, I would ask him, "Is there anything about yourself that you have been dreading having to say, that you just want to tell me right now, and get it over with?" Very often the candidate would mention one or two things, we would talk about them and the rest of the interview would proceed with much less stress. (It is similar to confessing your worse and most embarrassing sin first. The rest of the Confession is a piece of cake. But if you intentionally conceal a mortal sin in Confession, it invalidates the sacrament.)

Many years ago, at Mount St. Mary's Seminary in Emmitsburg, Maryland, a fourth-theology transitional deacon walked into a classroom for his final oral comprehensive exams. This man had been in seminary for eight years and he was about to field questions from a team of five professors for one hour on any topic of philosophy or theology covered during that expansive amount of time. It was a very intimidating exam. The man was extraordinarily nervous, but he was also confident. He had studied hard, prayed hard, and completely immersed himself in the formation process. He trusted that Jesus would help him. The Academic Dean asked the first question. He said, "On the table in front of you, there is a book. Please open that book to page 797 and go to paragraph 4. Read the paragraph in the Latin, translate it into English, and then comment on its meaning." Now that book was a very old, dog-eared copy of Denzinger's *Enchiridion Symbolorum*, a complete listing of every major moral and doctrinal declaration of the Catholic Church since the first century. The man opened the book to the designated page and went to paragraph 4. To his amazement, someone had scribbled in pencil an English translation in the margin of the very paragraph he had been asked to translate. He quickly looked at the Latin and then at the English scribbled in the margin and it seemed pretty accurate. His Latin was not great but it looked like a pretty good translation. So he just read what was written in pencil and then went on to comment about its meaning. The exam continued for the designated hour with the other professors also asking questions. At the end of the hour, the Academic Dean said, "Does anyone have any more questions?" Since no one did, the Dean said, "Okay, I guess you are free to go." The man stood up to leave. But then the Dean said, "Oh, by the way, before you go, I want to compliment you on your Latin. That was a perfect translation you made from the Latin to the English. Your Latin is excellent!" The man hesitated a moment, looking at the priest, and then he said, "Monsignor, my Latin is not very good. Someone had scribbled in pencil an English translation of the very paragraph you asked me to translate. It was just my lucky day. I checked the Latin quickly and the scribbled translation looked pretty close. So I just read that." And the Academic Dean looked at him intently and smiled, "I wrote that translation in the margin before you came in. I already knew that you knew your theology. I just wanted to know if you were a man of integrity before I sent you out to take care of the souls of God's people. Now I know that you are."

The Church desperately needs priests who are men of integrity. Demonstrate that you are a man of integrity by your complete honesty and self-disclosure during the application process.

CHAPTER 16

WHAT IS SEMINARY LIKE?

In this chapter I describe life within a major seminary during the four years of priestly formation. During this time, a man is studying theology and making final preparations for ordination. The atmosphere of a college seminary is similar in many ways to major seminary, though the academic curriculum is different.

I think that most people, including most Catholics, have an idea that a seminary is like a strict monastery. Perhaps they have seen a movie in which the monks are walking around in complete silence, fingering their rosary beads, chanting in Latin, and never smiling or laughing. That idea is not true even of a monastery, and it is certainly not true of a seminary. Seminaries in the U.S. are very much like specialized universities such as medical schools or law schools. They exist to train men to do a specialized work which requires not only academic knowledge, but also the development of the skills to do their work: to bring Jesus to people and people to Jesus. But priesthood is not just a job; it is a life. Seminarians must be formed not just to *do* something but to *be* someone — someone very extraordinary. Seminarians must be formed to be an *alter Christus* — another Christ.

It is true that a Catholic seminary is a place of deep prayer, and that necessitates a certain amount of silence, but it is also true that seminaries are places of great joy and excitement. Seminarians study hard, they pray hard, they serve other people, and teach them about Jesus. And they have fun. Laughter rings in the halls of our seminaries because the men are joyful. They are excited to be following Jesus and excited that they might be called to become priests. I always say that I consider it one of the greatest privileges of my life to live in a house with one hundred fifty men who are seriously trying to become like Jesus.

There are two foundational documents, already referenced in this book, which guide and structure priestly formation:

~ *Pastores Dabo Vobis* (PDV), translated as *I Will Give you Shepherds,* by Pope John Paul II

~ *The Program of Priestly Formation* (PPF), by the U.S. Conference of Catholic Bishops

Every seminary program in the U.S. is structured according to these two handbooks, both of which can easily be found online. The PPF is based largely on the wisdom of Pope John Paul II in PDV. It is not possible to talk about seminary formation today without reference to these two works.

Formation in Seminary

What is a seminary like these days? What do the men do? The next page shows a sample schedule for a week of major seminary. Each seminary will have its own specific schedule, but the schedules will usually be similar.

Sample Seminary Schedule

	Monday	Tuesday	Wed.	Thursday	Friday	Saturday	Sunday
7:00 .am.	Mass and Morning Prayer	Mass and Morning Prayer	Mass and Morning Prayer	Spanish Mass and Morning Prayer	Mass and Morning Prayer	Two Masses to choose from: 7:30 and 11 a.m.	
8:00 a.m.	8:00 a.m. Breakfast	8:00 a.m. Breakfast	8:00 a.m. Breakfast	8:00 a.m. Breakfast	8:00 a.m. Breakfast	Morning Prayer and Evening Prayer are done in private	Solemn Mass
9:00 a.m.	Classes Begin	Classes Begin	Classes Begin	Classes Begin	Classes Begin	Some men go to an all day PFE assignment	Some men go to PFE
Noon	12:00 Lunch	12:00 Lunch	12:00 Lunch	12:00 Lunch	12:00 Lunch	Free day to study, rest, pray, run errands	Free day for study, prayer, and rest
1:00 - 4:00 p.m.	Free time to study, rest, exercise, pray	Spiritual Direction (every two weeks)	Pastoral Field Ed. (PFE), i.e. Teaching in a Catholic school.	Free time to study, rest, exercise, pray	Free time to study, rest, exercise, pray		
4:00 p.m.	Holy Hour	Holy Hour	Holy Hour	Weekly Rector's Conference	Holy Hour		
5:00 p.m.	Evening Prayer	Evening Prayer	Evening Prayer	Evening Prayer	Evening Prayer		Solemn Sung Vespers
6:00 p.m.	Supper	Supper	Supper	Supper	5:30 Supper out with friends		Supper
7:00 p.m.	Study Time	Study Time	Study Time	Study Time	Movie or party-social time in recreation room	Movie offered in recreation room; social time	
8:00 p.m.	Study Time	Study Time	Study Time	Meeting with Formation Advisor			
9:00 p.m.	Rosary and Night Prayer	Rosary and Night Prayer	Rosary and Night Prayer	Rosary and Night Prayer	Rosary and Night Prayer	Rosary and Night Prayer	Night prayer with diocesan brothers (DB's)

Seminary formation has improved dramatically in the last five hundred years and even more since the year 2000. Seminaries were first mandated by the Council of Trent in its 1563 decree *Cum Adolescentium Aetas*. It immediately produced great fruit and priests were much better educated than previously. The establishment of seminaries in every nation has provided for a more standardized education and thorough formation of priests. Of course, seminary formation varied greatly from country to country. Until the 1960s in this country, seminaries were very strict and isolated; the monastic idea mentioned above would not have been too far off the mark.

After the Second Vatican Council, like the rest of the Church, seminaries went through great, sweeping changes and some of these changes were not good. Some U.S. seminaries in the seventies and eighties were not very healthy places for priestly formation. Thankfully, those days are gone. When I entered seminary in 1984, I thought that the formation was excellent, but formation today is far superior! It is a great time to go to seminary.

Why is it far superior? There are many reasons, but primarily because of *Pastores Dabo Vobis* and the *Program of Priestly Formation*. In addition, the Holy Father mandated Apostolic Visitations of all U.S. seminaries, first in the mid-1980s and again in 2005, in the wake of the sexual abuse scandal. A team of bishops, priests, and laypeople, personally selected by the Holy See, visited each seminary to complete a thorough audit of every area of formation and governance. The report that they generated was sent to Rome and eventually to the bishop in charge of each seminary. Finally, the seminaries received the reports and were instructed to make improvements accordingly. These Apostolic Visitations have done great work to clean up and strengthen nearly every diocesan seminary in the country.

The Four Pillars of Priestly Formation

In today's seminaries, priestly formation rests on four pillars which the Holy Father clearly outlined and explained in PDV. The four pillars of priestly formation are:

1. Human Formation
2. Spiritual Formation
3. Intellectual Formation
4. Pastoral Formation

The respective bishops of many individual nations of the world have produced their own Program of Priestly Formation, but they are all based on *Pastores Dabo Vobis* and include these four pillars.

Human Formation

The basic principle of human formation is to be found in PDV, #43: "The human personality of the priest is to be a bridge and not an obstacle for others in their meeting with Jesus Christ the Redeemer of the human race."

I always explain it like this: people usually buy a product because they like and respect the salesman. Thus they will listen to their priest and follow him to Jesus if they like him as a human person. Human formation includes instilling the virtues of prudence, justice, temperance, and fortitude. It includes developing humility, constancy, sincerity, patience, good manners and hygiene, and truthfulness. A man who has received good human formation can relate to others, even perfect strangers. He is a man of affective maturity, who works well with others, is free of prejudice, and who is a good steward of material possessions. He is joyful, he smiles and laughs, but he knows when to be serious. Human formation means that this man is ready to take on the role of a public person. It also includes a balanced and healthy sexuality and preparation for loving others, both men and women, in a life of celibacy.

Here are some examples of problems that human formation should work to overcome:

~ A priest walks up and shakes hands with another man, offering him a "wet fish" instead of a strong, manly handshake. This greatly turns off the other man because, in this culture, a firm handshake with another man is part of public propriety; it is fitting and proper.

~ A priest who has body odor, wears terrible-looking clothes, and has bad table manners. He always looks dirty and disheveled.

~ A priest who feels threatened by the very people he is supposed to be loving and serving, and is thus stern, unkind, and unapproachable.

~ A priest who does not understand appropriate boundaries in his friendships and relationships with both men and women. He becomes overly-involved with people.

Human formation addresses these problems and more. This is why PDV emphasizes that human formation is the "necessary foundation" of priestly formation. Just as St. Thomas Aquinas writes that "prudence is the charioteer of all the other virtues,"[60] so human formation is the charioteer of priestly formation. It must come first and be foremost, guiding the other three pillars of priestly formation.

Every seminarian is assigned a formation advisor who helps him address any human formation areas in which he needs to improve. In fact, the formation advisor has the job of mentoring and monitoring the seminarian in all four pillars. The formation advisor, though he is definitely a friend and supporter of the seminarian, must operate in the external forum. This means that he must give a regular report to the rector and formation team about a seminarian's progress in each area.

Spiritual Formation

PDV#45 summarizes the purpose of spiritual formation: "To live in intimate and unceasing union with God the Father through his Son, Jesus Christ, in the Holy Spirit." Spiritual formation is about falling in love with Jesus. It is about developing a personal relationship with each Person of the Most Blessed Trinity. It is about communion with the Church, the Body of the Lord. It is not enough that a Catholic priest know *about* Jesus and his Church; he must know Jesus personally, and be convinced of the Lord's unconditional love for him and for every person. *Nemo dat quod non habet.* One cannot give what one does not have.

Spiritual formation entails developing a life of prayer that will sustain the priest throughout his life and work. The PPF mentions specifically: devotion to the Mass and to the Holy Eucharist, the sacrament of Penance, liturgy of the hours, spiritual direction, the Bible (*lectio divina*), retreats, personal meditation, devotion to Mary, interceding for others, doing penance, obedience, celibacy, and simplicity of life. The seminary spiritual director is responsible for making sure that every area is appropriately treated.

The seminarians learn *how* to pray using many different methods. They learn both through their courses and their own struggles about the difficulties and obstacles to praying well. The purpose of this regimen of prayer is not just to come to know Jesus better personally, but to gain the ability to guide others in prayer and spiritual direction.

The seminarian is also required to do regular spiritual reading, since, as St. Teresa says, "a fire cannot burn without fuel." A man is supposed to "pray his theology." What he learns in his classes about Christ and the Church, he takes into the chapel and discusses with the Lord. Most seminarians in major seminary say that they pray between three and four hours a day, including holy Mass, holy hour, liturgy of the hours, rosary, and other devotions. But do not let this statistic frighten you. I see fifty new seminarians begin every year and 99 percent fall into this regimen of prayer eagerly, easily, and energetically.

Every seminarian chooses a personal spiritual director from among the approved list of priests given by the seminary. He meets with this priest regularly, often twice per month. This relationship is in the internal forum, meaning that the seminarian can talk confidentially about every area of his life. The spiritual director cannot disclose any part of these conversations to the formation advisor, the rector, or the formation team. The confidentiality of the internal forum is sacrosanct, but for the most grave emergency. For example, the spiritual director would only come forward with information if he felt that a man was a danger to himself or to others, and the man was unwilling to ask for help. The seminarian is also encouraged to go to Confession regularly to his spiritual director.

The seminary spiritual director also gives conferences to the entire seminary about the different aspects of the spiritual life of a priest. Finally, he is in charge of arranging for retreat masters to come in several times per year to give days of recollection and at least one week-long silent retreat.

I once heard a very saintly, elderly woman remark, "Father, we can tell if our priest prays. We can tell by the way he says Mass, the way he preaches, and the way he treats others." When a priest does not have an authentic, personal relationship with Jesus Christ, it is obvious to the people to whom he ministers. People want holy priests and they deserve holy priests. Spiritual formation is about forming holy priests.

Intellectual Formation

The PPF states: "The basic principle of intellectual formation for priesthood candidates is noted in PDV #51: 'For the salvation of their brothers and sisters, they should seek an ever deeper knowledge of the divine mysteries.' Disciples are learners. The first task of intellectual formation is to acquire a personal knowledge of the Lord Jesus Christ who is the fullness and completion of God's revelation and the one Teacher. This saving knowledge is acquired not only once, but it is continuously appropriated and deepened."

Intellectual formation entails acquiring the *scientia debita* (debt of knowledge) needed for effective pastoral ministry. Thus seminary classes are very challenging. Major seminary includes rigorous academic programs on par with master's-level programs in secular universities.

According to the PPF, intellectual formation specifically prepares seminarians to be:

~ Hearers of the Word (to know Scripture and biblical theology)

~ Proclaimers of the Word (preachers)

~ Catechists (teachers)

~ Followers of Christ (to acquire a personal knowledge of the Lord Jesus)

~ Faithful to the Church

~ Culturally aware (able to understand the world and diverse cultures in which the Gospel must be preached)

~ Historically aware (familiar with the two-thousand-year history of the Church and of societies in general)

~ Ministers of the sacraments

~ Promoters of marriage and family

~ Moral teachers and guides

~ Advocates of justice

~ Ecumenically sensitive

Seminary Curriculum

The PPF describes in detail the specific classes to be included at each level of seminary. Keep in mind that there is still some latitude, and the exact course of studies differs among seminaries. The following pages contain charts showing how the classes might be arranged during a college seminary program, a pre-theology program, and a theology program.

College Curriculum for Philosophy Majors

Year 1

Fall Semester	*Spring Semester*
Writing I	Western Civilization II
Western Civilization I	Elementary Latin II
Elementary Latin I	Byzantine/Eastern Christianity
Ancient Philosophy	Logic
Intro to Spirituality	Physical Education
Principles of Effective Speaking	

Year 2

Fall Semester	*Spring Semester*
Inter. Latin	Latin Prose & Poetry
Philosophy of Human Nature	Logic
Roman Catholic Tradition	Ethics
Our Lady of Guadalupe	Catholic Morality
Bowling	Elementary Spanish I
Writing II	

Year 3

Fall Semester	*Spring Semester*
American Experience I	Music History Appreciation
Latin American I/Col. Hist	Confessions of St. Augustine
Golf	Philosophy of God
Metaphysics	Phenomenological Tradition
Spanish II	Intermediate Spanish
Survey of Spanish Literature	Mysticism and Span. Lit.
Sacraments	

Year 4

Fall Semester	*Spring Semester*
Visions/Heaven & Hell I	Biology I
Koine Greek I	Intro. to Astronomy
Medieval Philosophy	Koine Greek II (Dis)
Early Modern Philosophy	U.S. History I
Intro. to Psychology	General College Math
	Late Modern Philosophy

Pre-Theology Curriculum

A man with a college degree who is sent to a two-year pre-theology program might take the following courses:

Year One

Fall Semester	*Spring Semester*
Greek or Latin	Greek or Latin
Logic	Ethics/Moral Philosophy
Ancient Philosophy	Medieval Philosophy
Catechism of Catholic Church I	Catechism of Catholic Church II
Formation Seminar	Formation Seminar
Intro. to Pastoral Music/Choir	Intro. to Pastoral Music/Choir
Pre-theology Placement	Pre-theology Placement

Year Two

Fall Semester	*Spring Semester*
Greek or Latin	Greek or Latin
Modern Philosophy	Contemporary Philosophy
Metaphysics	Epistemology/Phil. of Knowledge
Natural Theology	Philosophical Anthropology
Elective	Elective
Intro. to Pastoral Music/Choir	Intro. to Pastoral Music/Choir
Pre-theology Placement	Pre-theology Placement

Theology Curriculum

In the course of major seminary, candidates minimally earn the master of divinity degree. The chart is an example of how the classes can be arranged during the four-year program of theological studies.

First Theology

Fall Semester	*Spring Semester*
The First Millennium	Medieval/Renaissance Church
Introduction to Liturgy	Fundamental Moral Theology II
Fundamental Moral Theology I	Pentateuch & Historical Books
Biblical Study: Wisdom/Psalms	Christian Spirituality
Revelation, Faith, & Theology	Theology of Tri-personal God
Pastoral Music I & class choir	Pastoral Music I & Class Choir
1st Theology PFE Placement	1st Theology PFE Placement

Second Theology

Fall Semester	*Spring Semester*
Code of Canon Law	Christian Love & Justice
Modern/Contemp. Church	Matthew and Mark
Prophets	Ecclesiology I
Christology and Soteriology	Sacraments: Baptism, etc
Elective	Elective
Pastoral Music II & class choir	Pastoral Music II & Class Choir
2nd Theology PFE Placement	2nd Theology PFE Placement

Third Theology

Fall Semester	*Spring Semester*
Models of Preaching	Marriage Law
Luke and Acts of Apostles	Homiletics Practicum
Grace I	Johannine Writings
Holy Orders	Grace II
Deacon Practicum	Elective
Elective	Pastoral Music III & class choir
Pastoral Music III & class choir	3rd Theology PFE Placement
3rd Theology PFE Placement	

Fourth Theology

Fall Semester	Spring Semester
Church in United States	Marriage & Family
Catholic Med/Sexual Morality	Pastoral Counseling
Pauline Letters	Sacraments of Healing
Ecclesiology II: Ecumen/Misslgy	Penance Practicum
Elective	Holy Eucharist
Pastoral Music IV & Class Choir	Mass Practicum
4th Theology Parish Placement	Elective
Pastoral Music IV & Class Choir	4th Theology Parish Placement

Besides the Masters of Divinity degree, which is generally required for all men for priestly ordination, different seminaries offer other more advanced degrees which can also be earned during the same timeframe. These degrees include the M.A. degree in Theology with a concentration in a specific area, such as Systematic Theology, Scripture, History, Pastoral, Moral Theology, or Patristics. Other seminaries offer the STB and even the STL. The STL generally requires one or two additional years to attain after the four years of theology. It qualifies a man to teach that specific area of theology in a Catholic university or seminary. The terminal degree for a seminary or university professor is the STD, which is a doctoral-level degree. It requires several more years of study after the four years of theology and the STL.

The study of theology in seminary intellectual formation is truly to be *fides quaerens intellectum*, faith seeking understanding. The study of theology both begins and ends in faith. It is not enough for a seminarian to pass all of his classes. He must be able to apply the theology he has learned while preaching, teaching, counseling, and hearing confessions. Therefore seminarians must study diligently. Most seminarians spend two to three hours per day outside of class in reading, studying, and writing papers. This intensive study would be challenging enough by itself, but it is especially challenging while being attentive to the other three pillars of formation. Should this seem intimidating, I remind you of the words of Pope John Paul the Great: "Do not be afraid."[61] God will never send you where his grace cannot sustain you.

The intellectual pillar is an essential component of priestly formation, but it cannot exist without the other three pillars. We always say during orientation to our new men, "You can't just study your way through seminary. Nor can you just pray your way through seminary. There are four pillars and you must be fully engaged in all four." As the Academic Dean of Mount St. Mary's Seminary, Fr. Dan Mindling, always remarks to the new men during orientation: "Congratulations. You are about to embark on the most privileged education the Catholic Church has to offer — the education the Church gives to her priests." Truly, it is a great privilege to undergo priestly academic formation!

Pastoral Formation

The basic principle of pastoral formation is described in the PPF#238: "The whole training of the students should have as its object to make them true shepherds of souls after the example of the Lord Jesus Christ, teacher, priest and shepherd."

Priesthood is about getting people to heaven! All priestly formation culminates in pastoral skill: being able to shepherd people and help them to grow in holiness. We often say in formation work that "grace builds on nature." Though a priest will receive the grace to be a good shepherd at his ordination, that grace calls for the priest's personal commitment *to develop the knowledge and skills* to teach and preach well, to celebrate the sacraments properly and prayerfully, and to take care of people's spiritual needs.

The PPF emphasizes the following elements: proclamation of the word, celebration of the sacraments, having a missionary heart, building the community of faith, developing the skills for effective public ministry, an initiation to various apostolic works (practicums in hospitals, prisons, CCD classes, etc.), cultural sensitivity, learning to be a pastor in a parish, working with the poor, and development of leadership skills. All of these are covered in pastoral formation.

The seminary accomplishes this pillar with a coordinated program of Pastoral Field Education (PFE). The PFE director, always a priest, gives each seminarian a PFE assignment where he goes to learn a specific pastoral skill. The seminary has this program outlined in its handbook, and each seminary has an organized program for each year of theology. The following schema would be an example:

> **First Theology:** A teaching assignment in a CCD class or Catholic school
>
> **Second Theology:** A health care assignment in a hospital or nursing home
>
> **Third Theology:** A prison assignment, youth ministry, or some other pastoral area in which a specific man has not yet had any experience.
>
> **Fourth Theology:** Transitional deacons are ordinarily assigned to a local parish to preach, baptize, and witness marriages.

Each seminarian should receive practical pastoral experience in each area of pastoral ministry. If a seminarian arrives in the seminary with significant experience in youth ministry, for instance, then he will obviously not be sent to a youth ministry assignment. He needs to grow in other areas. Each pastoral placement is supervised, and the supervisor gives a written evaluation of the seminarian's performance. PFE assignments usually require three to four hours one day per week.

Pastoral formation brings together all aspects of formation. It is analogous to the graduate of medical school who finally starts to see patients during his residency. He must develop his bedside manner, learn what to look for and how to treat "real people."

Another example of pastoral formation is the Confession practicum, where the seminarians practice hearing Confessions, giving counsel, and assigning penances. There is also a Mass practicum, where they practice celebrating Holy Mass according to the rubrics of the Church. Most seminaries today have a special chapel for deacons, complete with video equipment, so seminarians can record themselves preaching, celebrating Holy Mass, and baptizing.

Priestly formation today is the best it has ever been in the history of the Church! It is a great time to go to seminary.

Setting Goals

Most seminaries require the men to set yearly formation goals for each of the four pillars of formation. These goals will vary as the men get closer to ordination, but the following will illustrate possible goals for a man who is in first theology.

Human Formation Goals

~ Because I am by nature shy and socially awkward, I will initiate a conversation with another seminarian or a stranger once per day by asking sincere questions about him or her, and then asking him if he has any special intention for which I can pray.

~ Because I am not good at public speaking and I get very nervous, I will take the seminary non-credit public speaking course to develop my public speaking skills now, before I begin my formal homiletics course in third theology.

Spiritual Formation Goals

~ Because I am just learning about the liturgy of the hours and incorporating them into my spiritual plan of life, I will pray the Office of Readings and Night prayer every day (in addition, of course, to morning prayer and evening prayer, which the seminary prays in common).

~ I will make a Holy Hour before the Blessed Sacrament every day, experimenting with different forms of prayer with the guidance of my spiritual director.

Intellectual Formation Goals

~ I will spend a minimum of two and half hours per day in study outside of class, six days per week, for a total of fifteen hours per week.

~ Because I do not take good notes, I will supplement my class notes by acquiring the notes of a very good student in my class and I will study these along with my own notes.

Pastoral Formation Goals

~ I will spend one or two hours on Saturday morning preparing the material for my 4th grade CCD class which I teach on Sunday morning.

~ I will memorize the names of every child in my class, find out at least a little information about them, and pray for them by name every single day.

Seminarians set goals such as these and they are held accountable to those goals in their regular meetings with their formation advisor and their spiritual director. Seminary formation is primarily "self formation." Seminarians must have the self-knowledge to see where they need to grow in each area, then to set goals to accomplish this growth.

The Train is Leaving the Station!

When the new seminarians arrive each year for orientation, I always tell them, "The train is leaving the station. Get on now — or within a few weeks, you will be running behind it trying to catch up." Many of these new men arrive wondering what they will be doing with all of their free time. Within four weeks, they are wondering how they will possibly finish all that is required. Priestly formation is a full-time job.

Consider that three hours of prayer, four hours of class, three hours of study, and one hour of PFE adds up to eleven hours. This does not include spiritual direction every two weeks, formation advising, meals, exercise, keeping up with current events, choir practice, and many other (albeit optional) meetings or events. Organization, time management, and good study habits are essential.

The Formation Advisor Report

At the end of each year, the seminarian's formation advisor will write a report which is sent to his vocation director and bishop. This report outlines the seminarian's strengths and weaknesses, his success attaining personal goals, and general progress in each of the four pillars. The report also contains the official vote of the formation team regarding advancement to the next year of theology or to ordination. The rector of the seminary attaches his official recommendation (or lack thereof) to this report. Canonically, only the rector has the authority to recommend a man to his bishop for advancement.

What Do Seminarians Wear?

Each seminary has its own policy regarding dress code and some are more formal than others. In most college seminaries, the men will wear casual clothes. Some have an official dress; for example, black pants, white button down shirt, black tie and black shoes. Most seminaries require that all seminarians possess a black cassock and white surplice, black clerical attire, and casual clothes. In more and more major seminaries, black clerical attire is often worn for Mass, classes, and field education assignments. Some major seminaries have their men wear the more formal cassock on a daily basis and others permit casual non-clerical clothing. You should not purchase a cassock, clerics, or any other clothing until you have read carefully the policies of the seminary you will attend. Some seminaries require a specific brand or style of cassock, for example.

What Do Seminarians Do in the Summer?

Most vocation directors give seminarians a special summer assignment. This assignment may be to work in a parish, to work with the poor, to study Spanish in an immersion program in a Spanish-speaking country, or to teach the faith in a Bible school program. Some dioceses have a structure similar to the PFE structure in the seminary; that is, each summer has a specific emphasis on a certain aspect of pastoral ministry. The summer assignment generally is not the decision of the seminary, but of the diocese. Still, whatever the assignment, the seminary requests a written evaluation of how the seminarian performed. Seminarians are not just on vacation in the summers, though they certainly do spend a couple of weeks on vacation. The summer assignment is an important part of their priestly formation.

Seminary Expenses

Priestly formation is expensive. It costs between $30,000 and $40,000 every year for one seminarian. This includes the seminary cost, health insurance, books, travel, and other necessities. Most dioceses pay all of this. Seminarians in major seminary are not allowed to have a job on the side because priestly formation is a full-time job.

Suppose a man goes to seminary for three years (two years of pre-theology and first theology), and then discerns that he is not called to priesthood. He has done a diligent discernment and his spiritual director agrees that he is making a good decision. Most dioceses do not require this man to repay the $120,000 they have spent on him in the last three years. If they did require this, some men might elect to stay in the seminary when they should not stay—rather than leave formation and face repaying this huge debt. In other words, the pressure of debt repayment could cause a seminarian to make a bad discernment decision.

Many dioceses have a very different financial policy for college seminarians than major seminarians. In my experience, many dioceses do *not* pay the full cost of college seminary. They do pay part of it and then ask the collegian to take out loans or get his family's support for the rest. Your vocation director will cover the financial policies of your diocese when you are in application.

Different Kinds of Seminaries

There are a number of differences in seminaries around the country, even among those who specifically train diocesan priests. Even though the Council of Trent mandated that, when possible, every diocese should have their own seminary, this is not possible for most dioceses. Running a seminary requires a huge investment of priests and money, and most dioceses do not have enough seminarians to warrant this investment. The larger archdioceses in the country usually have their own respective seminaries and they welcome seminarians from other dioceses as well. Some examples of diocesan seminaries are St. Charles Borromeo Seminary in Philadelphia, St. Joseph's Seminary in New York, St. John's Seminary in Boston, and Mundelein Seminary in Chicago.

Some religious orders have traditionally trained diocesan priests as one of their apostolates. The Benedictines are most prominent in this regard. Examples include St. Meinrad's Seminary in Indiana, which is part of St. Meinrad's Archabbey, and St. Vincent's Seminary in Latrobe, Pennsylvania, which is also run by the attached monastery. These seminaries accept seminarians from any diocese and they have provided a wonderful service to the Church in this regard for many years.

There are also national seminaries that accept candidates from any diocese in the nation, but they are not attached to a religious order or to a specific diocese. Examples of national seminaries are Mount St. Mary's Seminary in Emmitsburg, Maryland and the Pontifical College Josephinum in Columbus, Ohio.

There are also regional seminaries, which are created by several dioceses working together. For example, the bishops of the many dioceses in Florida worked together to create St. Vincent de Paul Seminary in Boynton Beach, Florida. In this way, financing and staffing the seminary is more evenly distributed. Any of these seminaries will happily accept candidates from outside their region.

There are special seminaries for older candidates. Places like Blessed John XXIII Seminary in Weston, Massachusetts, Holy Apostles Seminary in Cromwell, Connecticut, and Sacred Heart School of Theology in Hales Corner, Wisconsin have all specialized in training older men. Ss. Cyril and Methodius Seminary in Orchard Lake, Michigan specializes in training seminarians from Poland to work as priests in the U.S.

The North American College (NAC) in Rome, Italy is another special category of seminary. It is a U.S. seminary, but it is located in the center of Rome. Men who are appointed to study there receive their formation at the NAC, but take their theological courses in a local Roman university, usually in the Gregorian University which is operated by the Jesuits, or the Angelicum University which is operated by the Dominicans. Studying in Rome means that the seminarian must become fairly proficient in Italian, since many of the classes are taught in that language. Being appointed by one's bishop to study at the North American College is considered an honor. It is an invaluable experience to witness the universal Church firsthand and study with students from all over the world.

Leaving Seminary

How does a man leave the seminary once he has discerned that he is not called to become a priest? I have said that some men are called to go to seminary who are not being called to become priests. Seminary is part of the discernment process. God prepares some men to do an important work in the Church by calling them to seminary for a few years, and then calling them out.

In times past, it was considered shameful for a man to leave the seminary. People would whisper about him, "That is the man who went off to become a priest but left the seminary. What a shame. His poor family must be so embarrassed." This is an extremely unhealthy and uncharitable attitude. Unfortunately, in days past, seminary faculty sometimes contributed to this unhealthy attitude by insisting that the man who was leaving pack his bags in the middle of the night and be gone by morning, without even telling his friends and classmates that he was leaving. The rationale for this was that the faculty did not want to disturb the priestly formation of the other men. In my opinion, having men leave in the middle of the night without telling anyone is much more disturbing.

It is not shameful to leave the seminary. It is virtuous to leave the seminary when God calls you to leave—but it should be done in the right way. What is the right way? First of all, I always recommend that a man commit himself to seminary one year at a time. It is not appropriate for a seminarian who has a couple of bad weeks to pack his bags and leave. After all, the diocese has undertaken a considerable expense. He should stay the full year, even if he is convinced early in the year that he likely will leave. Seminary is the finest Christian formation in the world! A man should take advantage of it, even if he is not called to become a priest. God may be preparing him for something else. Secondly, just as a man should not *enter* seminary without having made a diligent discernment, he should not *leave* seminary without a diligent discernment. Leaving seminary is a decision which should be made with your spiritual director, during which you are praying very faithfully, with good information, and keeping your formation advisor, the rector, and your vocation director duly informed. If a man is doing all of the above, but he simply does not have peace, and that lack of peace persists over a long period of time, this is a sign that he is not being called to become a priest. Once this decision is made, the man informs his classmates and the larger seminary community (often via e-mail or a letter posted on the main bulletin board) and he leaves with the prayers and best wishes of all. Do you see how different this is from packing one's bags in the middle of the night and being gone by morning, having said nothing to anyone?

Every year in the spring, a handful of men make a private appointment with me to tell me that they are leaving priestly formation. They come to thank me and the seminary staff for helping them to make this important discernment. I always tell them how proud I am of them and how happy I am that they will be building the Kingdom of God in another way. I always say, "Thank you for listening to Jesus when he called you to come to seminary and thank you for listening to him when he called you to leave. Just keep doing whatever he tells you!"

Go Visit a Seminary

In this chapter, I have tried to describe seminary life. But the best way to understand seminary is to go visit one. Many seminaries have Come and See days when potential seminarians are invited to visit, attend some classes, and receive a mini-orientation to seminary life. Ask your vocation director to set up a visit with one of the seminaries used by your diocese. A seminary visit can really change a man's perspective entirely and clear up any discernment difficulties!

St. Vincent de Paul once wrote: "There is nothing more perfect than the formation of a good priest." In my opinion, priestly formation today is better than it has ever been in the history of the Church. It is not perfect, but it is excellent. It is a great time to go to seminary!

Is it time for you to go?

CHAPTER 17

PREREQUISITES AND IMPEDIMENTS TO DIOCESAN PRIESTHOOD

In trying to provide good, solid priests for the people of God, the Church has codified the minimum requirements for a man to be ordained a priest and she has declared certain actions or conditions to be impediments to ordination. These prerequisites and impediments are declared in the Canon Law of the Church, #1024-1052. It is the duty of the vocation director, the seminary, and ultimately the bishop, to ascertain if these requirements have been met before a man is ordained a deacon or priest.

An impediment is an obstacle, something which stands in the way of moving forward. If a man has or suspects he has any of the impediments mentioned in this chapter, he must be able to overcome this obstacle in order to become a priest. In addition to *canonical* impediments there are also *practical* impediments not covered in canon law, such as severe addictions and some physical handicaps. It is important to remember that if a man has an impediment to ordination, he should not assume that it is a permanent roadblock. A dispensation from some impediments can be attained from the local bishop or the pope.

Canonical Prerequisites for Priestly Ordination

The Code of Canon Law describes the following requirements for a man to be ordained a priest in the Catholic Church. These prerequisites are listed below, with commentary on those which are more difficult to understand. The canonical language has been simplified, but the list is based very closely on the applicable canons of Church law.

~ Only a baptized male may be ordained a priest (C. 1024).

This canon simply codifies the theology of the Church regarding an all-male priesthood. This infallible teaching is not open to discussion and is not able to be changed.

~ A man must complete a period of probation and training. He must not have any irregularity or impediment. His bishop must judge him to have the required qualities (C. 1025).

~ It is required that in the judgment of the bishop, the man is considered to be useful for the ministry of the Church (C. 1025, #2).

~ It is required that a man possess freedom in the decision to be ordained. He cannot be forced or coerced (C. 1026).

This canon refers to anyone or anything which might unduly influence a man to become a priest. Parents, relatives, teachers, and superiors can have a very strong influence on a man. For a valid ordination, it must be the free choice of the man.

~ The diocesan bishop must make sure that candidates are properly instructed, educated and formed before they can be ordained (C. 1028).

~ Before ordaining a man, the bishop must make the prudential judgment that the man possesses an integral faith, that he is motivated by the right reasons, that he possesses a good reputation, good morals, and proven virtues, and other necessary physical and psychological qualities (C. 1029).

No man becomes a priest for himself. A man is ordained a priest in order to serve the People of God. The bishop must be convinced that this man seeks ordination because he is motivated to serve others as a priest. In some nations and some cultures, priestly ordination is an extremely prestigious social elevation. It provides a man with a stable income, food, and housing. Personal security is not the correct motivation for priesthood. Rather, a man should desire to sacrifice himself to serve the People of God.

~ A man cannot be ordained a priest until he has completed the age of twenty-five and he has sufficient maturity. If he is moving towards priesthood, he cannot be ordained a transitional deacon until he is at least twenty-three (C. 1031).

~ A six-month interval is required between the diaconate and priesthood (C. 1031).

The Church is conscious that priesthood is a tremendous responsibility that can be undertaken only by a man with sufficient maturity. Men mature differently in different cultures, some sooner and some later, but the Code of Canon Law is written for the universal Church. When a man is ordained a priest at the age of twenty-five, people will sometimes jokingly call him a "boy-priest." What they are saying is that even a twenty-five-year-old man is young to carry this kind of responsibility! The CARA ordination survey indicates that 465 men were ordained priests in the U.S. in 2009 and the average age of these men was thirty-six (of the 310 who responded). Though some of these men were ordained priests at the minimum age of twenty-five, the majority of ordinands were older.[62]

To help prepare for the responsibility of priesthood, the Church requires a transitional deacon to do pastoral work for at least six months before ordination. This includes preaching, serving at Mass, teaching, visiting the sick, baptizing, and witnessing marriages.

~ A man moving towards priesthood cannot be ordained a transitional deacon until he has completed a five-year curriculum of philosophical and theological studies (C. 1032).

Based on this canon, the Program of Priestly Formation requires (after completing college) at least two years of philosophy and four years of theology before priestly ordination. This means that the man can be ordained a deacon, at the very earliest, after his fifth year of study, and be ordained a priest after his sixth year of study.

~ A man cannot be ordained a priest unless and until he has received the sacrament of Confirmation (C. 1033).

~ A man cannot be ordained either a permanent or transitional deacon until he has received the ministries of lector and acolyte and has exercised them for a suitable period of time. After the man has received acolyte, he must exercise this ministry for at least six months before he can be ordained a deacon (C. 1035).

The Church has always admitted men to Holy Orders through a series of smaller steps or ministries. Today, these ministries include lector and acolyte. The ministry of lector enables a man to officially read the Sacred Scriptures at Mass and the ministry of acolyte enables him to officially serve the Mass. This slow progression of different steps helps mark the man's level of formation and competence as he moves through the lengthy process of formation. It also helps the man and the Church to identify any serious problems or obstacles which might be present.

~ An unmarried man moving towards priesthood cannot be ordained a transitional deacon unless and until he has publicly promised before God and the Church the obligation of celibacy (C. 1037).

A man to be ordained a deacon and priest in the Latin rite must make a promise to live celibately, not to marry for the sake of the Kingdom of God. This promise is made during the diaconate ordination rite, prior to the laying on of hands and prayer of consecration.

~ Before ordination to diaconate or priesthood, a man must make a retreat for at least five days. The bishop must verify this before he ordains the man (C. 1039).

This "canonical retreat," as it is called, is generally to be five continuous days. It may be a silent retreat or led by a retreat master. It must be made both before ordination to diaconate and again before ordination to priesthood. Ordination confers an indelible mark on the soul which lasts forever! The Church wisely requires that a man spend five days in prayer with the Lord Jesus before taking this step.

Canonical Impediments to Priestly Ordination

~ A man cannot be ordained a priest if he has some form of insanity or other psychic defect which, in the opinion of a psychologist, would hinder him from doing priestly ministry (C. 1041).

Insanity is to be understood as a disorder which habitually impairs the use of reason. Each case must be judged individually by experts. This is why most dioceses require a psychological evaluation to insure that a candidate has the psychological, mental, and emotional stability to care for souls in priesthood. If a person is judged incapable of carrying out priestly ministry due to schizophrenia or bi-polar disorder, for instance, then he is obviously impeded from moving forward.

I know many priests who have some degree of mental illness (especially depression) and who do wonderful work as priests. I also know many seminarians who carry these crosses. Some of these men must see a psychologist or psychiatrist periodically to maintain their mental health. Some require medication. Mental and emotional health is very important for a priest. A priest must be able to look outward, caring for the needs of others. In order to do this, any inner psychological and emotional turmoil must be under control.

~ A man cannot be ordained a priest if he has committed apostasy, heresy or schism (C. 1041).

This law exists because candidates for priesthood should have a stable faith. A baptized Catholic man may incur this impediment if, for example, he receives sacraments in another church, formally joins another church, or joins an atheistic group. The law specifically refers to a man who converted to the Catholic Faith, then subsequently left the Church and finally, returns to it. However, if a man who was baptized and raised Catholic goes off to college, stops practicing his faith for a while, attends some protestant services, and then returns to the full practice of the Catholic faith, he would likely not have incurred this impediment. There are many reverts to the Church who are studying in Catholic seminaries or who are priests today. Your vocation director will guide you in this regard.

~ A man cannot be ordained a priest if he has ever been married, even civilly, unless and until his wife has died or he has received a declaration of nullity from the Church (C. 1041).

Some candidates for priesthood were previously married. Either their wives died, or they are divorced and have obtained a decree of nullity from the diocesan tribunal. If a man was married, even in a civil ceremony, and even if the marriage lasted only a very short time, this must be brought to the attention of the vocation director immediately. If there is an annulment, some vocation directors will want more information on the grounds for the annulment, since these can be important in evaluating a candidate for seminary.

~   A man cannot be ordained a priest if he has killed
    another person. This includes voluntary homicide and
    also abortion. If a man did not do this crime himself,
    but helped another person do it by positive
    cooperation, the impediment is still incurred (C. 1041).

If a man causes the death of another person, either directly or by cooperation, he would incur an impediment to ordination. This does not include accidents or legitimate self-defense. It certainly includes abortion, and some candidates for priesthood have a history in this area. If a man gave any assistance whatsoever in procuring a direct abortion—if he encouraged it, paid for it, or drove a woman to the abortion clinic—he should talk about this in full detail with his vocation director early in the admissions process. Another area which sometimes shows up in candidates is vehicular homicide or the death of another caused by driving under the influence of alcohol. Because of the gravity of this canon, obtaining a dispensation can be complicated and difficult.

~   A man cannot be ordained a priest if he has seriously
    and intentionally mutilated himself (or another person)
    or if he has attempted suicide (C. 1041).

The Church certainly understands more today about the psychological causes of serious depression or other mental illnesses which might lead a person to attempt suicide. Some candidates will acknowledge having made this attempt at a very difficult time in life. This impediment should be viewed in light of canon 1041-1 regarding psychological health. If a man ever attempted suicide or if he ever seriously considered it, this should be discussed in detail with the psychologist who conducts the exam. If the man did incur this impediment, and he now has the psychological and emotional health to function as a priest, a dispensation can be obtained. The same is true for mutilation, an action which deprives oneself of a bodily organ or its use. Having a vasectomy is one example of mutilation. Interestingly, Origin, a famous early Christian writer and mystic, would have incurred this impediment since he castrated himself in an attempt to gain sexual purity!

> ~ A man cannot be ordained a priest if he has intentionally impersonated a bishop or priest by attempting to celebrate Mass or any other sacrament (C. 1041).

Many young boys played Mass when they were children. Their parents encouraged this so as to help the boy consider a vocation to priesthood. This is a very good practice and quite a few priests remember doing it. But this canon is describing something else: a serious impersonation of sacred acts reserved for a bishop or priest. If a man who is not a priest, for example, were to intentionally and deceptively attempt to celebrate Mass (in a church, wearing vestments, with people present), or to hear Confessions, he would incur this impediment. It is hard for me to imagine why any man would ever attempt to do this, and the very fact that he does would show incapacity and impede him from ordination.

> ~ A man cannot be ordained a priest if he is a neophyte (C. 1042).

Any adult man who has only recently joined the Catholic Church either through Baptism or a profession of faith is impeded from Holy Orders until, in the judgment of his bishop, he has proven himself to be firm in the faith. Most bishops will require the neophyte to be a Catholic two or three years before they will allow him to begin seminary.

~ If any member of the Church, priest or layman, is aware of an impediment in a candidate or seminarian, he or she must report this to the bishop before the man's ordination (C. 1043).

A vocation director once told me that he received a phone call from a woman who claimed that she was the ex-wife of one of his seminarians! She explained that they were civilly married for a few years and had two children. They subsequently divorced and she had not heard from him since. He did not pay child support or alimony, and he had no contact with the children. One day she just happened to see his picture on the diocesan poster of seminarians. She realized that he was being deceptive. There was no annulment. The man had simply lied to his bishop and vocation director, because he knew he was bound in justice to take care of his children until they reached the age of emancipation. He knew that marriage was an invalidating impediment to Holy Orders. This man was a dead-beat dad and a dishonest seminarian — and likely would have been the same kind of priest. Thankfully, this woman called the vocation director and his ordination was called off permanently!

Sometimes a seminarian becomes aware of an impediment in another seminarian or candidate for priesthood about which the vocation director has not been informed. It is very important that this seminarian bring this information to the vocation director or rector immediately. He should not feel that he is betraying a friend or brother seminarian. If a person loves the Church, he or she should do all in his power to protect her and to help the Church produce holy, well-balanced priests. The canon obliges all of the faithful to reveal impediments if they become known.

~ A dispensation can be attained from most impediments from the pope or the local bishop, depending on what kind of impediment it is (C. 1047).

In other words, if a candidate is honest with his vocation director and bishop from the beginning, it is likely that the impediment can be dispensed, and the man can be ordained a priest. In my experience as a vocation director and seminary formator, many of the men who believe they may have an impediment had actually not incurred the impediment at all! If there is any question, the vocation director will ask the bishop and a canon lawyer to review the case.

Non-Canonical Impediments

Alcoholism or Substance Abuse

Can an alcoholic become a diocesan priest and expect to flourish and succeed? Substance abuse addictions have both a physical and a psychological/emotional element. I have known many excellent priests who carried this cross, though some have done so more successfully than others. If a candidate for seminary is already an alcoholic, he will need to disclose this completely to his vocation director along with his record of sobriety. He will need to demonstrate an extended period of sobriety and an ability to remain sober even in times of great stress. If accepted to study for priesthood, this issue will be monitored carefully during his years of formation, with any lapses in sobriety duly noted. Whether or not to accept a man who is an alcoholic, though sober for a sufficient time, will be a prudential judgment made by the bishop.

Most bishops, at some point during their episcopacy, have had to send one or more of their priests off to a special program for alcohol-related problems. This is painful for all involved. These programs, while often very effective, are also expensive. When a priest enters such a program it can be embarrassing to him, to the parish, and to the diocese.

The stress and pressure of diocesan priesthood can really push a man at times to self-medicate in order to "take the edge

330

off." This is why a previous addiction to alcohol or to another substance is something your vocation director and bishop will take very seriously.

Although every diocese and seminary has had seminarians who were alcoholics, I think the more common problem in seminaries today is the condition which Alcoholics Anonymous describes as ACOA—Adult Child of an Alcoholic. Children who grow up in homes or families with one or more alcoholic parents can have residual psychological and emotional issues such as depression, low self-esteem, anxiety, and anger. Many of these men do attend counseling and ACOA groups to deal with these residual effects and they can become excellent priests. However, quite often, these candidates must be strongly encouraged to avail themselves of this counseling.

Addiction to Gambling

Every priest who becomes the pastor of a parish is the administrator and steward of a great deal of money. Some parishes have multi-million dollar budgets and this money belongs to God's people, given for the building up of the Kingdom. It seems obvious that if a man has an addiction to gambling, this must be dealt with definitively before he can study for priesthood. Almost every diocese has had cases of financial mismanagement by priests, a scandal which is very harmful to the Church. I am not saying that a man with a gambling problem cannot ever become a priest, but the addiction must be very solidly under control and this must be demonstrated consistently over an appropriate amount of time.

Addiction to the Internet

There is much ink being spilt about the technological revolution and how the Internet and other electronic gadgets are changing the world. Instant communication has become a part of our culture. The men who grow up in this culture can become very dependent upon technology, even obsessed by it. I have seen candidates who spend an inordinate amount of time e-mailing, texting, blogging, gaming, and updating their Facebook and Twitter accounts. Seminary formators constantly have to remind seminarians to balance their time online. Priests bring Jesus Christ to others primarily through face-to-face contact. Sometimes internet communication can prevent or limit a man from socially engaging others—and thus can limit his ministry. If a man has a history of Internet addiction or even an obsessive tendency to stay online for long hours, this must be dealt with definitively prior to ordination.

Addiction to Pornography

Online pornography is a serious problem that has grown astronomically since the advent of the Internet and continues to grow worse. Sadly, it is fast becoming very much a part of our culture. Most young men growing up these days have viewed internet pornography at least a few times and many have serious addictions. Growing towards sexual integration is an important part of Christianity, and pornography can seriously impede this growth. Many priests I know say that this is the most commonly confessed sin of young men. If a man has a bad habit or an addiction to internet pornography, this will certainly impede his progress towards priesthood, unless and until he can bring it under control. Like all addictions, a person must ask for help! Go to your spiritual director and vocation director and they will assist you in overcoming this serious obstacle.

Prone to Addictions

Through advances in modern psychology, it is now known that some people are simply more prone to addictions than other people. Some call this an "addictive personality" and there are tests to identify men with a high chance of developing an addiction of some kind. These tests are often done as part of the battery of psychological tests for priesthood candidates. Having parents or relatives who are addicts is certainly one contributing factor. If tests show that a man has a very high likelihood of developing an addiction, this will have to be weighed with all of the other information in the application dossier. If the man has a history of addictions and he does not have a history of sobriety from his addictions, he is not ready to enter seminary.

Gross Obesity

Gross obesity is defined as weighing more than twice your ideal weight or being more than one hundred pounds overweight. Men who are obese are limited in their energy level. It is likely that their life span is limited as well. Each bishop has to make the decision to accept such a man on a case-by-case basis. Some of the seminarians with whom I have worked through the years have reminded me that St. Thomas Aquinas also had this problem. His stomach was so large that they had to cut out the front of his desk to enable him to sit comfortably. But where would Catholic philosophy and theology be today without this saint and doctor of the Church? Their point is well-made. That being said, when a man is morbidly obese, sometimes a vocation director will postpone acceptance pending the loss of a certain amount of weight. Or, at the very least, his acceptance is conditional as long as he does not gain any more and that he make a concerted effort to control his weight problem. I do know some seminarians and priests who have undergone gastric-bypass surgery and have done quite well in maintaining a stable weight afterward. If a man has a serious obesity problem, he will be advised in seminary to make weight loss one of his formal goals; often he is encouraged to use a program like Weight Watchers, combined with regular exercise. Obesity is a heavy cross for these men, yet many of them make very fine priests for the Church.

Physical Disabilities

Can a diocesan priest have a physical disability and still do the work required of him? The local bishop and vocation director will have to make this decision based on specific information about the handicap and information about the diocese. For example, an extensive public transportation system in an urban diocese may make it possible for a priest who is visually impaired or in a wheelchair to function relatively well, whereas it may not be possible in a rural diocese with no public transportation. Sometimes older churches do not yet have convenient handicap access (the law of the land notwithstanding), so a disabled priest might be able to be assigned only to certain parishes.

Other possible impediments are illnesses like cancer, AIDS, tuberculosis, and congenital disorders such as heart disease. If a man has congenital heart disease, it could severely limit both his ability to work and his life span. I have known some candidates with these types of concerns who were accepted by the bishop and subsequently made wonderful priests. If God wants you to become a diocesan priest, he can make it happen regardless of your physical limitations.

Your bishop will want to ascertain how long you will be able to serve the Church as a priest. He will have to make a prudential judgment to spend more than $150,000 in seminary formation in exchange for your priestly service. This is a difficult decision if a man may live only a few years. Some people take offense at this line of reasoning. They say, "Money should have nothing to do with it. Priesthood is about saving souls. Who can measure what God can do with a holy, humble, fervent priest? In fact, God often seems to do the greatest things with the weakest priests." While I certainly acknowledge this sentiment, the bishop is charged to be a good steward of the people's money. The physical health of a candidate will be an important consideration in his decision.

Full Disclosure to Your Vocation Director

A vocation director once told me that he preached the five-day canonical retreat for a group of transitional deacons who were to be ordained priests the next week. Between the conferences, he met with some of the men for the sacrament of Confession and spiritual direction. He said that he very much enjoyed the meetings and he was impressed with the quality of the men. During one private meeting, one of the men casually mentioned that he had once attempted suicide by taking an overdose of some medication. It was many years before when he was a teenager, after a terrible divorce between his parents. Thankfully, he was unsuccessful. His mother took him to the hospital and she promised that she would never tell anyone about it, since it was a source of embarrassment to the man. The retreat master said to the man, "But of course you told your vocation director about that when you first applied to seminary?" He replied that he had never told anyone about it. The retreat master had to explain that, according to canon law, attempted suicide is an impediment to his ordination, and that he would need to tell his bishop and vocation director immediately since he was scheduled to be ordained a priest the next week. The deacon called his vocation director and with much difficulty the appropriate dispensation was attained. The retreat master recalled that the man had to be ordained a transitional deacon again before he could be ordained a priest.

I relate that story not to denigrate that young man in any way. I am sure that he was a fine man and that he became a wonderful priest. I tell it to emphasize the importance of full disclosure to your vocation director and bishop about any possible impediment, canonical or practical, from the beginning.

An impediment can invalidate your ordination. It is serious business.

Impediments? Do Not Despair!

Please do not finish this chapter having despaired of ever becoming a priest. If you believe that you might have one or more of these impediments, be it a canonical or a practical impediment, bring it to the attention of your vocation director. God has the power to overcome any and all impediments, if he is calling you to become a priest. Remember that many of these impediments, if they have even been incurred, can be dispensed from by the proper ecclesiastical authority.

Be completely honest. Bring it to the Church. She is your mother and she loves you greatly.

CHAPTER 18

SPECIAL ASSIGNMENTS FOR DIOCESAN PRIESTS

What are the duties of the vicar general, the chancellor, and the judicial vicar?

How does a priest become the vocation director or begin teaching in a seminary?

I was thinking about becoming a military chaplain. Can I still do this if I become a diocesan priest?

I knew a diocesan priest who became a foreign missionary and served ten years in South America. I would like to do that, but would I be permitted?

These are all very good questions that bring up an important aspect of diocesan priesthood: specialized ministry. Some diocesan priests serve for a time in a special job like one of those mentioned above. Some even serve for their entire priesthood. But these specialized jobs were not what they envisioned while they were in seminary. Instead, they were studying to become diocesan priests who would work in parishes taking care of people. To use a medical analogy, diocesan priests are like general practitioners; they normally are not the orthopedic surgeons or neurologists. The vast majority of parish priests work in parishes. But because of the structure of the Church, every diocese needs a certain number of priests to work in a special job, often outside of a parish. In this chapter, I will describe some of those specialized ministries.

First of all, we all know that God gives different gifts to different people, including priests. Some priests have a great gift for languages; they pick up foreign languages quickly and can move back and forth between languages with ease. If the bishop needs someone to work as a port chaplain, speaking to sailors from many different countries, a language specialist would be a good choice. Other priests are tremendous administrators. They have the gifts and experience to manage a large institution such as a diocese or Catholic college.

I have heard it said that one of the most important duties of a bishop is to be a talent scout. A bishop looks for the gifts and talents of his priests (and seminarians) and at the needs of his diocese and the universal Church. His job is to tap into these resources so that all the needs of the Church are filled.

How does a diocesan priest end up in one of these specialized ministries? The short answer is that his bishop assigns him to it. But there is usually a longer answer. Sometimes, the priest feels drawn to do a certain work and he communicates this to the bishop. But in other circumstances, the priest was very happy working in his parish and the bishop asks him to do a special job. Like Simon of Cyrene, he is pressed into service to do something he never desired to do. Yet he promised obedience to his bishop, and so he begins his new job.

Some dioceses require every priest to fill out a short questionnaire annually for the bishop and personnel committee. Many priests jokingly refer to this form as a "dream sheet." The form asks questions like these:

Would you like a change of assignment or are you content to stay where you are?

Do you prefer rural or urban ministry?

Of the following special assignments, check the ones in which you might be interested: high school or college work, prison ministry, Hispanic ministry, vocation ministry, military chaplaincy, etc.

Is there anything else about yourself (health, family, etc.), that you would like the bishop to know as he contemplates assignments for the coming year?

This form can be helpful to the bishop as he tries to match up the available priests with the needed assignments. And it can also remind the bishop that a certain priest feels drawn to do a certain specialized ministry. When that ministry comes open, he will often be the obvious choice. I said in chapter 2 that there is a third level of personal vocation. Just as a married man may be called to the occupation of teacher, a priest may be called to a special ministry such as working with the poor, teaching in a high school, or working in the pro-life arena.

I know a priest who has spent thirty-five years teaching in a diocesan high school. He is a legend in his diocese. The students love and respect him tremendously. They are on waiting lists to get into his courses. Years after they have graduated, hundreds of his former students have asked him to witness their marriages. This priest clearly has special gifts and talents to do this work, and yet, in his case, he never asked to do it or even especially desired it. The bishop assigned him to teach high school as a young priest, and he was so successful that he has been there ever since.

I heard of another priest who was a disaster as a pastor. Even though he was ordained a diocesan priest, he was not skilled at parish ministry and was a poor administrator. This priest, through a process of trial and error which caused both he and his bishop much suffering, ended up being assigned to full-time hospital ministry. And he is one of the best hospital chaplains one could hope for. He has a great gift of compassion. The sick, dying, and bereaved to whom he ministers think he is the best priest in the world.

On the other hand, I know some priests who are bitter because they have asked the bishop repeatedly to assign them to a certain specialized ministry and he has not done so. It is sad and unfortunate that they are bitter, because the will of God for a diocesan priest is always shown through the bishop to whom he promised obedience.

Wearing Several Different Hats

Some diocesan priests do indeed receive a special assignment from the bishop, but at the same time, they also remain active as pastors or associates in parishes. In other words, they have more than one full-time job. They must work hard to take care of themselves and avoid getting burned out. For example, a priest might serve simultaneously as pastor of a medium-sized parish, the vocation director, and the master of ceremonies for the bishop. Juggling several jobs is quite common today. It is not easy. This is one of the many reasons why the Church needs more priests.

Now let's look at some of these specialized ministries to which some diocesan priests are appointed. I will describe positions in the diocesan curia, then special jobs outside the curia.

Vicar General

A vicar general is the principal deputy of the bishop. He exercises administrative authority over the whole diocese, and thus has the highest official position after the bishop himself. He is the bishop's right-hand man, the second in command. In the Catholic Church, a diocesan bishop must appoint at least one vicar general for his diocese, but he may appoint more. Larger dioceses or archdioceses routinely have two or even three. A vicar general must be a priest or bishop. Generally, the vicar general has an advanced degree (licentiate or doctorate) in canon law or theology. In his administrative role, the vicar general spends much of his time helping the bishop handle problems. Though it is a job with great power and responsibility, it is often not the most pleasant job in the Church. Many a bishop was first a vicar general before being named to the episcopacy.

Episcopal Vicar

An episcopal vicar shares in the bishop's ordinary executive power like the vicar general, except for the fact that the episcopal vicars' authority normally extends over only a particular part of the diocese. A large archdiocese, for example, might have four auxiliary bishops or priests who are appointed episcopal vicars for the four different quadrants of that diocese. These episcopal vicars essentially run the Church in that quadrant. The majority of U.S. dioceses are not large enough to necessitate episcopal vicars over geographic areas. More commonly, a bishop names an episcopal vicar not to a geographic area, but to an area of pastoral ministry. For example, there may be an episcopal vicar in charge of properties, hospitals, or senior clergy. An episcopal vicar must be either a priest or a bishop.

Judicial Vicar (also called Officialis)

The judicial vicar is an officer of the diocese who has ordinary power to judge cases in the diocesan ecclesiastical court. Although the diocesan bishop can reserve certain cases to himself, the judicial vicar and the diocesan bishop are a single tribunal. The judicial vicar ought to be someone other than the vicar general, unless the smallness of the diocese or the limited number of cases suggest otherwise (C. 1420). The judicial vicar is most well known for running the diocesan marriage tribunal, which grants annulments, permission for mixed marriages and dispensations in other cases so that marriages in the Catholic Church will be valid and licit. A judicial vicar must be a priest of good repute, must be at least thirty years old, and must hold a doctorate or licentiate in canon law (C. 1420).

Chancellor

Historically, the chancellor is the principal record-keeper of a diocese. The chancellor is a notary, so that he may certify official documents, and often has other duties at the discretion of the bishop of the diocese. He may be in charge of some aspect of finances or of managing the personnel connected with diocesan offices. His office is normally within the chancery, or diocesan headquarters. Normally, the chancellor is a priest or deacon, although in some circumstances a lay person may be appointed to the post.

Secretary to the Bishop

Bishops usually have one or two lay secretaries, but some bishops, especially those of larger dioceses, appoint a priest as secretary to assist in their pastoral work. The priest secretary handles the most confidential correspondence. Often he lives with the bishop, travels with him, drives for him at times, and also functions as his master of ceremonies at Confirmations and other special liturgies. Almost all Cardinals and Archbishops will have a priest secretary, though many diocesan bishops of smaller dioceses do not. This is usually a position filled by a younger priest for four or five years, who is then moved to a parish, with another younger priest taking his place.

Vicar for the Clergy

The vicar for clergy is usually an episcopal vicar who serves as a liaison between the bishop and the priests of the diocese. Since the bishop is not always available and can't always give the priests the priority they need and deserve, the vicar for clergy meets regularly with priests, evaluates their needs and gives them support. He maintains close ties with the retired priests, keeping them informed about what is happening in the diocese. He makes sure that the needs of the younger priests are met. The vicar for the clergy is often the chair of the priests' personnel committee so he has considerable influence as to where each priest is assigned. He also helps plan continuing education "clergy days" and the annual priests' retreats. The vicar for clergy will almost always be a priest or auxiliary bishop. I mention this particular type of an episcopal vicar because it is a very important job in most dioceses.

Vocation Director

The vocation director is the priest in charge of the entire vocations program for the diocese, specifically to recruit and train future diocesan priests. He visits the Catholic schools and colleges to teach the youth about vocations. He preaches at different parishes regularly, inviting men to consider the vocation of priesthood. He is in charge of advertisements, mailings to candidates, prayer campaigns, and running vocation retreats. He also supports the Serra Clubs and Knights of Columbus vocations programs.

The vocation director guides men over a period of years as they discern diocesan priesthood, go through the application process, and go to seminary. He annually visits the seminarians in their seminaries and receives updates from the seminary formation team. He makes the seminarians' summer assignments and maintains the seminarians' files until they are ordained priests. Some vocation directors recruit seminarians from other countries and bring them to the U.S. The vocation director almost always is a priest, though whether he is full-time or part-time depends on the diocese. Some vocation directors remain pastors of parishes. The vocation director is a very important ministry in a diocese because his work greatly influences the makeup of the presbyterate for years to come. Vocation directors usually serve in this capacity for five to ten years, but they rarely do it for their entire priesthood.

Other Specialized Ministries Outside of the Diocesan Curia

Prison Chaplains

Most dioceses will have one or more prisons within their boundaries with Catholic inmates who are in need of Mass and the sacraments. Depending on the availability of priests and the size of the prison, these needs may be met by a local parish priest who comes into the prison once per week for Mass, catechism, and the other sacraments. Sometimes a full-time prison chaplain may be named. This is a very important specialized ministry because the Lord Jesus said: "When I was in prison, you visited me" (Matthew 25:36).

Hospital Chaplains

Catholic hospitals are one of the most prominent and traditional apostolates of the Catholic Church. Hospital work fulfills a number of the spiritual and corporal works of mercy. In the U.S. today, there are 557 Catholic hospitals caring for 83 million patients per year. These hospitals often have at least one full-time Catholic priest celebrating Mass each day in the hospital chapel and caring for the spiritual needs of the patients and health care workers. Some diocesan priests are asked to become full-time hospital chaplains.

Chaplains and Teachers in Catholic High Schools and Colleges

The education and formation of young people is another traditional apostolate of the Church. Having priests present in our Catholic schools to do Christian formation and to promote priestly vocations is of utmost importance. In the U.S. today, there are 1,352 Catholic high schools educating 680,000 students and 236 Catholic colleges educating 794,000 students! Some bishops always assign their newly ordained priests to teach in one of the Catholic high schools for a few years, which teaches the new priest how to work with youth and to promote vocations. Likewise, chaplains in our Catholic colleges are instrumental in guiding the college students at critical times in their vocational journeys. College students are making important decisions about practicing their faith. The Church needs good, holy priests guiding and caring for these young students.

Port Chaplains

Many U.S. dioceses have port cities, which receive thousands of international ships into their harbors every year. The bishop will often assign a priest to the port, typically one who is gifted with several languages. A port chaplain visits the ships, says Mass for the crew, and otherwise attends to the spiritual needs of the sailors. If the sailors are not being treated fairly and humanely, he will report this to the port authorities. This may be a part-time or a full-time position.

Police and Fire Chaplains

Though usually not a full time position, many priests in the U.S. are asked to function as chaplains to the local police or fire department. These priests will minister to the needs of the police officers and fire fighters, especially in times of disaster. Sometimes the bishop will assign a priest to this ministry, and at other times, the priest is asked to serve by a local station. These jobs can come with some nice perks! I know one priest who had his own squad car—and anytime he had a funeral, a police motorcade would come to escort the funeral procession to the cemetery.

Foreign Missionaries: The St. James Society

Some diocesan priests are sent to work for a few years in a poor nation as a foreign missionary. Many dioceses sponsor a parish in an impoverished area of the world which they support financially and by sending priests to serve. This is an arrangement worked out between the two bishops, and it is a blessing to both parties. The Missionary Society of St. James the Apostle was founded by Richard Cardinal Cushing in 1958 specifically to send diocesan missionary priests to volunteer a minimum of five years in Peru, Bolivia and Ecuador. Priests who serve in this society come back to their respective dioceses fluent in Spanish and with a renewed heart to work with the poor. Again, this may be a specialized ministry assigned directly by the bishop, or it may be a ministry to which the priest feels especially called. There are also other ways that a diocesan priest can become a foreign missionary for a season.

Specialized Cultural Ministry

Though it is still parish ministry, some U.S. diocesan priests are needed to work with special national and cultural groups of Catholics, especially African-Americans, Hispanics, Vietnamese, and Koreans. These national groups often have their own ethnic parishes, and Mass and the sacraments are celebrated in their own language. The priest assigned to this parish will need not only to speak the language, but also to know the culture and customs. Some bishops actually require their seminarians to learn Spanish or another language if it is extensively used in their diocese.

Seminary Professors

The Holy See has repeatedly asked the bishops of the world to release some of their best priests to serve as seminary professors and formators. The formation of our future priests is obviously very important work with huge ramifications for the future! Some priests have been given amazing intellectual gifts; they love the intellectual life and are talented teachers. Some of these priests are sent for further studies in a certain area of theology, and may end up teaching in seminaries. Many spend most of their lives in this third level of vocation. Others teach for a designated term and then return to parish ministry. Some priests are sent to work in seminaries as rectors, spiritual directors, directors of field education, and deans of men. A seminary faculty is composed of both professors and non-professor formators.

The Sulpicians

The Society of St. Sulpice is an organization of diocesan priests who permanently leave their dioceses (with their bishop's permission and blessing) in order to spend the rest of their priesthood forming future priests in seminaries around the world. Founded more than 300 years ago by Fr. Jean Jacques Olier, who was influenced by St. Vincent de Paul in his passion for training priests, this society has done invaluable work in assisting bishops by establishing and running seminaries. Sulpicians almost always send their priests for further studies so that they will have a terminal degree in theology in order to teach in seminaries. The Sulpicians are not a religious community. They are an organization of diocesan priests who have been permanently released from their dioceses to do seminary work. In the U.S., the Sulpicians own and operate several seminaries, including St. Mary's Seminary in Baltimore, Maryland (the oldest seminary in the U.S.), Theological College of the Catholic University of America in Washington D.C., and St. Patrick's Seminary in Menlo Park, California.

Military Chaplains

The U.S. military has an enormous need for Catholic priest chaplains. The shortage of priests in this country has been acutely felt by our Catholic service men and women. According to the Archdiocese for Military Services, there are 1.5 million Catholics in the U.S. Armed Services. This includes 300,000 active duty service people, in addition to their spouses and families. It also includes the Catholics at the five Service Academies. The Naval Academy alone, in Annapolis, Maryland, is more than 50 percent Catholic. Finally, this 1.5 million includes Catholics who are in service of the federal government overseas and Catholic patients in VA facilities in the U.S. and Puerto Rico. Especially during war time, these faithful Catholics need and deserve spiritual support. They need priests! When the Archdiocese of the Military Services was first established, the rule of thumb suggested was that every diocese endeavor to give 1 percent of their priests to serve as military chaplains. Some dioceses have been able to do more in this regard than others.

There are several different ways that a diocesan priest might end up in this specialized ministry. Most Catholic military chaplains first serve as diocesan priests, then receive the bishop's permission to serve a certain number of years in the military. Some of these priests are permitted to complete a full twenty-year career as military chaplains, while others serve only the minimum, usually at least three years.

The Archdiocese for the Military Services has its own program of recruitment and formation, and sponsors several different avenues of entry into the military chaplaincy, besides that mentioned above. Some seminarians join the Archdiocese for the Military Services at the same time that they join their own diocese, in what is called the Military Co-Sponsorship Program. The interested seminarian must fill out an application and submit the required admissions documentation to both his own bishop and to the archbishop for the Military Services. Usually, both bishops will interview this man before acceptance. In this program, the seminarian will spend some summers doing military chaplaincy training in a certain branch of the Service and then some summers in diocesan assignments. The Military Archdiocese pays up to half of the expenses for the training of this priest. When he is ordained a priest, he serves his own diocese for at least three years and then he is released to serve as a military chaplain for a designated term.

Another avenue offered by the military is the Chaplain Candidate Program (C.C.P.). This program entails less commitment than the Co-Sponsorship. A seminarian who joins the C.C.P. investigates the military chaplaincy through summer pastoral experiences in the military (for which he is well-paid). The hope is that he will become interested in being a military chaplain. But he is not committed to serve after ordination, as he would be if he were in the co-sponsorship program.

Finally, some seminarians and priests serve in the military reserves. This usually involves a few weeks per year of service and training, or one Saturday per month. If a bishop gives a priest permission to serve in the reserves, the bishop understands that in the case of war, the priest can be called into active service for an indefinite period of time.

Remember that every priest serving in the military is on loan from a diocese or religious order. There are no permanent priests in the military. The majority of Catholic chaplains began serving later in their priesthood. They did not complete the co-sponsorship program nor the C.C.P. The number of years these priests serve in the military is decided by the bishop and the priest, but as indicated above, the minimum is three years. Because the first year is spent becoming accustomed to military life, several years of service is most productive. However, with waivers, a priest can spend as little as two years. The Military Archdiocese is not part of the military as such; their purpose is to provide chaplains to Catholics in the military. A priest has to have a Masters of Divinity degree minimum to serve as a chaplain in any capacity.

If a young man discerning diocesan priesthood feels a strong attraction to serve as a military chaplain, he should let his vocation director know this from the beginning. If the bishop is not open to that possibility, and if his spiritual director agrees that military service is likely a calling from God, the young man may want to seek out a diocese that is more open to it.

The Bishop's Decision

How do bishops make the difficult decision of whether to release a priest for specialized ministry, especially outside of his diocese?

These are not easy decisions. Every bishop is conscious of his responsibility to support the universal Church, not only his own particular diocese. Nonetheless, he understands that his first priority is to take care of the Catholic people under his jurisdiction. He is the local shepherd. His duty is to supply Mass, the sacraments, and spiritual care to his people. When the bishop is already short of priests—especially if he has priestless parishes—these decisions become even more challenging. The people are writing him letters saying, "Bishop, please send us a priest!" Some bishops are tempted to write back and say, "Priests don't grow on trees. Please send me some seminarians from your parish!"

Remember that bishops must also send a certain number of priests for further studies in specialties like Canon Law and Scripture. The bishop must remember to plan for the future in having priests in his own diocese with the credentials to become vicar general, judicial vicar, etc. If the bishop has his own diocesan seminary, then he is even more obliged to send some of his priests to get doctorates in these areas of theology so as to have seminary professors in the future.

Priests (and seminarians) should keep all of this in mind when they write their bishop to say that they feel called by God to serve in a specialized ministry. This might be a very valid discernment. But as one bishop replied, "Tell God to tell me, and then I will release you."

I have been in a specialized ministry almost all of my life as a priest. I was vocation director for ten years and I have served as vice rector of a seminary for five years. I do love this work. I love being a part of the formation of our future priests. But, as I have told my spiritual director at times, "I really miss being in a parish. I love being a parish priest. I miss the families, going to the kid's ball games, celebrating weddings, baptisms, and funerals. That's what I signed up for!"

And my spiritual director has reminded me, very gently, "No, you signed up to do the will of God. Go where you are sent, do what you are asked, and stay until your bishop sends you elsewhere."

The Greatest Priestly Work of All

Archbishop Timothy Dolan, Archbishop of New York, tells this true story in his book *Priests For the Third Millenium.*

> George Lodes, a priest of my home diocese of St. Louis, who, while in Rome in 1962, had the privilege of an audience with Pope John XXIII. He recalled that there were about ten other priests in the *sala,* and he was last in line to greet the pontiff. Each of the priests before him introduced himself to John XXIII, told him what he did as a priest, and then knelt to kiss the fisherman's ring.
>
> "I am a university president," the first one reported, and then knelt to kiss the pope's ring; "I teach in a college," the next said, genuflecting for the *baciamano*; "I am a hospital chaplain", declared the next, dutifully genuflecting; "Holy Father, I am chancellor of my diocese," the next said, and then knelt to kiss the ring.
>
> Well, reported my brother priest from St. Louis, as Pope John came to him he felt rather lowly, for, so he thought, his priestly work was hardly as exalted as those nine before him, so he almost inaudibly whispered, "Holy Father, all I am is a parish priest."

Whereupon, to his consternation, Pope John genuflected before him, kissed his hands, and stood to say, "That's the greatest priestly work of all!"[63]

CHAPTER 19

ORDINATION DAY

There is one Sunday morning that I will never forget for the rest of my life. It is the Sunday morning that I woke up the day after being ordained a Catholic priest.

I remember opening my eyes and thinking, "Oh my goodness. I am a priest. I was ordained a priest yesterday. My soul is ontologically changed into the image of Jesus Christ and that change will last forever. I will be a priest forever! I can hear Confessions and forgive sins. And this morning, I am going to celebrate Mass for the first time. I am going to offer the sacrifice of Jesus Christ and confect bread and wine into the very Body and Blood of Christ. I better get up, say my prayers, and get myself a cup of coffee!"

The day of ordination and the day of his first Mass are two of the greatest days in the life of every priest. Priestly formation is a long, arduous process than can last eight years or longer, and it all culminates on a Saturday morning in late May or early June in the diocesan cathedral — with the man lying face down on the marble floor, praying to be a good and faithful priest.

Ordination is a Day but Priesthood is Forever

In Pre-Cana courses, it is stressed to a young couple preparing for marriage: "The wedding is a day; the marriage is a lifetime." It is an expression to remind the couple that they should carefully prepare to live the sacrament of marriage and not spend all of their time preparing for the one-hour wedding ceremony. The same is true for those to be ordained priests. The ordination is a day, but priesthood is forever. Both preparations must be made, but the second is much more important and extensive. I have described in earlier chapters some of the formation the

Church gives the men who would be priests. Now I want to briefly describe the months, weeks and days leading up to the day of ordination and some things about that very solemn Mass.

Mass and Penance Practicums

The last year of seminary is the most enjoyable and exciting of all the years, in my opinion. Formation becomes very practical. The seminarian has already been ordained a transitional deacon and he is usually serving on weekends in a local parish, preaching the homily, baptizing, and witnessing marriages. He has just returned from spending a summer in a parish acting as a deacon. He knows that he is moving quickly toward his goal. Usually in the fourth year of theology the man takes the Mass and Penance practicums to practice celebrating these sacraments. Many seminaries have "practice chapels," or "deacon chapels," where the men practice celebrating Mass. Some even have video systems so that the deacons can review their performance, note errors, and correct them.

"If it's in black, say it. If it's in red, do it!" This expression describes how to use the Sacramentary, the large red book which a priest uses to celebrate Mass. The Sacramentary has the words printed in black and the rubrics printed in red. The men love doing practice Masses and many do one every day in their last months before ordination.

The Penance practicum class is also enjoyable as the seminarians hear one another's practice Confessions, then give good spiritual counsel, a penance, and absolution. In the seminary where I work, the fourth-year men know that at any time during their final semester, any faculty member can walk up to them and say, "I feel sinful. Absolve me." And the man must be able to say the words of sacramental absolution from memory! They are also required to have memorized the words for the sacrament of Anointing of the Sick and the Apostolic Pardon (a special plenary indulgence that a priest can give a person who is dying). By the last year of seminary, the men will have had practicums in all the other sacraments as well—Baptism, Marriage, Anointing of the Sick—everything except Holy Orders and Confirmation, the two sacraments reserved for bishops. Often when I stop a man in the hall and ask to make a practice Confession, he will say, "Okay, Father, I will absolve you. But remember that I am not ordained yet. I'm still shooting blanks."

Called by the Church

A fourth-year seminarian must write a letter to his bishop petitioning to be ordained a priest. This letter is written in the seminarian's own handwriting and signed. It is sent to the bishop, accompanied by the seminarian's own self-evaluation and the evaluation and recommendation of the seminary formation team and rector. The bishop will then send a dismissorial letter to the seminarian, formally calling him to priesthood. Receiving this letter is an exciting day and many seminarians tape it to their doors so as to share the news with their seminarian brothers. Once this letter has been received, and not before, the seminarian may send out invitations to his ordination.

Canonical Retreat

Canon 1039 stipulates that before a man can be ordained a deacon or priest, he must make a retreat lasting a minimum of five days. In the final year of studies, this retreat is planned carefully. Some men make their "canonical retreat" with the seminary community, since every seminary has a retreat of this length at least once per year, but others go away for a special retreat. Receiving the sacrament of Holy Orders, being ordained a priest forever, is certainly not something to undertake lightly. The canonical retreat helps the man to reflect with Jesus one final time about his vocation, before the laying on of hands.

Preparing for the Ordination Day

The last year of seminary is also the time when preparations must be made for the ordination itself. Typically a man works with the other seminarians who will be ordained that day to select hymns, Scripture readings, lectors, and gift bearers. The bishop's master of ceremonies is usually in charge of all aspects of the ceremony, but he seeks the input of the ordinandi. Invitations must be ordered and mailed. Most priests have an ordination card printed for people to take home, usually with a religious image on one side and the priest's name and ordination date on the other. It almost always says at the bottom, "Please pray for me!"

Depending on their financial resources, or those of their family, some priests will purchase a new chalice or have a beautiful older chalice refurbished. It will be inscribed with his name and ordination day. This is certainly not required, since every parish has a number of chalices available, but some priests prefer to have their own. Some also will purchase a first Mass vestment. Most of these things are given to the new priest as gifts by their family and friends. Finally, there is usually some kind of a reception or supper for family and guests, similar to a wedding banquet or celebration. Once again, these things are not required and traditions differ from culture to culture and country to country. An ordination celebration does not have to cost a fortune—and it should not. But it is a great day when a man is ordained a priest of Jesus Christ; people want to celebrate!

The Rite of Ordination

The ordinandi has processed into the cathedral and he is seated with his family in the first pew, vested in a white alb and his deacon stole. Immediately after the proclamation of the Gospel, the man (or men) to be ordained is called forward. The Deacon of the Word says: "Let those to be ordained priests come forward. John Michael O'Quinn." The man replies, "Present," and steps forward. Each man to be ordained is called forward. It is usually the vocation director who speaks next. Referring to the bishop, who is seated on his cathedra, he says:

> **Vocation Director:** Most Reverend Father, holy mother Church asks you to ordain these, our brothers, to the responsibility of the priesthood.

> **Bishop:** Do you know them to be worthy?

> **Vocation Director:** After inquiry among the Christian people and upon the recommendation of those responsible, I testify that they have been found worthy.

> **Bishop:** Relying on the help of the Lord God and our Savior Jesus Christ, we choose these, our brothers, for the Order of the Priesthood.

All present say "Thanks be to God." The people of God are often invited at this time to show their approval and a thunderous applause ensues! The bishop has given the formal call of the Church. Now, finally, this man *knows* that he is called to become a priest. It has been confirmed in his heart through prayer and spiritual direction. It has been confirmed by the seminary formation team, the rector, by the people and pastors of his various assignments, by his vocation director, and now finally and most profoundly, by his bishop. He has been called by God and by the Church. He knows that his God pre-determined vocation is priesthood. Often the bishop has to ask the people to stop the applause or it would continue for several minutes. The people of God sense that this is a very powerful moment.

After the bishop gives a homily and instruction to the candidates, the ordination rite proceeds. The bishop examines the men about their freedom and readiness for ordination by asking them several questions which the men answer, "I do." It is interesting and noteworthy that the men are not asked to make the promise of celibacy and prayer in the Liturgy of the Hours, because they already have made these promises at their diaconate ordination. However, the men are asked to *repeat* their promise of obedience, which they also made at diaconate! The men now kneel in front of the bishop one by one, and they place their folded hands between the hands of the bishop.

Bishop: Do you promise respect and obedience to me and my successors?

Candidates: I do

Bishop: May God who has begun the good work in you bring it to fulfillment.

I consider these last words some of the most profound in the rite of ordination, probably because I work in priestly formation. After many years of intense priestly formation, on the day of ordination, the Church is declaring that God has only *just begun* the good work he is doing in this priest! This man will leave the cathedral a Catholic priest, but God will continue to work in and through him, forming him more and more into the image of Jesus Christ. And the priest will understand that he will remain in formation throughout his life. As we say to our seminarians: "Ordination is not emancipation from formation."

Finally, the ordinandi are asked to prostrate themselves on the floor, lying face down on the marble. The congregation is asked to kneel and the Litany of Saints is sung. The Church is asking the intercession of all the saints in heaven, for the moment has come—a man is to be ordained a priest. Immediately afterward, with the people of God still kneeling, the ordinandi arise from the floor and kneel before the bishop. In silence, the bishop lays his hands on their heads (the essential *matter* of priestly ordination). Every priest present then processes forward in turn and lays his hands on the ordinandi's head also, a sign of the unity of the presbyterate. The final essential part of the rite of ordination is the prayer of consecration by the bishop (the *form* of priest-ly ordination). When the people say "Amen" after this prayer, the man is a priest of Jesus Christ. The matter and form of the sacra-ment of Holy Orders, the things that must happen for validity, consist in these two actions.

There are several other beautiful parts of the rite before the ordination Mass ends. The bishop will anoint the hands of the new priests with sacred chrism, they will be vested by a brother priest in their priestly vestments (the stole and chasuble), and they will receive the bread and wine from the bishop which they will thenceforth be using in the offering of the sacrifice of Christ. Finally, with the bishop as celebrant, the new priest concelebrates his first Mass with all the other priests present.

Before the final blessing, the bishop kneels before the newly ordained priests to receive his first blessing. In some dioceses, the priest is also invited to give his first blessing to his parents and family.

What is the Maniturgium?

Before the liturgical revisions of the Second Vatican Council, the maniturgium was part of the rite of ordination. The Latin word means "to bind the hands." The maniturgium was a small linen strip which was used to tie the newly-ordained priest's hands together immediately after the anointing with sacred chr-ism. Later in the ceremony, they would be untied and the linen was soaked with the sweet smell of the chrism. The tradition de-veloped that this maniturgium was kept as an important memen-to and given to the mother of the priest at the end of the first Mass. When the mother died, the tradition was that her hands would be tied together with the chrism-soaked maniturgium in her casket—a powerful remembrance that she had given one of her sons to be a priest.

Though the maniturgium is no longer used in the actual or-dination rite, some priests like to maintain a form of the tradition during the ordination by simply wiping the chrism from their hands on a specially-sewn linen cloth, sometimes inscribed with the date and name of the priest. Though it is not used to bind the priest's hands, it is still given to the mother at the first Mass, with the understanding that it will be placed in her casket with her when she dies. This is not part of the ordination rite and it is certainly not required, though some priests choose to do it. Mothers like this sort of thing!

First Assignment as a Priest

At the end of the ordination Mass, in some dioceses, the bishop will announce to the entire congregation where the new priests will be assigned. Procedures differ from diocese to diocese in this regard. Some new priests learn their first assignment at the same time as the congregation, others have been previously informed and some are simply given an envelope with this information inside. It is an exciting announcement, not only because the man is now an ordained priest of Jesus Christ, but also because he knows where he will spend the next several years of his life! In the dioceses where the bishop makes this announcement at the ordination, the people usually respond with a thunderous applause, especially if they are from the parish where the new priest has been assigned.

In High Demand

One newly ordained priest told me that he could hardly remember what happened on his ordination day. From the moment he left the cathedral after being ordained a priest, he was giving first blessings, receiving congratulations, blessing objects, and hearing Confessions for many hours. There was a *prie-dieu* at the reception for people who wanted to kneel and receive the first blessing and he stood there for a long time receiving and blessing people. The line of people continued all afternoon. He told me, "I was reminded of the title of Bishop Sheen's book, *The Priest is Not*

His Own." I said to him, "Father, when you give a blessing or say the words of absolution, you're not shooting blanks anymore — and the people of God know it!"

How Much Does the Ordination Cost and Who Pays for It?

The ordination Mass itself usually does not cost the ordinandi or his family anything. The diocese pays for whatever expenses might be incurred with regard to music, flowers, and other incidentals of the liturgy. The diocese also hosts a reception for all immediately following the Mass. There are some expenses incurred regarding out-of-town guests, invitations, holy cards, and the post-ordination dinner or party, but this all depends on the preference and taste of each ordinandi. Though the celebration is every bit as solemn and important as a wedding, the costs to the family are usually significantly less for an ordination than for a wedding.

Celebrating the Mass of Thanksgiving

The newly-ordained priest concelebrates his own ordination Mass, but most priests will celebrate the Holy Mass for the first time as celebrant the day after ordination. It is normally celebrated in a man's home parish, where he grew up, or in another parish to which he has a significant attachment.

The first Mass is a great day for the priest. It is well-planned, complete with special music and flowers. Some priests ask one of their brother seminarians or a priest to function as the master of ceremonies, because the new priest may be nervous about celebrating the liturgy correctly. Usually he invites a priest friend who was instrumental in his vocational journey to give the homily at this Mass.

Why is he so nervous? Because a newly ordained priest knows that the Holy Mass is the very sacrifice of Jesus Christ, the Son of God. He can say the words of consecration in the Eucharistic Prayer and the sacrifice of Jesus will be offered and bread and wine transformed into the Body and Blood of Jesus. This priest has knelt and worshipped Jesus during Eucharistic Adoration every day for at least six years, and now the Eucharist will be confected through his own hands. Yes, a new priest is nervous at his first Mass; this is why the presence of a master of ceremonies is consoling.

Plenary Indulgence

The faithful can receive a plenary indulgence by attending the first Mass of a newly ordained priest. (If they fulfill the other conditions for a plenary indulgence: Confession, receiving Holy Communion, praying for the intentions of the Holy Father, and being truly sorry for all one's sins.) It is wonderful to receive the first blessing of a newly ordained priest and this blessing will certainly bring a person many graces, but it is attendance at the first Mass that gives one the plenary indulgence. I have seen many graces come to family members and friends by attending the ordination and first Mass of a newly ordained priest. It is a grace-filled weekend, and in many instances, people return to the sacraments and the practice of their Catholic faith as a result.

"There is nothing more perfect than the formation of a good priest"

These words were penned by St. Vincent de Paul, for whom priestly formation was very important. He realized that men have to be *formed* into good priests and this is why he spent so much time working to improve seminaries. God will not form a man into a good priest without the man's knowledge and permission—and the man must make a heroic effort. Grace builds on nature. I once attended the ordination and preached at the first Mass of a newly-ordained priest from Savannah. I said in the homily that "Priestly formation is 99.9 percent God's grace and .1 percent human effort."

After the Mass, the new priest said to me, "Father, you mean to tell me that these past six years in the seminary, working, studying and praying—all of that was only .1 percent of the process?" I replied, "Well, I'm probably over-estimating your part. It's probably less, but I realize that the .1 percent you contributed was an enormous effort. And I am very proud of you. Thank you for saying yes to Jesus."

As we walked out of the sacristy after the first Mass, I said to him, "So where are you going now?" He looked at me and said, "I'm a priest. I'm going to work, with the help of God, to save a thousand souls!"

I replied, "May God who has begun the good work in you bring it to fulfillment."

ROSARY FOR DISCERNING DIOCESAN PRIESTHOOD

For each mystery, say one Our Father, ten Hail Marys, and one Glory Be. Then end each decade with this prayer:

O God, I want to want what you want.
Help me to want to be what you want me to be.
Here I am Lord; I come to do your will.
Jesus, I love you.

The Joyful Mysteries

+ The Annunciation

"Hail Mary, full of grace, the Lord is with you" (Luke 1:28). The angel Gabriel was sent to the Blessed Virgin with an important question from God: will you become the mother of the Savior? The angel announced that it was God's will that Mary be the vehicle to bring Jesus to earth, to save his people. It was clearly a request, not a command. It was a calling, a vocation. Mary was understandably troubled to be visited by the angel of God: "Do not be afraid Mary, for you have found favor with God" (Luke 1:30). The most pure, trusting Virgin asked for a little more information: "How can this be since I do not know man?" (Luke 1:34) But she realized that it would all become clear in time, in God's time. The angel waited for Mary's answer. God is waiting for your answer.

If you are called to become a priest, you will be a powerful vehicle to bring Jesus to earth every day in the Holy Mass and the Eucharist. If this is your vocation, then you must give an answer. Even though you do not understand why God would call you, even if you have many fears and doubts, trust him. It is good to ask for more information; follow the Blessed Virgin's way. But remember, the angel is waiting. God is waiting! "I am the handmaid of the Lord. Let it be done unto me according to thy word" (Luke 1:38).

Holy Archangel Gabriel, pray for me that I may say yes to the will of God.

The purpose of a priest is to bring people to Jesus and Jesus to people.

365

+ The Visitation

Elizabeth cries out, "Blessed are you among women and blessed is the fruit of your womb" (Luke 1:42). All generations will call the Virgin Mary blessed both because she was called by God to bring Jesus to earth and because she said yes. Immediately after receiving Jesus herself, Mary knew she must bring him to others. Elizabeth was very old and John the Baptist was very young (an unborn child), but both said yes to God in their turn. Every vocation is different. Every vocation is a mystery. At the sound of Mary's voice, St. John the Baptist leapt for joy while still in his mother's womb, answering God's call for him early and enthusiastically! Everyone is filled with great joy during the Visitation.

You too will be called blessed in the Kingdom if you say yes to your vocation. If you are called to be a diocesan priest, you will spend your life bringing people the only hope that will ever fill the emptiness within them: Jesus. This will bring great joy to both you and them! Whether you are old or young, answer now! To be filled with Jesus as Mary was (and as you are), will always move us to bring him to others. Are you doing this now?

St. Elizabeth and St. John the Baptist, pray for me that I may say yes to the will of God.

The purpose of a priest is to bring people to Jesus and Jesus to people.

+ The Birth of Jesus

The Blessed Mother and St. Joseph could have complained to God: "Is this how you treat your friends?" Nine months pregnant, in labor, after a long ride on a donkey, the time to give birth to the Son of God had arrived—and there was no private place provided. Mary and Joseph continued to trust and wait, though they also did their part. Jesus was born according to God's perfect will, humbly, in a stable. The Savior has come. The salvation of the world is upon us. The angels are singing. The shepherds marvel. The Christ child sleeps. How can anyone doubt God's love? "And Mary kept all these things, reflecting on them in her heart" (Luke 2:19).

St. Joseph went about knocking on doors, asking for a room, praying, trying to trust. God can't drive a parked car! God will never lead you where his grace cannot sustain you. He is faithful and he will provide. Difficulty is always a part of discerning one's vocation. You have to keep trusting and waiting, even when life is hard and things are unclear, but you must also do your part. You must knock on doors, gather information, and keep moving. The time came for the child to be born... there was no more delaying. Has the time come for you to answer God's call? Reflect in your heart.

Baby Jesus, please give me the grace. St. Joseph, pray for me that I may say yes to the will of God.

The purpose of a priest is to bring people to Jesus and Jesus to people.

+ The Presentation

"Behold this child is destined for the fall and rise of many in Israel, and to be a sign that will be contradicted (and you yourself a sword will pierce) so that the thoughts of many hearts will be revealed" (Luke 2:34-35). Simeon had been promised that he would not die until he had seen the Savior, and God kept that promise. Taking the Christ Child in his arms, he prophesied that not everyone would welcome Jesus and the Christian message. He also foretold that the Blessed Mother would suffer intently as the perfect disciple of her Son. Jesus is *Lumen Gentium*, the light of the nations, though some people will harden their hearts and choose to remain in their darkness. Yes, the presence of Jesus in the world reveals the "thoughts of men's hearts." Every person must choose to be with him or against him.

The Gospel must be preached so that people can come to know Jesus. Most of the world today has never heard the Gospel. How tragic that most people living today have never known the love and mercy of Jesus! Will they die without ever having seen him or known him? Who shall go to them? If you are called to be a priest, you will bring Jesus and his Gospel to the world. He is the answer to which every human heart is the question. Is Jesus revealing the thoughts of your heart regarding your vocation?

St. Simeon, pray for me that I may say yes to the will of God.

The purpose of a priest is to bring people to Jesus and Jesus to people.

+ Finding in the Temple

"After three days, they found him in the temple, sitting in the midst of the teachers, listening to them and asking them questions, and all who heard him were astounded at his understanding and his an-

367

swers" (Luke 2:46-47). Poor Mary and Joseph looked for Jesus in sorrow for three days, terrified that they might have lost him. Jesus said: "Why were you looking for me? Did you not know that I must be in my Father's house?" (2:49) If only everyone were looking for Jesus as Mary and Joseph did, seeking him as if their very lives depended on finding him. Jesus is the key to eternal life! And he has chosen to bring his teaching and grace through the sacraments to all people through the Holy Catholic Church.

Listen to your heart. If you are called to be a diocesan priest, then your place is in the Father's house and you must be there. Because a priest is present at Mass every Sunday, the people can come searching for Jesus and they find him, powerfully present in the Word and in the Eucharist. They find his mercy in Confession and they see his care and kindness in your priestly hands. When you read the words, "Did you not know that I *must be* in my Father's house?" does something resonate in your heart?

Blessed Mother, pray for me that I may say yes to the will of God.

The purpose of a priest is to bring people to Jesus and Jesus to people.

The Sorrowful Mysteries

+ The Agony in the Garden

Jesus prayed, "My Father, if it is possible, let this cup pass from me; yet not as I will but as you will" (Matthew 26:42). Jesus prayed intently not only to know the Father's will but to have the strength to do it. He made the first Holy Hour in the Garden of Gethsemane, beseeching his apostles to do the same: "My heart is sorrowing, even unto death. Can you not stay awake and watch with me for one hour?" Jesus was suffering greatly and he was asking only that his closest friends stay with him and watch. "He was in such agony and he prayed so fervently that his sweat became like drops of blood falling on the ground" (Luke 22:44).

Discerning a vocation to diocesan priesthood can be an agony. Many men have prayed, "My Father, if it is possible, let this cup pass from me..." Perhaps to be a priest would not be your first choice. But a vocation is not about what you want. Keep watch with Jesus to hear what he wants! Praying before the Blessed Sacrament will be an important way for you to come to know the will of God. It will strengthen you to say yes to the Father's will. As you kneel with Jesus in his agony, pray with him: "My Father, if it is not possible that this cup pass without my drinking it, your will be done." An angel from heaven comes to strengthen you.

Holy Guardian Angel, pray for me that I may say yes to the will of God.

The purpose of a priest is to bring people to Jesus and Jesus to people.

+ The Scourging at the Pillar

"Then he released Barabbas to them, but after he had Jesus scourged, he handed him over to be crucified" (Matthew 27:26). Already Jesus is saving others through the shedding of his blood. Barabbas did not deserve to be saved, yet then again, neither do we. "The Son of God loved me and gave himself for me" (Galatians 2:20). Jesus poured out his blood for me. The blood of Jesus Christ is easily the most precious thing in the universe! It has the power to give everlasting life. Before it, the demons shriek and flee. "For one drop of his blood which for sinners was spilt, is sufficient to cleanse the whole world from its guilt."[64]

If you are called to be a priest, you will feed people with the very body and blood of Jesus. They cannot be fed *except* through the hands of a priest! If you become a priest, you will handle the most precious thing in the universe. The blood of Jesus has the power to give everlasting life. Kneel with Jesus at the scourging and ask him for the gift of generosity. Pray for the gift of mercy for Barabbas, for yourself, and for all others who do not deserve to be saved. "And the whole people said in reply: 'May his blood be upon us and upon our children'" (Matthew 27:25). This ancient curse is now our prayer.

Holy Souls in Purgatory, pray for me that I may say yes to the will of God.

The purpose of a priest is to bring people to Jesus and Jesus to people.

+ The Crowning with Thorns

"Weaving a crown out of thorns, they placed it on his head, and a reed in his right hand. And kneeling before him, they mocked him saying, 'Hail, King of the Jews.' They spat upon him and took the reed and kept striking him on the head." (Matthew 27:29-30). One day, when Je-

369

sus comes again on the clouds of heaven, to judge the living and the dead, every knee will bend and every head will bow and every tongue will proclaim that he is Lord! That day will be a day unsurpassed in glory in the entire history of the world. Come Lord Jesus! But today is a different day. The same God of infinite glory has been beaten bloody, crowned with thorns, and spat upon. Jesus is a patient God. Look at his magnanimity, his greatness of soul. He endures all this, saying nothing. Though one glance would annihilate the entire Roman army, he will not use his infinite power to protect himself.

Jesus suffered humiliation and derision as he worked out his vocation to do the Father's will, so you should expect nothing less. If you are called to become a priest, some will ridicule you and say that you are wasting your life. Even your family may deride you. Be like Jesus and show mercy to those who persecute you. Pray for them. Jesus died for them too, and he knows that your priesthood will affect them powerfully. "Father forgive them; they know not what they do" (Luke 23:43). Do not be afraid of those who scoff at your vocation. Jesus may not use his infinite power to protect himself, but he will use it to protect you! Trust him.

All holy priests in heaven, pray for me that I may say yes to the will of God.

The purpose of a priest is to bring people to Jesus and Jesus to people.

+ The Carrying of the Cross

"And when they had mocked him, they stripped him of the purple cloak, dressed him in his own clothes, and led him out to crucify him. They pressed into service a certain passer-by, Simon of Cyrene… to carry his cross" (Luke 23:26). St. Simon of Cyrene *just happened to be passing by*. Though in reality, it was all part of God's plan. Simon was called by God to help Jesus in his moment of agony; to literally walk beside him and support him, because the cross was impossibly heavy in his weakened state.

The people of God carry very heavy crosses of all shapes and sizes. Carrying their crosses is their way to heaven, but sometimes they cry out and fall; the cross is just too heavy. A priest is a Simon of Cyrene for these people. He goes to them in the hospitals, the nursing homes, and the prisons to pray for them, to console them and to lighten their burdens. If you are called to be a priest, you will be a Simon of Cyrene for others. "Whatsoever you do for one of these least brothers of mine, you do for me" (Matthew 25:40). Perhaps you *are just passing by*, minding your own business, and are being pressed into service... God may be calling you to become a priest! If so, what a blessed man you are!

St. Simon of Cyrene, pray for me that I may say yes to the will of God.

The purpose of a priest is to bring people to Jesus and Jesus to people.

+ The Crucifixion and Death

"They brought him to the place of Golgotha (Place of the Skull). They gave him wine drugged with myrrh, but he did not take it. Then they crucified him and divided his garments by casting lots for them to see what each should take" (Mark 15:22-24). St. John, the beloved disciple, was the only one who stayed with the Blessed Mother at the foot of the cross. All the other disciples fled. The Son of God spoke to him these wonderful words, in the very moment of the redemption of the world: "'Behold your mother.' And from that hour, the disciple took her into his home."

If you are called to become a priest, you will boldly proclaim the mystery of faith: "Christ has died, Christ has risen, Christ will come again." Keeping our eyes fixed on the cross always provides the strength needed to do the will of God. The temptation is so strong to run away like the apostles, not to embrace it, not to accept the will of God. Any Christianity without the cross is a sterile heresy which saves no one! The holy priest, St. John, because he stayed close to Mary, stayed close to the cross also.

St. John, Apostle and Priest, pray for me that I may say yes to the will of God.

The purpose of a priest is to bring people to Jesus and Jesus to people.

The Glorious Mysteries

+ The Resurrection

Jesus asked Mary Magdalene, "Woman, why are you weeping? Who are you looking for?" (John 20:15) Jesus Christ has risen! The great feast of Christianity, the cause of our joy, is the Resurrection of Christ.

Jesus has won the infinite victory, the victory over sin and death. The war is won; all that is left now is to fight the smaller battles until Jesus comes—but these battles must be fought, for they still can be lost. Jesus has called certain men, his priests, to lead this charge. "Peace be with you. As the Father has sent me, so I send you. And when he had said this, he breathed on them and said to them: 'Receive the Holy Spirit. Whose sins you forgive are forgiven them, and whose sins you retain are retained'" (John 20:23).

If Jesus is calling you to be a priest, you will lead an entire parish of Catholic Christians into the battle for holiness. You will be a living Easter candle, bringing the light, the love, and the power of Jesus to the world. Do not be intimidated. All people are looking for Jesus, even if they do not realize it. The Lord said: "Without me, you can do nothing." The priest functions *in persona Christi capitis,* in the person of Jesus Christ, risen, the head of the Church. The sacred power given to a priest at ordination is none other than the very presence of the risen Savior! And there is no snatching out of his hands. The war is won. Preaching Jesus Christ, crucified and risen, is our victory call. Christ has risen! Alleluia. Do not be afraid.

St. Mary Magdalene, pray for me that I may say yes to the will of God.

The purpose of a priest is to bring people to Jesus and Jesus to people.

+ The Ascension of Jesus

"Then he led the apostles out as far as Bethany, raised his hands, and blessed them. As he blessed them, he parted from them and was taken up to heaven. They did him homage and then returned to Jerusalem with great joy" (Luke 24:50-52). After his resurrection, Jesus spent forty days with the apostles, teaching and forming them to be heralds of the Gospel, preparing them for the day when they would be sent out. He promised to send the Holy Spirit to give them strength. After the forty days were over, the Lord ascended to heaven, where he is seated at the right hand of the Father, from which he will come to judge the living and the dead.

Jesus said, "When I am raised up from the earth, I will draw all people to myself" (John 12:32). Raised up on the cross, and then raised up into heaven, the Lord has begun this work of drawing people to himself, and he often does this through his priests. People see Jesus in their priests and are drawn to him! The people of God often can see that a priest is an *alter christus* even more so than the priest himself.

If you are called to be a priest, trust that Jesus will arrange for you to be properly formed and instructed before you are sent out to teach and preach to others. Trust in the grace he provides through the seminary. The Holy Spirit will come upon you at your ordination and you will be strengthened and empowered to do the work of a priest.

St. Peter, St. Paul and all the Apostles, pray for me that I may say yes to the will of God.

The purpose of a priest is to bring people to Jesus and Jesus to people.

+ The Descent of the Holy Spirit

"And suddenly there came from the sky a noise like a strong driving wind, and it filled the entire house…Then there appeared to them tongues as of fire, which parted and came to rest on each one of them. And they were filled with the Holy Spirit and began to speak in different tongues" (Acts 2:1-4). Mary and the apostles received the Holy Spirit and they were clothed with power from on high. As the Holy Spirit descended, the Body of Christ, the Church, came to life and the first priests were sent to work! There were three thousand converts that first day (Acts 2:41).

If you are called to be a priest, the grace of Holy Orders will strengthen you to do whatever is needed to build the Kingdom. The choir will sing *Veni Creator Spiritus* as the bishop lays his hands on your head, and the Holy Spirit rushes down upon you with great power. God will enable you to do what a priest does, through his natural gifts to you, through your seminary training, and through the supernatural grace of Holy Orders. You will be amazed at God's power working in you (the *sacra potestas*) as you begin to teach and preach and forgive the sins of others. Don't trust in yourself! That is frightening. Trust in Jesus. The Holy Spirit is the Sanctifier and the Advocate. Trust that the Holy Spirit of God will give you the grace to do whatever he asks you to do, and to do it well!

Holy Spirit, strengthen me that I may say yes to the will of God.

The purpose of a priest is to bring people to Jesus and Jesus to people.

+ The Assumption of Mary into Heaven

At the end of her earthly life, the Blessed Virgin Mary was taken up body and soul into heaven, surrounded by the angels. This should not be surprising, since Jesus promised all of us that our earthly bodies will rise from their graves, glorified and beautiful, when he comes again! For Mary, this great miracle of resurrection has already happened, due to her sinless conception and life. The rest of us will have to die, be buried, and wait for the Lord to come. Our Blessed Mother prays for us throughout our lives, and at the moment of our death. She will continue to guide and protect us from her place in heaven until the day of Resurrection.

The Blessed Mother's intercession is often a pivotal moment in many vocations to diocesan priesthood. God uses her powerfully in the process of discernment, and she will help you too! Ask her to pray for you right now. Ask her to pray that you will know whether or not God wants you to be a priest, and that if he does, you will have the grace to follow your vocation. She is in heaven in glory united in body and soul, as we will one day be. She has the ear of God. She is the Mother of Priests.

Our Lady of the Assumption, pray for me that I may say yes to the will of God.

The purpose of a priest is to bring people to Jesus and Jesus to people.

+ The Coronation of the Blessed Virgin Mary, Queen of Heaven and Earth

From all eternity, it was the plan of God that Mary be the Queen of heaven and earth. It was all part of her vocation. God called her to be the mother of Jesus. He permitted her to care for him and he desired that she be his first disciple—and the only perfect disciple. He willed that she faithfully stand beneath the cross and that her heart be pierced with a sword of sorrow. It was God's plan that Mary be assumed body and soul into heaven and that she be crowned Mother and Queen. She did not ask for any of this! She simply loved God, prayed, and sought his will. God called her, and she humbly said yes.

God is also calling you. From all eternity, God has known to which vocation you would be called and he has created you with that in mind. Your vocation, like every vocation, will have both joys and sorrows. If you are called to become a priest, you might say, "I did not ask for this. God called me. He asked me." Nonetheless, you must give an answer. Imitate the humility and docility of the Blessed Virgin Mary. God will reward all of those who generously say yes to his call with a crown in heaven.

Regina Coeli (Queen of Heaven), pray for me that I may say yes to the will of God.

The purpose of a priest is to bring people to Jesus and Jesus to people.

The Luminous Mysteries

+ The Baptism of Jesus

John the Baptist said: "I need to be baptized by you and yet you are coming to me?" (Matthew 3:14) "After Jesus was baptized, he came up from the water and behold, the heavens were opened for him and he saw the spirit of God descending like a dove and coming upon him. And a voice came from the heavens saying, 'This is my beloved son, with whom I am well pleased'" (Matthew 3:16-17). Jesus was baptized not because he needed baptism but because we needed it! Before he began his mission, he showed us what is necessary for us to begin ours. When you were baptized, the Holy Spirit descended upon you with sanctifying grace; with faith, hope and love. You became a beloved son of God, and God's plan for your life and mission began.

If you are called to be a priest, you will baptize hundreds, maybe thousands. You will be the instrument by which people become beloved sons and daughters of God, temples of the Holy Spirit, and heirs to everlasting life. Baptism is God's plan for the salvation of his people, and he uses his priests to execute this plan. What a privilege it is to be God's instrument in this way! Like St. John the Baptist, you may not feel worthy: "I need to be baptized by you and yet you are coming to me?" You may say, "I am not worthy to be a priest." Jesus said in reply, "Allow it now, for thus it is fitting for us to fulfill all righteousness" (Matthew 3:15). Are you listening to the voice coming from the heavens with regard to your vocation?

St. John the Baptist, pray for me that I may say yes to the will of God.

The purpose of a priest is to bring people to Jesus and Jesus to people.

+ The Wedding Feast at Cana

"When the wine ran short, the mother of Jesus said to him, 'They have no wine.' And Jesus said to her, Woman, how does your concern affect me? My hour has not yet com" (John 2:4). Jesus did his first miracle at a wedding feast, at the request of his mother. She said to the servers, "Do whatever he tells you" (John 2:5). Jesus changed the water into wine—a huge amount of wine—as an eschatological sign that the Kingdom of God is upon us. From that day, "his disciples began to believe in him."

If you are called to become a priest, you will witness many marriages. You will have the privilege of catechizing young couples on God's plan for marriage, sexuality, and family life. You will teach them how to grow in faith together. A wedding day is one of the greatest days in a young couple's life, and a priest is a big part of it! You will also witness many miracles as a priest, as you see grace move in people's lives. You will watch with amazement as God gently draws people to himself. But are you called to become a priest? *Has your hour come to make a move?* The Blessed Mother is looking at you, smiling gently and pointing to Jesus. She says: "Do whatever he tells you."

Holy Mary, pray for me that I may say yes to the will of God.

The purpose of a priest is to bring people to Jesus and Jesus to people.

+ The Proclamation of the Kingdom of God

"After John had been arrested, Jesus came to Galilee proclaiming the Gospel of God: 'This is the time of fulfillment. The Kingdom of God is at hand. Repent, and believe in the Gospel'" (Mark 1:14-15). It was immediately after Jesus began to proclaim the Kingdom that he called his first disciples: "Come after me and I will make you fishers of men" (Mark 1:17). They immediately left their nets and their father to follow him! The call of Jesus is powerful and it is urgent. This is the time of fulfillment. Repentance means changing your heart, or rather, giving God permission to change your heart.

If you are called to become a priest, you will be charged with the *primum officium*, the primary duty of a priest, to preach the Gospel. With God's grace and your priestly formation, you will learn how to preach and teach about Jesus Christ and his holy Catholic Church. You will stand in the pulpit every Sunday and explain the mysteries of the Kingdom of God to many people. Jesus said, "He who obeys these things and teaches others to obey them will be called great in the Kingdom of God" (Matthew 5:19). The call of Jesus is powerful and it is urgent. Repent! Give God permission to change your heart to be truly open to his will. "In his will is your peace," wrote Dante. "Come follow me, and I will make you fishers of men." This is the time of fulfillment. The Kingdom must be proclaimed!

Jesus, my great High Priest and Lord, help me that I may say yes to the will of God.

The purpose of a priest is to bring people to Jesus and Jesus to people.

+ The Transfiguration

"Jesus took Peter, James and John and led them up a high mountain by themselves. And he was transfigured before them; his face shone like the sun and his clothes became white as light. And behold, Moses and Elijah appeared to them... behold, a bright cloud cast a shadow over them, then from the cloud came a voice that said, This is my beloved Son, with whom I am well pleased. Listen to him" (Matthew 17:1-2, 5) Ever since Adam and Eve disobeyed God, we have been disfigured by original sin. Ever since Jesus came and obeyed God, we have been transfigured by grace. One day, we shall shine like the sun with Jesus in heavenly glory, and we should keep our eyes fixed on the prize. But in the meantime, as Moses and Elijah remind us, we must carry our cross up the hill of Calvary.

If you are called to become a priest, you will have the privilege of being with people at some of the most joyful times of their lives: the birth of a child, baptisms, weddings, and anniversaries. But you will also walk with them in the valleys of suffering, sickness and death. A priest is a constant reminder to God's people that their treasure is in heaven. God's grace will transfigure a dysfunctional and disfigured people into the image of his priestly Son. The Father is speaking to you now from the cloud, for he knows that you are discerning: "This is my beloved Son. Listen to him."

Moses and Elijah, pray for me that I may say yes to the will of God.

The purpose of a priest is to bring people to Jesus and Jesus to people.

+ The Last Supper

"Jesus took bread, said the blessing, broke it, and gave it to his disciples saying, 'This is my body which will be given for you. Do this in memory of me.' And likewise the cup after they had eaten, saying, 'This cup is the new covenant in my blood, which will be shed for you'" (Luke 22:19-20). At the last supper before he died, Jesus ordained the apostles the very first priests. He commissioned them to offer the holy Mass and to feed his people with word and sacrament by saying, "Do this in memory of me." Jesus also showed the depth of his love and humility by washing the feet of his disciples, modeling that a priest is called to serve others, not to be served by them. After washing their feet, he asked, "Do you understand what I have done for you?" St. Peter did not understand. He said: "You shall never wash my feet" (John 13:8).

If you are called to become a priest, you will offer the sacrifice of Jesus every day in holy Mass and you will feed people with his body and blood. It is a tremendous honor and privilege to stand *in persona christi capitis* at the altar of God. Even though priesthood is an honor and privilege, men are not called to priesthood for that reason. Jesus taught us to serve others, humbly and simply. A priest shows people God's love for them by laying down his life to serve them, as Jesus did. Perhaps you have come to the realization that God is calling you to become a priest. If so, the Lord asks: "Do you understand what I have just done for you? Do you understand the honor that has been bestowed upon you?"

St. Peter, please pray for me that I may say yes to the will of God.

The purpose of a priest is to bring people to Jesus and Jesus to people.

O God, I want to want what you want.
Help me to want to be what you want me to be.
Here I am Lord; I come to do your will.
Jesus, I love you.

NOTES

[1] Widely attributed to Padre Pio

[2] John Rosengren, "Father Stan Rother: American Martyr in Guatemala," Website of The Franciscans and St. Anthony Messenger Press, http://www.americancatholic.org/Messenger/Jul2006/Feature1.asp

[3] l'Abbé Bernard Nodet, "Le Sacerdoce, c'est l'amour du cœur de Jésus," in *Le Curé d'Ars. Sa Pensée – Son Cœur*, éd. Xavier Mappus, (Foi Vivante, 1966), 101

[4] Ibid., 100

[5] Fr. John Ciahak, "Priestly Hands," www.qvdays.org/linksandarticles/priestlyhands.htm

[6] l'Abbé Bernard Nodet, "Le Sacerdoce, c'est l'amour du cœur de Jésus," in *Le Curé d'Ars. Sa Pensée – Son Cœur*, éd. Xavier Mappus, (Foi Vivante, 1966), 105

[7] Jacobus de Voragine (1275), *The Life of Saint Francis of Assisi in The Golden Legend Volume 5*, Trans. William Caxton (1483), in the Medieval Sourcebook, http://www.fordham.edu/halsall/basis/goldenlegend/gl-vol5-francis.html

[8] Pope Benedict XVI , Pastoral visit in Poland. Address by the Holy Father Meeting with the Clergy. Warsaw Cathedral, May 25, 2006; par. 5. www.vatican.va/holy_father/benedict_xvi/speeches/2006/may/docum ents/hf_ben-xvi_spe_20060525_poland-clergy_en.html

[9] Abbé Bernard Nodet, *Le Curé d'Ars, Pensées* (Desclée de Brouwer, Foi Vivante, 2000), 97

[10] From a commencement speech by Albert Schweitzer

---

[11] Widely attributed to St. Bonaventure

[12] Pope John Paul II, General Audience, L'Osservatore Romano Weekly Edition in English, 21 September 1978, 1

[13] John Cardinal Newman, "Meditations on Christian Doctrine with a Visit to the Blessed Sacrament before Meditation, Section 2, March 7, number 2" in Meditations Part III, in *The Newman Reader*, http://www.newmanreader.org/works/meditations/meditations9.html

[14] Widely attributed to St. Augustine

[15] Widely attributed to St. Bonaventure

[16] St. Ignatius, *The Spiritual Exercises of Saint Ignatius*, trans. Anthony Mottola (New York: Doubleday, 1989), 82

[17] From a World Youth Day speech, May 13, 1984

[18] St. Catherine of Siena, *Letters of St. Catherine of Siena*, trans. Suzanne Noffke (New York: Medieval & Renaissance Texts & Studies, 1988), 149

[19] Pope Benedict XVI, *Address to the German Pilgrims Who Had Come to Rome for the Inauguration Ceremony of the Pontificate* (Monday, 25 April 2005) in Vatican Papal Archives

[20] Thomas Merton, *No Man is an Island* (New York: Harcourt Brace Jovanovich, Publishers, 1983), 131

[21] Albert Einstein, "Part One, the World as I See It" in *The World as I See It*, trans. Alan Haris (New York: The Wisdom Library, 1949), 1

[22] Pope Benedict XVI, Apostolic Journey to Munchen, Altotting and Regensburg (September 9-14, 2006). Marian Vespers with the Religious and Seminarians of Bavaria. Homily of the Holy Father. Basilica of Saint Anne, Altotting. September 11, 2006. Par. 1.

23 Thurston and Atwater, *Butler's Lives of the Saints*, vol. 4 (Westminster, Maryland: Christian Classics, 1988), 509

24 Thurston and Atwater, *Butler's Lives of the Saints*, vol. 4 (Westminster, Maryland: Christian Classics, 1988), 568

25 John Paul II, *Pastores Dabo Vobis* [I Will Give You Shepherds] (Boston, MA: St. Paul Books & Media), par. 11

26 Widely attributed to Oliver Wendell Holmes

27 Blessed Mother Teresa of Calcutta, *My Life for the Poor*, ed. Jose Luis Gozalez-Balado and Janet N. Playfoot (San Francisco: Harper and Row, Publishers, 1985), 37

28 Blessed Julian of Norwich, *Revelations of Divine Love*, trans. Grace Warrack (1901), Chap XV, http://www.ccel.org/ccel/julian/revelations.html

29 C. J. Devine, "Father Isaac Jogues: Missionary to the Iroquois" in *These Splendid Priests*, ed. James J. Walsh (New York: Books for Libraries Press, 1926), 185-200

30 Lawrence G. Lovasik, *Treasury of Catechism Stories* (Pittsburg, PA: Marian Action Publications, 1966), story 118

31 Walker Percy, "Commencement Address at St. Joseph Abbey and Seminary College 1983" in *Signposts in a Strange Land* (The Noonday Press, 1991), 316-325

32www.vatican.va/archive/hist_councils/ii_vatican_council/documents/vat-ii_decree_19651207_presbyterorum-ordinis_en.html

33 St. Jerome, *Commentary on Isaiah*, Prol.: PL 24,17.

34 Aristotle, *Nicomachean Ethics*, trans., J. A. K. Thomson (1953), revised, Hugh Tredennick (New York: Penguin Books, 1976) 249

---

35 St. Bernard of Clairvaux, Epistle 87, par. 7

36 Thomas Aquinas, *Summa Theologica*, I, 20, 2

37 Blaise Pascal, *Pensees*, trans. W.F. Trotter "Pascal's Pensees and the Provincial letters" (New York: The Modern Library, 1941), 90

38 St. Ignatius, *The Spiritual Exercises of Saint Ignatius*, trans. Anthony Mottola (New York: Doubleday, 1989), 132

39 John Paul 11, Message for the XXX World Day of Prayer for Vocations at Castle Candolfo, 8 September 1992 Nativity of the Blessed Virgin Mary (Section 5) http://www.vatican.va/holy_father/john_paul_ii/messages/vocations/documents/hf_jp-ii_mes_08091992_world-day-for-vocations_en.html

40 Pierre Coste, *The Life and Work of St. Vincent de Paul*, (Newman Press, 1952), 14

41 Ibid., 14

42 Widely attributed to Thomas Merton

43 Widely attributed to Will Rogers

44 T.S. Eliot, *Murder in the Cathedral* (Orlando, FL: Harcourt Brace Jovanovich, 1963), 44

45 Second Vatican Ecumenical Council, *Gaudium et Spes* [Pastoral Constitution on the Church in the Modern World], par. 48

46 St. Ignatius, *The Spiritual Exercises of Saint Ignatius*, trans. Anthony Mottola (New York: Doubleday, 1989), 37

47 Dante, *Paradiso*, Canto III, line 85

48 Sophocles, "Chorus" Acrisius 61, *Sophocles Fragments*, ed. Trans. Hugh Lloyd- Jones (Cambridge: Harvard University Press, 1996), 29

[49] Widely attributed to Marie Curie

[50] Saint Teresa of Avila, *The Life of St. Teresa of Jesus, of the Order of Our Lady of Carmel*, trans. David Lewis (New York: Benziger Bros., 1904), Chapter X., http://www.ccel.org/ccel/teresa/life.html

[51] St. Augustine, *Homilies on the Gospel of St. John Tractate XXIX*, Chapter VII, 14-18, article 6

[52] Frederick M. Jones, *Alphonsus Liguori: Selected Writings* (New York: Paulist Press, 1999), 20

[53] Erasmus, "Letter to Ulrich von Hutten dated 23 July, 1517, Antwerp" in *The Epistles of Erasmus*, Vol. 3, trans. Francis Morgan Nichols (New York: Russell & Russell Inc., 1962), 393-4

[54] See St. Thomas Aquinas, *Summa Theologica*, IIa IIae q. 151 a 4

[55] St. Augustine, *Confessions*, trans. Henry Chadwick (Oxford: Oxford University Press 1992), 145

[56] St. Augustine, *In Jo. ev.* 12,13:PL 35,1491

[57] St. Thomas Aquinas, *Summa Theologica*, II, II, 152

[58] Ignacio Larranaga, *Brother Francis of Assisi*, trans. Jennie M. Ibarra (Sherbrooke, QC: Mediaspaul, 1994), 213

[59] St. Thérèse of Lisieux, *The Story of a Soul: the Autobiography of St. Therese of Lisieux*, ed. Rev. T.N. Taylor (London: Burns, Oates & Washbourne, 1912; 8th ed., 1922)

[60] Thomas Aquinas, *Summa Theologica*, IIa IIac q. 47 a. 6. Reply to objection 3

[61] John Paul II, Homily of His Holiness John Paul II for the Inauguration of His Pontificate St. Peter's Square. Sunday 22 October 1978. Article 5.

http://www.vatican.va/holy_father/john_paul_ii/speeches/1978/docu
ments/hf_jp-ii_spe_19781022_inizio-pontificato_en.html

[62] Applied Research in the Apostolate, "The Class of 2009: Survey of
Ordinands to the Priesthood: A Report to the Secretariat of Clergy,
Consecrated Life & Vocations, United States Conference of Catholic
Bishops" (Washington, D.C. 2009)

[63] Archbishop Timothy Dolan, Priests for the Third Millennium
(Huntington, IN: Our Sunday Visitor, 2000), 267

[64] From the children's poem, "A Good Night Prayer to the Blessed
Mother"

RECOMMENDED READING

Vocation Discernment

Personal Vocation: God Calls Everyone By Name
Dr. Germain Grisez and Russell Shaw

What Does God Want
Fr. Michael Scanlon

Discovering Your Personal Vocation
Herbert Alphonso, S.J.

Is Jesus Calling You To Be A Catholic Priest? A Helpful Guide
Fr. Thomas Richter, published by the NCDVD

Radical Surrender; Letters to Seminarians
Fr. Michael Najim

Paths of Love: The Discernment of Vocation According to the Teaching of Aquinas, Ignatius, and Pope John Paul II
Joseph Bolin

Could You Ever Become a Catholic Priest?
Christopher J. Duquin & Lorene Hanley Duquin

Called by Name: The Inspiring Stories of 12 Men Who Became Catholic Priests
Christine Mugridge

Priesthood

Priests for the Third Millennium
Archbishop Timothy Dolan

The Priest is Not His Own
Archbishop Fulton J. Sheen, 2004

Those Mysterious Priests
Archbishop Fulton J. Sheen, 2005

The Joy of Priesthood
Msgr. Steve Rosetti

Reclaiming our Priestly Character
Fr. David Toups

Maurice and Therese: The Story of a Love
Saint Therese of Lisieux

Short Catechism on the Priesthood
St. John Vianney

The Grace of Ars
Fr. Frederick Miller

Together on the Road: A Vision of Lived Communion for the Church and the Priesthood
Massimo Camisasca

Dear Father: A Message of Love to Priests
Catherine De Hueck Doherty

Be Holy! God's First Call to Priests Today
Thomas Forrest, C.Ss.R.

A Celebration of Priestly Ministry: Challenge, Renewal, and Joy in the Catholic Priesthood
Cardinal Walter Kasper

Magisterial Documents

Presbyterorum Ordinis (Order of Priests), 1965

Sacerdotii Nostri Primordia (From the Beginning of Our Priesthood) 1959

Pastores Dabo Vobis (I will Give You Shepherds), 1992

Program of Priestly Formation (5th Edition), U.S. Conference of Catholic Bishops, 2005

Celibacy

The Courage to be Chaste
Fr. Benedict Groeschel

When God Asks for an Undivided Heart
Fr. Andrew Apostoli

Sacerdotalis Caelibatus (Priestly Celibacy)
Pope Paul VI, 1967

Virginity
Fr. Raniero Cantalamessa

"...And You are Christ's" The Charism of Virginity and the Celibate Life
Thomas Dubay, S.M.

Biographies or Autobiographies of Priests

Parish Priest: Father Michael McGivney and American Catholicism
Douglas Brinkley and Julie M. Fenster

The Cure D'Ars: St. Jean-Marie-Baptiste Vianney
F. Trochu

A Priest Forever
Fr. Benedict Groeschel

He Leadeth Me
Fr. Walter J. Ciszek, S.J.

Edmund Campion
Evelyn Waugh

From Slave to Priest: A Biography of the Reverend Augustine Tolton (1854 - 1897): First Black American Priest of the United States
Caroline Hemesath

Treasure in Clay
Archbishop Fulton Sheen

The Grunt Padre
Fr. Daniel Mode

A Shepherd in Combat Boots: Chaplain Emil Kapaun of the 1st Cavalry Division
William L. Maher

Holy Man: Father Damien of Molokai
Gavan Daws

The Shadow of His Wings: The True Story of Fr. Gereon Goldmann, OFM
Gereon Karl Goldmann

INDEX OF QUESTIONS

Chapter 2: The Sacred Power of Priesthood

Chapter 3: What is a Vocation in the First Place?

Chapter 4: God said Go and I said No

Chapter 5: Signs of a Vocation to Priesthood

Chapter 6: Developing a Spiritual Plan of Life

Chapter 9: The Seven Stages of a Diligent Discernment

Chapter 10: Practical Ideas for Discerning Diocesan Priesthood

Chapter 14: My Path to Priesthood; When Do I Start?

Chapter 15: The Application and Admissions Process

Chapter 17: Prerequisites and Impediments to Diocesan Priesthood

161. At what point in the process does a man make the promise of celibacy? p. 324

162. What is the "canonical retreat" which is required before ordination to the diaconate and priesthood? p. 325

163. How can canonical impediments be removed so that a man can be ordained? p. 329

164. If a person suffers from a degree of mental illness, does this mean that he can never become a priest? p. 325

165. If a man ever abandoned the Catholic Faith and joined another church, does this mean that he cannot become a priest? p. 326

166. How can a man who was married and divorced still become a priest? p. 326

167. If a man was involved in an abortion, does this mean he cannot become a priest? p. 327

168. If a man ever attempted suicide, does this mean he cannot become a priest? p. 327

169. Can a man who is an alcoholic or drug addict become a priest? p. 330

170. Can a man who has an addiction to gambling or the internet become a priest? p. 331

171. Can a man who has an addiction to pornography become a priest? p. 332

172. If a man suffers from gross obesity, can he ever become a priest? p. 333

184. What is the most essential part of the ordination rite—the matter and form of the sacrament of Holy Orders—which is necessary for a man to be validly ordained? p. 356

185. At what point in the process does a man promise obedience to his bishop? p. 357

186. What is the matter and form of the sacrament of Holy Orders? p. 358

187. How much does the ordination cost and who pays for it? p. 361

188. What is the maniturgium? p. 359

189. What is the Mass of Thanksgiving? p. 361

190. What is the plenary indulgence which the faithful can receive by attending a priest's first Mass of Thanksgiving? p. 362

VIANNEY VOCATIONS

Effective Strategies to Increase Priestly Vocations

Order additional copies of this book at

www.vianneyvocations.com